The Tutorverse
MAKING THE UNIVERSE BRIGHTER, ONE STUDENT AT A TIME

Upper Level SSAT®
1500+ Practice Questions

Upper Level SSAT®: 1500+ Practice Questions
February 2023

Published in the United States of America by:

The Tutorverse, LLC

222 Broadway, 19th Floor

New York, NY 10038

Web: www.thetutorverse.com

Email: hello@thetutorverse.com

For information about buying this title in bulk or to place a special order, please contact us at hello@thetutorverse.com.

ISBN-13: 978-1-7321677-0-4
ISBN-10: 1-7321677-0-2

SSAT® is a registered trademark of the Secondary School Admission Test Board, Inc., which was not involved in the production of, and does not endorse, sponsor, or certify this product.

Neither the author or publisher claim any responsibility for the accuracy and appropriateness of the content in this book, nor do they claim any responsibility over the outcome of students who use these materials.

The views and opinions expressed in this book do not necessarily reflect the official policy, position, or point of view of the author or publisher. Such views and opinions do not constitute an endorsement to perform, attempt to perform, or otherwise emulate any procedures, experiments, etc. described in any of the passages, excerpts, adaptations, cited materials, or similar information. Such information is included only to facilitate the development of questions, answer choices, and answer explanations for purposes of preparing for the SSAT®.

Table of Contents

Upper Level SSAT® 1500+ Practice Questions

Welcome

Dear Students, Parents, and Educators,

Welcome to The Tutorverse!

Congratulations on taking the first steps towards conquering the Upper Level SSAT! This workbook contains the key to scoring well on the test: high-quality practice materials. While test-taking strategies are certainly helpful, we believe that high-performance is built on a foundation of core learning and subject-matter proficiency.

That's why this workbook contains over 10 exams' worth of questions – over 1,500 questions in total! We identified the core concepts tested on the Upper Level SSAT and crafted questions that introduce these ideas, build on the fundamentals, and increase in difficulty. Our goal is to help students master their skills, increase their knowledge, and build their confidence leading up to test day. To help with this, detailed answer explanations for every question are available online at **www.thetutorverse.com**.

Ready to get started? Whether you use this workbook for independent study or with a professional teacher or tutor, we believe these learnings will benefit you on the Upper Level SSAT and beyond!

Good luck!

The Team at The Tutorverse

The Tutorverse

How to Use This Book

Overview

The purpose of this workbook is to provide students, parents, and educators with practice materials relevant to the Upper Level SSAT. This workbook assumes its users have a working knowledge of the exam, including its structure and content. Though it contains tips, strategies, and suggestions, the primary goal of this workbook is to provide students with extensive practice by introducing new words, skills, and concepts. A brief overview of the exam is shown below.

Scoring	Section	Number of Questions	Time Limit
Unscored Section (sent to schools)	Writing Sample	1	25 minutes
Scored Section	5-Minute Break		
	Section 1: Quantitative	25	30 minutes
	Section 2: Reading	40	40 minutes
	10-Minute Break		
	Section 3: Verbal	60	30 minutes
	Section 4: Quantitative	25	30 minutes
	Total Scored Exam (Sections 1-4)	**150**	**2 hours, 10 minutes**
Unscored Section	Section 5: Experimental	16	15 minutes

Organization

This workbook is organized into six main sections. Each section is designed to accomplish different objectives. These sections and objectives are as follows:

🐦 Diagnostic Practice Test (Form A)

The first full-length practice test is designed to help students identify the topics that require the most practice. It mirrors the length and content of the actual Upper Level SSAT in order to ensure that students become accustomed to the duration of the real test. This diagnostic practice test should be used to gauge the amount of additional practice needed on each topic, **not** as an estimate of how a student will score on the actual Upper Level SSAT. **NOTE:** the diagnostic practice test includes 16 questions in a mock-experimental section and, while they are useful practice, they are included only to emulate the full duration of the actual test.

🐦 Quantitative

The main concepts covered in this section are Number Concepts and Operations; Algebra; Geometry & Measurement; and Data Analysis & Probability. All of these concepts are further divided into sub-categories, which can be found in the table of contents.

The Tutorverse

☞ Reading

This section tests a student's ability to read passages and answer questions about them. Passages include non-fiction persuasive and informative pieces, as well as excerpts from fictional works, including poems, novels, and short stories. Questions center around understanding main idea and themes, making inferences, and understanding how details contribute to the meaning of the passage.

☞ Verbal

The material in this section covers word similarities and relationships through synonym and analogy questions. Students will encounter many new words in this section.

☞ Writing Sample

This section provides information about the writing prompts (creative writing and essay-type), and includes several practice prompt pairs.

☞ Practice Test (Form B) & Final Practice Test (Form C)

This workbook ends with two additional full-length practice tests. They are similar to the diagnostic practice test in length and content and should be taken once students have completed the diagnostic practice test and have spent sufficient time answering the appropriate questions in the practice sections. **NOTE:** each practice test includes 16 questions in a mock-experimental section and, while they are useful practice, they are included only to emulate the full duration of the actual test.

Note: The Experimental section is designed by the SSAT Test Development Team to test new questions, in order to make sure they are appropriate for use on future SSAT exams. Since this section is **not** scored, this workbook will not include content related to the Experimental section (except in the Practice Test sections). Students need **not** worry about attempting these questions on the actual exam.

At the beginning of each of the above-listed sections are detailed instructions. Students should carefully review these instructions, as they contain important information about the actual exam and how best to practice.

Strategy

Every student has different strengths and abilities. We don't think there is any one strategy that will help every student ace the exam. Instead, we believe there are core principles to keep in mind when preparing for the Upper Level SSAT. These principles are interrelated and cyclical in nature.

☞ Evaluate

A critical step in developing a solid study plan is to have a clear idea of how to spend your time. What subjects are more difficult for you? Which types of questions do you frequently answer incorrectly? Why? These and many other questions should be answered before developing any study plan. The diagnostic practice test is just one way to help you evaluate your abilities.

☞ Plan

Once you've taken stock of your strengths and abilities, focus on actions. How much time do you have before the test? How many areas do you need to work on during that time? Which areas do you need to work on? How many questions (and of which type) do you need to do each day, or each week? The answers to these and other questions will help you determine your study and practice plan.

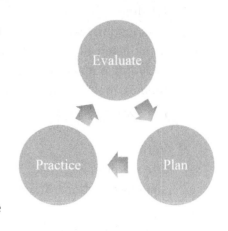

- Practice

    Once you settle on a plan, try to stick with it as much as you can. To study successfully requires discipline, commitment, and focus. Try turning off your phone, TV, tablet, or other distractions. Not only will you learn more effectively when you're focused, but you may find that you finish your work more quickly, as well.

- Reevaluate

    Because learning and studying is an ongoing process, it is important to take stock of your improvements along the way. This will help you see how you are progressing and allow you to make adjustments to your plan. The practice test at the end of this workbook is designed to help you gauge your progress.

Need Help?

Feeling overwhelmed? That's perfectly normal! Preparing for a standardized test is often a daunting task. While students should strive to meet the challenge of the test, it's also important for students to recognize when they need extra help.

First, know that since the Upper Level SSAT is given to students in various grades, students may find some material in this workbook difficult or entirely new. It's ok! That is to be expected, as certain material may not have been taught to all students yet. Students will only be scored against other students in their grade (9th graders vs. other 9th graders, for example). Even so, mastering advanced materials often provides a competitive advantage in achieving higher scores. Give it a try!

Second, students should know that they are not alone. We provide detailed answer explanations online at **www.thetutorverse.com** (students should ask a parent or guardian's permission before going online). We also encourage students to reach out to trusted educators to help them prepare for the Upper Level SSAT. Experienced tutors, teachers, mentors, and consultants can help students with many aspects of their preparation – from evaluating and reevaluating their needs, to creating an effective plan to help them make the most of their practice.

Looking for a tutor?

Look no further – we're The Tutorverse for a reason! Have a parent or guardian send us an email at hello@thetutorverse.com and get started with a **free consultation**!

The Tutorverse

Diagnostic Practice Test (Form A)

Overview

The first step to an effective study plan is to determine a student's strengths and areas for improvement. This first practice test assesses a student's mastery of certain skills and concepts that may be seen on the actual exam.

Keep in mind that this practice test will be scored differently from the actual exam. On the actual Upper Level SSAT, certain questions will **not** count towards a student's actual score (i.e. the experimental section), and the student's score will be determined by comparing his or her performance with those of other students in the same grade. On this practice test, however, every question is scored in order to accurately gauge the student's current ability level. Therefore, this practice test should **NOT** be used as a gauge of how a student will score on the actual test. This test should only be used to help students develop a study plan, and may be treated as a diagnostic test.

Format

The format of this diagnostic practice test is similar to that of the actual exam and includes 16 questions in a mock-experimental section. **For practice purposes only, students should treat the mock experimental section of the diagnostic practice test as any other.**

The format of the diagnostic practice test is below.

Scoring	Section	Number of Questions	Time Limit
Unscored Section (sent to schools)	Writing Sample	1	25 minutes
Scored Section	5-Minute Break		
	Section 1: Quantitative	25	30 minutes
	Section 2: Reading	40	40 minutes
	10-Minute Break		
	Section 3: Verbal	60	30 minutes
	Section 4: Quantitative	25	30 minutes
	Total Scored Exam (Sections 1-4)	**150**	**2 hours, 10 minutes**
Unscored Section	Section 5: Experimental	16	15 minutes

Answering

Use the answer sheet provided on the next page to record answers. Students may wish to tear it out of the workbook.

The Tutorverse

Section 1: Quantitative

1 Ⓐ Ⓑ Ⓒ Ⓓ Ⓔ	6 Ⓐ Ⓑ Ⓒ Ⓓ Ⓔ	11 Ⓐ Ⓑ Ⓒ Ⓓ Ⓔ	16 Ⓐ Ⓑ Ⓒ Ⓓ Ⓔ	21 Ⓐ Ⓑ Ⓒ Ⓓ Ⓔ
2 Ⓐ Ⓑ Ⓒ Ⓓ Ⓔ	7 Ⓐ Ⓑ Ⓒ Ⓓ Ⓔ	12 Ⓐ Ⓑ Ⓒ Ⓓ Ⓔ	17 Ⓐ Ⓑ Ⓒ Ⓓ Ⓔ	22 Ⓐ Ⓑ Ⓒ Ⓓ Ⓔ
3 Ⓐ Ⓑ Ⓒ Ⓓ Ⓔ	8 Ⓐ Ⓑ Ⓒ Ⓓ Ⓔ	13 Ⓐ Ⓑ Ⓒ Ⓓ Ⓔ	18 Ⓐ Ⓑ Ⓒ Ⓓ Ⓔ	23 Ⓐ Ⓑ Ⓒ Ⓓ Ⓔ
4 Ⓐ Ⓑ Ⓒ Ⓓ Ⓔ	9 Ⓐ Ⓑ Ⓒ Ⓓ Ⓔ	14 Ⓐ Ⓑ Ⓒ Ⓓ Ⓔ	19 Ⓐ Ⓑ Ⓒ Ⓓ Ⓔ	24 Ⓐ Ⓑ Ⓒ Ⓓ Ⓔ
5 Ⓐ Ⓑ Ⓒ Ⓓ Ⓔ	10 Ⓐ Ⓑ Ⓒ Ⓓ Ⓔ	15 Ⓐ Ⓑ Ⓒ Ⓓ Ⓔ	20 Ⓐ Ⓑ Ⓒ Ⓓ Ⓔ	25 Ⓐ Ⓑ Ⓒ Ⓓ Ⓔ

Section 2: Reading

1 Ⓐ Ⓑ Ⓒ Ⓓ Ⓔ	9 Ⓐ Ⓑ Ⓒ Ⓓ Ⓔ	17 Ⓐ Ⓑ Ⓒ Ⓓ Ⓔ	25 Ⓐ Ⓑ Ⓒ Ⓓ Ⓔ	33 Ⓐ Ⓑ Ⓒ Ⓓ Ⓔ
2 Ⓐ Ⓑ Ⓒ Ⓓ Ⓔ	10 Ⓐ Ⓑ Ⓒ Ⓓ Ⓔ	18 Ⓐ Ⓑ Ⓒ Ⓓ Ⓔ	26 Ⓐ Ⓑ Ⓒ Ⓓ Ⓔ	34 Ⓐ Ⓑ Ⓒ Ⓓ Ⓔ
3 Ⓐ Ⓑ Ⓒ Ⓓ Ⓔ	11 Ⓐ Ⓑ Ⓒ Ⓓ Ⓔ	19 Ⓐ Ⓑ Ⓒ Ⓓ Ⓔ	27 Ⓐ Ⓑ Ⓒ Ⓓ Ⓔ	35 Ⓐ Ⓑ Ⓒ Ⓓ Ⓔ
4 Ⓐ Ⓑ Ⓒ Ⓓ Ⓔ	12 Ⓐ Ⓑ Ⓒ Ⓓ Ⓔ	20 Ⓐ Ⓑ Ⓒ Ⓓ Ⓔ	28 Ⓐ Ⓑ Ⓒ Ⓓ Ⓔ	36 Ⓐ Ⓑ Ⓒ Ⓓ Ⓔ
5 Ⓐ Ⓑ Ⓒ Ⓓ Ⓔ	13 Ⓐ Ⓑ Ⓒ Ⓓ Ⓔ	21 Ⓐ Ⓑ Ⓒ Ⓓ Ⓔ	29 Ⓐ Ⓑ Ⓒ Ⓓ Ⓔ	37 Ⓐ Ⓑ Ⓒ Ⓓ Ⓔ
6 Ⓐ Ⓑ Ⓒ Ⓓ Ⓔ	14 Ⓐ Ⓑ Ⓒ Ⓓ Ⓔ	22 Ⓐ Ⓑ Ⓒ Ⓓ Ⓔ	30 Ⓐ Ⓑ Ⓒ Ⓓ Ⓔ	38 Ⓐ Ⓑ Ⓒ Ⓓ Ⓔ
7 Ⓐ Ⓑ Ⓒ Ⓓ Ⓔ	15 Ⓐ Ⓑ Ⓒ Ⓓ Ⓔ	23 Ⓐ Ⓑ Ⓒ Ⓓ Ⓔ	31 Ⓐ Ⓑ Ⓒ Ⓓ Ⓔ	39 Ⓐ Ⓑ Ⓒ Ⓓ Ⓔ
8 Ⓐ Ⓑ Ⓒ Ⓓ Ⓔ	16 Ⓐ Ⓑ Ⓒ Ⓓ Ⓔ	24 Ⓐ Ⓑ Ⓒ Ⓓ Ⓔ	32 Ⓐ Ⓑ Ⓒ Ⓓ Ⓔ	40 Ⓐ Ⓑ Ⓒ Ⓓ Ⓔ

Section 3: Verbal

1 Ⓐ Ⓑ Ⓒ Ⓓ Ⓔ	13 Ⓐ Ⓑ Ⓒ Ⓓ Ⓔ	25 Ⓐ Ⓑ Ⓒ Ⓓ Ⓔ	37 Ⓐ Ⓑ Ⓒ Ⓓ Ⓔ	49 Ⓐ Ⓑ Ⓒ Ⓓ Ⓔ
2 Ⓐ Ⓑ Ⓒ Ⓓ Ⓔ	14 Ⓐ Ⓑ Ⓒ Ⓓ Ⓔ	26 Ⓐ Ⓑ Ⓒ Ⓓ Ⓔ	38 Ⓐ Ⓑ Ⓒ Ⓓ Ⓔ	50 Ⓐ Ⓑ Ⓒ Ⓓ Ⓔ
3 Ⓐ Ⓑ Ⓒ Ⓓ Ⓔ	15 Ⓐ Ⓑ Ⓒ Ⓓ Ⓔ	27 Ⓐ Ⓑ Ⓒ Ⓓ Ⓔ	39 Ⓐ Ⓑ Ⓒ Ⓓ Ⓔ	51 Ⓐ Ⓑ Ⓒ Ⓓ Ⓔ
4 Ⓐ Ⓑ Ⓒ Ⓓ Ⓔ	16 Ⓐ Ⓑ Ⓒ Ⓓ Ⓔ	28 Ⓐ Ⓑ Ⓒ Ⓓ Ⓔ	40 Ⓐ Ⓑ Ⓒ Ⓓ Ⓔ	52 Ⓐ Ⓑ Ⓒ Ⓓ Ⓔ
5 Ⓐ Ⓑ Ⓒ Ⓓ Ⓔ	17 Ⓐ Ⓑ Ⓒ Ⓓ Ⓔ	29 Ⓐ Ⓑ Ⓒ Ⓓ Ⓔ	41 Ⓐ Ⓑ Ⓒ Ⓓ Ⓔ	53 Ⓐ Ⓑ Ⓒ Ⓓ Ⓔ
6 Ⓐ Ⓑ Ⓒ Ⓓ Ⓔ	18 Ⓐ Ⓑ Ⓒ Ⓓ Ⓔ	30 Ⓐ Ⓑ Ⓒ Ⓓ Ⓔ	42 Ⓐ Ⓑ Ⓒ Ⓓ Ⓔ	54 Ⓐ Ⓑ Ⓒ Ⓓ Ⓔ
7 Ⓐ Ⓑ Ⓒ Ⓓ Ⓔ	19 Ⓐ Ⓑ Ⓒ Ⓓ Ⓔ	31 Ⓐ Ⓑ Ⓒ Ⓓ Ⓔ	43 Ⓐ Ⓑ Ⓒ Ⓓ Ⓔ	55 Ⓐ Ⓑ Ⓒ Ⓓ Ⓔ
8 Ⓐ Ⓑ Ⓒ Ⓓ Ⓔ	20 Ⓐ Ⓑ Ⓒ Ⓓ Ⓔ	32 Ⓐ Ⓑ Ⓒ Ⓓ Ⓔ	44 Ⓐ Ⓑ Ⓒ Ⓓ Ⓔ	56 Ⓐ Ⓑ Ⓒ Ⓓ Ⓔ
9 Ⓐ Ⓑ Ⓒ Ⓓ Ⓔ	21 Ⓐ Ⓑ Ⓒ Ⓓ Ⓔ	33 Ⓐ Ⓑ Ⓒ Ⓓ Ⓔ	45 Ⓐ Ⓑ Ⓒ Ⓓ Ⓔ	57 Ⓐ Ⓑ Ⓒ Ⓓ Ⓔ
10 Ⓐ Ⓑ Ⓒ Ⓓ Ⓔ	22 Ⓐ Ⓑ Ⓒ Ⓓ Ⓔ	34 Ⓐ Ⓑ Ⓒ Ⓓ Ⓔ	46 Ⓐ Ⓑ Ⓒ Ⓓ Ⓔ	58 Ⓐ Ⓑ Ⓒ Ⓓ Ⓔ
11 Ⓐ Ⓑ Ⓒ Ⓓ Ⓔ	23 Ⓐ Ⓑ Ⓒ Ⓓ Ⓔ	35 Ⓐ Ⓑ Ⓒ Ⓓ Ⓔ	47 Ⓐ Ⓑ Ⓒ Ⓓ Ⓔ	59 Ⓐ Ⓑ Ⓒ Ⓓ Ⓔ
12 Ⓐ Ⓑ Ⓒ Ⓓ Ⓔ	24 Ⓐ Ⓑ Ⓒ Ⓓ Ⓔ	36 Ⓐ Ⓑ Ⓒ Ⓓ Ⓔ	48 Ⓐ Ⓑ Ⓒ Ⓓ Ⓔ	60 Ⓐ Ⓑ Ⓒ Ⓓ Ⓔ

Section 4: Quantitative

1 Ⓐ Ⓑ Ⓒ Ⓓ Ⓔ	6 Ⓐ Ⓑ Ⓒ Ⓓ Ⓔ	11 Ⓐ Ⓑ Ⓒ Ⓓ Ⓔ	16 Ⓐ Ⓑ Ⓒ Ⓓ Ⓔ	21 Ⓐ Ⓑ Ⓒ Ⓓ Ⓔ
2 Ⓐ Ⓑ Ⓒ Ⓓ Ⓔ	7 Ⓐ Ⓑ Ⓒ Ⓓ Ⓔ	12 Ⓐ Ⓑ Ⓒ Ⓓ Ⓔ	17 Ⓐ Ⓑ Ⓒ Ⓓ Ⓔ	22 Ⓐ Ⓑ Ⓒ Ⓓ Ⓔ
3 Ⓐ Ⓑ Ⓒ Ⓓ Ⓔ	8 Ⓐ Ⓑ Ⓒ Ⓓ Ⓔ	13 Ⓐ Ⓑ Ⓒ Ⓓ Ⓔ	18 Ⓐ Ⓑ Ⓒ Ⓓ Ⓔ	23 Ⓐ Ⓑ Ⓒ Ⓓ Ⓔ
4 Ⓐ Ⓑ Ⓒ Ⓓ Ⓔ	9 Ⓐ Ⓑ Ⓒ Ⓓ Ⓔ	14 Ⓐ Ⓑ Ⓒ Ⓓ Ⓔ	19 Ⓐ Ⓑ Ⓒ Ⓓ Ⓔ	24 Ⓐ Ⓑ Ⓒ Ⓓ Ⓔ
5 Ⓐ Ⓑ Ⓒ Ⓓ Ⓔ	10 Ⓐ Ⓑ Ⓒ Ⓓ Ⓔ	15 Ⓐ Ⓑ Ⓒ Ⓓ Ⓔ	20 Ⓐ Ⓑ Ⓒ Ⓓ Ⓔ	25 Ⓐ Ⓑ Ⓒ Ⓓ Ⓔ

Section 5: Experimental

1 Ⓐ Ⓑ Ⓒ Ⓓ Ⓔ	5 Ⓐ Ⓑ Ⓒ Ⓓ Ⓔ	9 Ⓐ Ⓑ Ⓒ Ⓓ Ⓔ	13 Ⓐ Ⓑ Ⓒ Ⓓ Ⓔ
2 Ⓐ Ⓑ Ⓒ Ⓓ Ⓔ	6 Ⓐ Ⓑ Ⓒ Ⓓ Ⓔ	10 Ⓐ Ⓑ Ⓒ Ⓓ Ⓔ	14 Ⓐ Ⓑ Ⓒ Ⓓ Ⓔ
3 Ⓐ Ⓑ Ⓒ Ⓓ Ⓔ	7 Ⓐ Ⓑ Ⓒ Ⓓ Ⓔ	11 Ⓐ Ⓑ Ⓒ Ⓓ Ⓔ	15 Ⓐ Ⓑ Ⓒ Ⓓ Ⓔ
4 Ⓐ Ⓑ Ⓒ Ⓓ Ⓔ	8 Ⓐ Ⓑ Ⓒ Ⓓ Ⓔ	12 Ⓐ Ⓑ Ⓒ Ⓓ Ⓔ	16 Ⓐ Ⓑ Ⓒ Ⓓ Ⓔ

The Tutorverse

Writing Sample

Schools would like to get to know you through an essay or story that you write. Choose one of the topics below that you find most interesting. Fill in the circle next to the topic of your choice. Then, write a story or essay based on the topic you chose.

Ⓐ If you could do one thing to improve your community, what would it be?

Ⓑ He ran as fast as he could.

Use this page and the next page to complete your writing sample.

_____

_____

_____

_____

_____

_____

_____

_____

_____

_____

_____

_____

_____

_____

_____

_____

_____

_____

_____

_____

_____

_____

The Tutorverse

SECTION 1

25 Questions

There are five suggested answers after each problem in this section. Solve each problem in your head or in the space provided to the right of the problem. Then, look at the suggested answers and pick the best one.

Note: Any figures or shapes that accompany problems in Section 1 are drawn as accurately as possible EXCEPT when it is stated that the figure is NOT drawn to scale.

Sample Question:

$11 \times 12 =$ ●ⒷⒸⒹⒺ
(A) 132
(B) 144
(C) 1,112
(D) 1,332
(E) 1,444

DO WORK IN THIS SPACE

1. $10\frac{1}{5} + 6\frac{1}{3} - 3\frac{7}{15} =$
   (A) $14\frac{1}{3}$
   (B) $13\frac{2}{5}$
   (C) $13\frac{4}{15}$
   (D) $13\frac{1}{15}$
   (E) $12\frac{1}{15}$

2. The triangle shown below has a perimeter of 36 centimeters. What is the area, in centimeters, of the triangle?
   (A) $12\sqrt{2}$
   (B) 36
   (C) $36\sqrt{3}$
   (D) 72
   (E) $72\sqrt{2}$

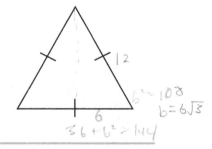

3. If 25% of a number is 12, then 70% of that same number is
   (A) 21
   (B) 33.6
   (C) 38.5
   (D) 42
   (E) 48

GO ON TO THE NEXT PAGE.

The Tutorverse

DO WORK IN THIS SPACE

4. What is the average amount of money in the savings account between the years 2014 and 2018, rounded to the nearest thousand dollars?
   (A) $6,000
   (B) $16,000
   (C) $17,000
   (D) $21,000
   (E) $83,000

Money in Savings Account

5. Which of the following could be the lengths of the sides of a triangle?
   (A) 2, 2, 6
   (B) 4, 4, 8
   (C) 1, 2, 3
   (D) 4, 6, 8
   (E) 4, 4, 12

6. A car dealership has six different car models on its lot. The prices of the first five are $15,000, $9,000, $12,000, $15,000, and $13,000. The price of the sixth car is the mode of the first five cars. What is the median price of all six cars?
   (A) $6,000
   (B) $13,000
   (C) $13,166
   (D) $14,000
   (E) $15,000

7. Joe's plant grows by 13% each month. Which expression represents the plant's new height after h months?
   (A) $h + 0.13$
   (B) $13h\%$
   (C) $0.13h$
   (D) $0.87h$
   (E) 1.13^h

8. John runs a food truck that sells sandwiches for $6 each. Supplies to make each sandwich cost $2. Which set represents a list of the possible number of sandwiches John can make and sell to earn more than $300?
   (A) {74, 76, 78, 85}
   (B) {71, 75, 77, 81}
   (C) {70, 72, 81, 85}
   (D) {74, 75, 77, 78}
   (E) {76, 77, 79, 82}

GO ON TO THE NEXT PAGE.

The Tutorverse

DO WORK IN THIS SPACE

9. A certain basketball player shot 663 free throws during the regular season and made 503 of them. Which is closest to the percentage of free throws the player made?
   (A) 60%
   (B) 65%
   (C) 75%
   (D) 80%
   (E) 85%

10. Simon has x baseball cards. Julie has twice as many cards as Simon. In terms of x, how many cards does Julie have?
    (A) $2x$
    (B) $x + 2$
    (C) x^2
    (D) $x - 2$
    (E) x

11. On a field trip, the ratio of chaperones to students is $\frac{3}{20}$. How many more students than chaperones were on the field trip if there were 12 chaperones?
    (A) 80
    (B) 68
    (C) 36
    (D) 9
    (E) 8

12. One bag of rice holds 22 gallons. A shipping container contains 35 bags of rice. How many pints of rice does one shipping container hold?
    (1 gallon = 8 pints)
    (A) 96.25
    (B) 770
    (C) 5,600
    (D) 6,160
    (E) 61,600

13. Which of the following is a possible value for x for which $3x(x - 5) = 0$?
    (A) −5
    (B) −3
    (C) 3
    (D) 5
    (E) 15

14. How many solutions does the equation $5x + 2.4 = 5(x + 2.4)$ have?
    (A) 0
    (B) 1
    (C) 2
    (D) 3
    (E) Infinitely Many

GO ON TO THE NEXT PAGE.

The Tutorverse

DO WORK IN THIS SPACE

15. Which inequality represents all possible solutions of $\frac{x}{3} \le -2$?

(A) $x \le -6$

(B) $x \ge -6$

(C) $x \le -5$

(D) $x \le 6$

(E) $x \ge -1$

16. The legs of a right triangle are formed by the sides of two squares. The first square has an area of 64 square feet and the other has an area of 17 square feet. The hypotenuse of the triangle is formed by the side of a square with an area equal to x^2 square feet. What is the value of x?

(A) 9 ft

(B) $15\sqrt{2}$ ft

(C) 27 ft

(D) 47 ft

(E) 81 ft

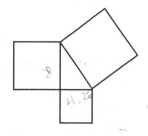

Not drawn to scale.

17. If the first term of a sequence is 100, and each successive term is 7 less than the preceding one, what is the first negative term of the sequence?

(A) –1

(B) –2

(C) –3

(D) –4

(E) –5

18. Which expression is equivalent to $x^4 - x^3 - 6x^2$?

(A) $x^2(x + 2)(x + 3)$

(B) $x^2(x + 2)(x - 3)$

(C) $x(x + 1)(x - 6)$

(D) $x(x - 1)(x - 6)$

(E) $x^2(x - 1)(x - 6)$

19. Amanda, Beatrice, Caroline, and Danielle are sitting in a row. If Amanda and Danielle insist on sitting next to each other, in how many ways can the four girls arrange themselves?

(A) 6

(B) 12

(C) 16

(D) 18

(E) 24

20. Which expression is equivalent to $\left(\frac{2}{x + 3}\right)\left(\frac{3}{x + 5}\right)$?

(A) $\frac{3x + 9}{2x + 5}$

(B) $\frac{6}{x^2 + 8x + 15}$

(C) $\frac{6}{x^2 + 8}$

(D) $\frac{5}{2x + 8}$

(E) $\frac{6}{x^2 + 3x + 15}$

GO ON TO THE NEXT PAGE.

The Tutorverse

DO WORK IN THIS SPACE

21. Which expression has a value three times that of 8.7×10^3?
    - (A) 8.7×10^3
    - (B) 8.7×10^9
    - (C) 2.61×10^4
    - (D) 2.61×10^5
    - (E) 2.61×10^{-4}

22. In the xy-coordinate plane, what is the slope of a line that is perpendicular to the line with the equation $3x + 2y = 10$
    - (A) $-\dfrac{3}{2}$
    - (B) $-\dfrac{2}{3}$
    - (C) $\dfrac{2}{3}$
    - (D) 3
    - (E) 5

23. A box contains 4 cherry candies, 5 green apple candies, 8 blueberry candies, and 3 banana candies. If 2 candies are randomly selected without replacement, what is the probability that a cherry candy and then a green apple candy are selected, in that order?
    - (A) $\dfrac{1}{20}$
    - (B) $\dfrac{1}{19}$
    - (C) $\dfrac{1}{16}$
    - (D) $\dfrac{1}{4}$
    - (E) $\dfrac{9}{20}$

24. Which expression is equivalent to $(x + 5)(x^2 + 3x + 2)$?
    - (A) $x^2 + 4x + 7$
    - (B) $x^2 + 3x + 10$
    - (C) $x^3 + 8x^2 + 17x + 10$
    - (D) $x^3 + 3x^2 + 15x + 10$
    - (E) $x^3 + 5x^2 + 15x + 7$

25. How many squares are drawn in the figure shown?
    - (A) 2
    - (B) 4
    - (C) 6
    - (D) 8
    - (E) 10

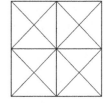

STOP

IF YOU FINISH BEFORE TIME IS UP,
CHECK YOUR WORK IN THIS SECTION ONLY.
YOU MAY NOT TURN TO ANY OTHER SECTION.

The Tutorverse

SECTION 2
40 Questions

Carefully read each passage and then answer the questions about it. For each question, select the choice that best answers the question based on the passage.

> The trees bend down along the stream,
>   Where anchored swings my tiny boat.
> The day is one to drowse and dream
>   And list the thrush's throttling note.
> 5   When music from his bosom bleeds
> Among the river's rustling reeds.
>
> No ripple stirs the placid pool,
>   When my adventurous line is cast,
> A truce to sport, while clear and cool,
> 10   The mirrored clouds slide softly past.
> The sky gives back a blue divine,
> And all the world's wide wealth is mine.
>
> A pickerel leaps, a bow of light,
> The minnows shine from side to side.
> 15   The first faint breeze comes up the tide—
> I pause with half uplifted oar,
> While night drifts down to claim the shore.

1. The mood evoked by the passage is best described as which of the following?
   (A) annoyance
   (B) amusement
   (C) melancholy
   (D) restlessness
   (E) tranquility

2. In line 7, the word "placid" most nearly means
   (A) bubbly
   (B) calm
   (C) cold
   (D) rough
   (E) watery

3. Line 11 is an example of
   (A) meter
   (B) metonymy
   (C) parallelism
   (D) personification
   (E) simile

4. What the author means in line 12 is that
   (A) he is inheriting a great fortune from his family
   (B) his talent as a fisherman has brought him wealth
   (C) the sky's brilliance is like that of precious gems
   (D) the land is rich with natural resources that can be sold
   (E) his appreciation for nature provides immaterial wealth

5. The author is primarily concerned with
   (A) telling about the sport of fishing
   (B) describing a beautiful experience
   (C) explaining how to accumulate great wealth
   (D) arguing in favor of a particular opinion
   (E) documenting different types of wildlife

GO ON TO THE NEXT PAGE.

The Tutorverse

Whoever coined the phrase "It's better late than never" would have relished the opportunity to meet the self-taught artist Bill Traylor. Born into slavery in 1854 in Benton, Alabama, Traylor spent the majority of his life working on a plantation. Even after the conclusion of the Civil War and the abolition of slavery, Traylor continued working in

5   Benton as a sharecropper, where he eventually married and raised nine children. It wasn't until 1935, at the ripe age of 82, that Traylor finally left his hometown for Montgomery, Alabama. It was then that his artistic career began to take flight.

Why such a sudden change in the twilight years of one's life? Asked to explain his rather unexpected move, Traylor responded bluntly, "My white folks had died and my

10   children had scattered." Arriving in Montgomery with limited means and no artistic training, Traylor nevertheless became a prolific artist. He would work with whatever supplies he had on hand, going so far as to draw sketches on salvaged cardboard pieces. His subjects ranged from the animals and livestock that populated the rural areas of town to the mix of passersby on Montgomery's busiest streets. One of these pedestrians was an

15   established, white painter named Charles Shannon, whose admiration of Traylor's work led him to become a staunch supporter of the former sharecropper. Aided by Shannon's professional networks, Traylor soon found his work exhibited at museums throughout the country, including the prestigious Museum of Modern Art in New York City.

Unfortunately, the bulk of Traylor's success did not come until around thirty years

20   after his death. It was only in the late 1970s, due in large part to fluctuating tastes in the art world, that modern audiences came to revere Traylor's genius. Traylor's works were initially considered to be an exemplar of "folk art," a term used to describe artwork that exists outside the mainstream. Now, however, the artist's works are deemed to fit squarely within the canon of contemporary, twentieth-century American art.

6. After meeting Charles Shannon, Traylor
   (A) gained a better understanding of modern art trends
   (B) enjoyed unprecedented fame for a Southern artist
   (C) was able to showcase his work at a variety of museums
   (D) became a master of Impressionistic sketches
   (E) finally quit his job as a sharecropper.

7. The tone of this passage is best described as
   (A) casual and admiring
   (B) academic and instructive
   (C) conversational and critical
   (D) formal and disdainful
   (E) analytical and questioning

8. In line 22, "exemplar" most nearly means
   (A) study
   (B) miracle
   (C) survey
   (D) criticism
   (E) representation

9. It can be inferred from the passage that today's audiences would likely see Traylor's art as
   (A) inferior in quality when compared to Traylor's peers
   (B) an adequate depiction of American art in the 1900s
   (C) undeserving of praise from modern audiences
   (D) a perfect reflection of artwork produced by mainstream artists
   (E) being at the forefront of American art trends for over a century

10. The passage is primarily about
    (A) the artistic pursuits of a former sharecropper
    (B) modern trends in the art world
    (C) race relations in the American South during the 1900s
    (D) the generosity of a successful, white painter
    (E) farming practices during the 20th century

GO ON TO THE NEXT PAGE.

The Tutorverse

Ever notice how it becomes oddly quiet outside when it snows? Many would assume that this is solely because there are fewer people than usual out and about when temperatures drop below freezing. What many don't know is that snow itself is also responsible for making things seem more quiet than usual.

5   Sound vibrations travel through the air much like ripples do on the surface of a pond. When those vibrations enter the ear, they are processed by the brain as sounds. Like ripples on a body of water, sound vibrations travel outwardly until they dissipate completely or are reflected off of a surface. When sound vibrations strike a surface, they create "echoes" – reflected sound waves that create additional sound. Harder surfaces can

10   reflect vibrations with greater force than softer surfaces, and thus are able to generate louder echoes.

       Imagine walking down a city street surrounded by tall buildings made of steel, concrete, and glass. What makes this environment so noisy is not just the abundance of cars and people, but also the number of hard, reflective surfaces that bounce sound

15   vibrations back and forth, creating a cacophony. Snow, on the other hand, has the opposite effect as these building materials. Because snowflakes are porous, they do not reflect sound as effectively as denser materials. In fact, there are so many holes in an individual snowflake that snow actually absorbs a bulk of the sound vibrations that ripple through the air. In addition, accumulated snow covers up what hard reflective surfaces

20   there are, further limiting the ability of sound to propagate around a space.

11. As used in line 15, the word "cacophony" most nearly means
 (A) silence
 (B) sound wave
 (C) hum
 (D) racket
 (E) ringing

12. It can be inferred from the passage that the effect of snow on sound waves is similar to the effect of which of the following on a ripple in water?
 (A) a large stone
 (B) a speck of dust
 (C) a small feather
 (D) a piece of metal
 (E) a thin sheet of cloth

13. The author of the passage is primarily concerned with
 (A) describing a cold winter's day
 (B) how ripples spread across water
 (C) how snow affects sound waves
 (D) the way in which echoes are created
 (E) how the brain processes sound

14. This passage is written in a style most like that of a(n)
 (A) poem
 (B) editorial
 (C) news article
 (D) fictional novel
 (E) science textbook

15. According to the passage, all of the following can alter noise levels outside EXCEPT the
 (A) hardness of exposed surfaces
 (B) number of people outdoors
 (C) presence of porous materials
 (D) number of reflective surfaces
 (E) reflective quality of air

GO ON TO THE NEXT PAGE.

The Tutorverse

"He wasn't more than thirteen; bound for the docks, you could tell at a glance; and by the way he looked about you could tell as easily that he'd set foot on London stones for the first time. God knows how it struck him – the slush and drizzle, the ugly shop-fronts, the horses slipping in the brown mud, the crowd on the pavement pushing him this side

5   and that. The poor little chap was standing in the middle of it with dazed eyes, like a hare's, when the omnibus pulled up. His eyelids were pink and swollen; but he wasn't crying, though he wanted to. Instead, he gave a gulp as he came on board with stick and bundle, and tried to look brave as a lion.

"I'd have given worlds to speak to him, but I couldn't. On my word, sir, I should

10 have cried. It wasn't so much the little chap's look. But to the knot of his bundle there was tied a bunch of cottage flowers, and the sight and smell of them in that stuffy omnibus were like tears on thirsty eyelids.

"It's the young that I pity, sir. It's the young faces, set toward the road along which we have travelled, that trouble me. Sometimes, sir, I lie awake in my lodgings and listen,

15 and the whole of this London seems filled with the sound of children's feet running, and I can sob aloud...As I kept glancing at the boy and his kit and his bunch of flowers, my mind went back to the January morning, sixty-five years back, when the coach took me off for the first time from the village where I was born...I remembered this, and how I stretched out my hands to the place from the coach-top; and how at Reading, where we stopped, I

20 spent the two shillings that I possessed on a coconut and a bright clasp-knife; and how, when I opened it, the nut was sour; and how I cried myself to sleep, and woke in London."

16. In line 3, "it" refers to the
(A) boy's inexperience
(B) sound of feet running
(C) pink and swollen eyelids
(D) powerful memory of childhood
(E) overwhelming chaos of the city

17. From the details, you can tell that the narrator is unable to speak to the boy (line 9) because
(A) the boy is crying too fiercely
(B) he is trying to open a coconut
(C) he is overcome with emotions
(D) he is too busy driving the omnibus
(E) the boy reminds him of his own child

18. Which of the following best summarizes the narrator's sentiment throughout the passage?
(A) The omnibus is a poor way to travel.
(B) Living in the countryside is preferable to living in cities.
(C) Flowers are a powerful symbol of childhood innocence.
(D) The loss of youth and innocence is tragic and unavoidable.
(E) Gaining worldly experience is a valuable and joyful process.

19. The narrator's use of which of the following phrases is an example of hyperbole?
(A) "tell as easily" (line 2)
(B) "brave as a lion" (lines 7-8)
(C) "given worlds" (line 9)
(D) "bright clasp-knife" (line 20)
(E) "like tears on...eyelids" (line 12)

20. It can be inferred from the passage that the narrator's story about the coconut (lines 18-21)
(A) is a memory that has faded with time
(B) embodies the hopeful potential of youthful energy
(C) shows how it pays off to take chances and try new things
(D) tells us that the narrator is an unreliable character
(E) illustrates that growing up is difficult and filled with disappointments

21. Which words best describe how the narrator feels as he recounts his own experience (lines 18-21)?
(A) tired yet optimistic
(B) gleeful and satisfied
(C) hopeful yet resigned
(D) melancholy and bitter
(E) unrepentant yet determined

GO ON TO THE NEXT PAGE.
The Tutorverse

Twice a year, people around the world dutifully turn their clocks forward or backward by an hour. And twice a year, nobody seems to understand why. This is the issue of Daylight Saving Time, a worldwide phenomenon that should go the way of the dinosaurs.

5   Daylight Saving Time, or DST, was first conceived of in the late 19th century. Yet, it was not implemented on a wide scale until 1916, when it was used by the then-German Empire as a way to conserve resources during World War I. The thinking was this: if clocks could be manipulated seasonally such that evening sunlight lasted longer, come nighttime, people could save on the resources used to produce artificial light.

10   But here's the kicker: despite having been adopted by multiple countries and employed for over a century, DST has never been proven to actually save energy! While studies show that turning our clocks forward or backward can foster minute energy savings, any conservation is offset by related instances of energy consumption. For example, in Indiana, the subject of a 2008 study, DST caused residents to save on

15   electricity used for lighting. However, these gains became negligible when accounting for the increased use of electricity used for heating and cooling – the former due to colder mornings, the latter due to hotter evenings.

What's more, due to a lack of data concerning energy consumption trends before the application of DST, it's nearly impossible to quantify its effects on a national, let alone

20   global, scale.

It's time to put an end to changing the time. Let's turn back the clock on DST.

22. The tone of the passage can best be described as
(A) informal yet passionate
(B) educational and passive
(C) abstract and determined
(D) heightened and theoretical
(E) casual and ambivalent

23. The author would most likely agree with which of the following statements?
(A) Any effort is worthwhile if it means saving energy.
(B) A practice that was useful in the past will also be useful in the present.
(C) Increasing the length of daylight is more important than saving energy.
(D) People should not follow traditions if those practices do not make sense.
(E) There is not enough evidence to rely on a case study when making a decision.

24. It can be inferred from the passage that the German Empire employed DST because
(A) artificial light was a precious weapon
(B) they sought to trick their enemies during World War I
(C) they needed to see during nighttime combat
(D) they possessed the fewest resources of all major empires
(E) it helped them conserve electricity for use on other wartime activities

25. The 2008 study in Indiana resulted in what conclusion about DST?
(A) DST is a necessity for countries during wartime.
(B) DST is responsible for substantial energy savings.
(C) Energy saved from lighting is negated by other energy uses.
(D) It is impossible to utilize energy data compiled before DST.
(E) DST allows residents to conserve energy used on air conditioning.

GO ON TO THE NEXT PAGE.

The Tutorverse

I speak as briefly as possible because too much harm has already been done with irresponsible words of bitterness and selfish political opportunism. I speak as simply as possible because the issue is too great to be obscured by eloquence. I speak simply and briefly in the hope that my words will be taken to heart.

5   I speak as a Republican; I speak as a woman. I speak as a United States Senator. I speak as an American.

The United States Senate has long enjoyed worldwide respect as the greatest deliberative body in the world. But recently that deliberative character has too often been debased to the level of a forum of hate and character assassination sheltered by the shield

10   of congressional immunity...

I think that it is high time for the United States Senate and its members to do some soul searching - for us to weigh our consciences - on the manner in which we are performing our duty to the people of America - on the manner in which we are using or abusing our individual powers and privileges.

15   I think that it is high time that we remembered that we have sworn to uphold and defend the Constitution. I think that it is high time that we remembered; that the Constitution, as amended, speaks not only of the freedom of speech but also of trial by jury instead of trial by accusation.

Whether it be a criminal prosecution in court or a character prosecution in the

20   Senate, there is little practical distinction when the life of a person has been ruined.

Those of us who shout the loudest about Americanism in making character assassinations are all too frequently those who, by our own words and acts, ignore some of the basic principles of Americanism –

The right to criticize;

25   The right to hold unpopular beliefs;

The right to protest;

The right of independent thought.

The exercise of these rights should not cost one single American citizen his reputation or his right to a livelihood nor should he be in danger of losing his reputation

30   or livelihood merely because he happens to know someone who holds unpopular beliefs. Who of us doesn't?

26. This passage was probably written to
    (A) issue a rebuke
    (B) provide a warning
    (C) tell a relatable story
    (D) teach a valuable lesson
    (E) share factual information

27. In line 3, "the issue" refers to
    (A) illegal behavior
    (B) the right to a trial by jury
    (C) making amendments to the Constitution
    (D) the treatment of those who have unpopular beliefs
    (E) a criminal prosecution of unconstitutional behavior

28. According to the author, "Americanism" (line 23) consists of all of the following EXCEPT
    (A) the right to publicly dissent
    (B) the right to uphold the Constitution
    (C) the right to form one's own opinion
    (D) the right to a belief that is different from others
    (E) the right to vocalize one's disagreement

29. According to the passage, the United States Senate is losing respect because
    (A) of overseas conflict
    (B) the Constitution is weakening
    (C) citizens disagree with the laws
    (D) senators are abusing their power
    (E) the political parties cannot agree

GO ON TO THE NEXT PAGE.
The Tutorverse

Internationally, climate change is already causing humanitarian disasters and resource scarcity that accelerate instability, contribute to political violence, and undermine weak governments. Examples of these repercussions are being seen around the world today. Climate change-induced drought in the Middle East and Africa is leading
5   to conflicts over food and water, escalating longstanding regional and ethnic tensions into violent clashes. Rising sea levels are putting people and food supplies in vulnerable coastal regions at risk, threatening to displace countless people.

The increasing scarcity of resources in regions across the globe is stressing governments that are trying to provide basic needs for their citizens. In already volatile
10   regions of the world, these are highly dangerous conditions that can enable terrorist activity and exacerbate refugee crises. As these threats around the world continue to multiply due to climate change, the U.S. is forced to extend our limited resources in humanitarian aid and military security to more locations in an effort to keep the peace, protect our interests and allies, and avoid major conflicts.
15   It is not just the scientist and policymaker sounding the alarm. The Department of Defense itself declared that the threat of climate change will affect the Pentagon's ability to defend the Nation and poses immediate risk to U.S. national security. The CIA and the Department of State have already identified climate change as a national security challenge, yet Congress continues to refuse to act on this issue.
20   We are already experiencing the impacts of climate change, from superstorms in the U.S. to devastating droughts in the Middle East. As climate change continues to strain economies and societies across the world, it will only create additional resource burdens and impact the way our military executes its missions, forcing our military to spend more on crisis prevention, humanitarian assistance, and government stabilization. We must act
25   now.

30. The primary goal of the passage is to
(A) chide
(B) commend
(C) convince
(D) inform
(E) refute

31. The passage contains information to answer all of the following questions EXCEPT
(A) Why does climate change lead to conflict?
(B) How does climate change lead to violence?
(C) How does climate change affect the U.S.?
(D) What does the government think about climate change?
(E) What can average citizens do to fight climate change?

32. The attitude of the author toward Congress (line 19) is best described as
(A) admiring
(B) critical
(C) deferential
(D) mischievous
(E) reverent

33. The writer's style is best described as
(A) circuitous
(B) emphatic
(C) euphemistic
(D) lyrical
(E) ornate

34. According to the author, climate change should be taken seriously because
(A) the problem affects mostly America
(B) scientists have made repeated warnings
(C) Congress declared it a security challenge
(D) it is worsened by political instability
(E) various government agencies already agree about its seriousness

35. Which of the following best states the main idea of the passage?
(A) Climate change is inevitable.
(B) Pollution worsens climate change.
(C) America must address climate change.
(D) The country must stop spending on aid.
(E) America should provide more aid to those displaced by rising sea levels.

GO ON TO THE NEXT PAGE.

The Tutorverse

> Two days later, toward noon, Sandy began to show signs of excitement and feverish expectancy. She said we were approaching the ogre's castle. I was surprised into an uncomfortable shock. The object of our quest had gradually dropped out of my mind; this sudden resurrection of it made it seem quite a real and startling thing for a moment,
> 5 and roused up in me a smart interest. Sandy's excitement increased every moment; and so did mine, for that sort of thing is contagious. My heart got to thumping. You can't reason with your heart; it has its own laws, and thumps about things which the intellect scorns. Presently, when Sandy slid from the horse, motioned me to stop, and went creeping stealthily, with her head bent nearly to her knees, toward a row of bushes that
> 10 bordered a ditch, the thumpings grew stronger and quicker. And they kept it up while she was gaining her ambush and getting her glimpse over the hedges; and also while I was creeping to her side on my knees. Her eyes were burning now, as she pointed with her finger, and said in a panting whisper:
> "The castle! The castle! Lo, where it looms!"

36. Why was the narrator surprised in line 2?
    (A) The ogres had crept around stealthily.
    (B) The horses stopped suddenly and uncomfortably.
    (C) Sandy's reaction unexpectedly reminded him of his mission.
    (D) The narrator did not expect to accomplish his goals so quickly.
    (E) Sandy was surprised by the row of bushes that appeared in front of them.

37. Without changing the author's meaning, "smart" (line 5) could be replaced by
    (A) dull
    (B) keen
    (C) clever
    (D) neutral
    (E) intelligent

38. The mood of the narrator can best be described as
    (A) pensive
    (B) nostalgic
    (C) brooding
    (D) infuriated
    (E) exhilarated

39. "Her eyes were burning" (line 12) probably means that Sandy was
    (A) filled with anger and hatred
    (B) surprised after being ambushed
    (C) irritated by something in her eyes
    (D) completely captivated by what she saw
    (E) upset with the narrator's incompetence

40. In the passage, "creeping," "ambush," and "whisper" (lines 9, 11, and 13) suggest that
    (A) Sandy and the narrator wish to remain unnoticed
    (B) Sandy and the narrator's horses are very nervous
    (C) Sandy and the narrator are unable to contain themselves
    (D) Sandy and the narrator desire to be friends with the ogres
    (E) Sandy and the narrator wish to avoid the ogres completely

STOP
IF YOU FINISH BEFORE TIME IS UP,
CHECK YOUR WORK IN THIS SECTION ONLY.
YOU MAY NOT TURN TO ANY OTHER SECTION.

The Tutorverse

SECTION 3
60 Questions

There are two different types of questions in this section: synonyms and analogies. Read the directions and sample question for each type.

Synonyms

Each of the questions that follow consist of one capitalized word. Each word is followed by five words or phrases. Select the one word or phrase whose meaning is closest to the word in capital letters.

Sample Question:

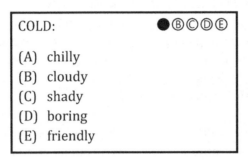

```
COLD:                    ●ⒷⒸⒹⒺ

(A)  chilly
(B)  cloudy
(C)  shady
(D)  boring
(E)  friendly
```

---

1. ATYPICAL:
    (A) extensive
    (B) ominous
    (C) regular
    (D) irresistible
    (E) strange

2. PROFESSIONAL:
    (A) honest
    (B) skillful
    (C) unstable
    (D) ceremonial
    (E) rudimentary

3. JUSTIFY:
    (A) tear down
    (B) support
    (C) judge
    (D) dominate
    (E) abhor

4. VEHEMENT:
    (A) passionate
    (B) disinterested
    (C) exotic
    (D) relaxed
    (E) tolerant

5. TECHNIQUE:
    (A) tool
    (B) supervisor
    (C) method
    (D) schematics
    (E) equipment

6. NUISANCE:
    (A) misbehaving child
    (B) special event
    (C) accidental occurrence
    (D) irritating circumstance
    (E) convenient location

7. AUTHENTIC:
    (A) genuine
    (B) duplicate
    (C) forged
    (D) autographed
    (E) enhanced

8. LITERAL:
    (A) long
    (B) exact
    (C) misspelled
    (D) uninteresting
    (E) entertaining

GO ON TO THE NEXT PAGE.

The Tutorverse

9. PREDICT:
   (A) confide
   (B) forecast
   (C) recollect
   (D) err
   (E) surprise

10. VARIATION:
    (A) confusion
    (B) penalty
    (C) constant
    (D) difference
    (E) biology

11. ABDICATE:
    (A) impoverish
    (B) give up
    (C) inspire
    (D) send away
    (E) tell how

12. DIPLOMACY:
    (A) strong disagreement
    (B) intense debate
    (C) tactful behavior
    (D) unwilling compromise
    (E) total immunity

13. PHILANTHROPIC:
    (A) destitute
    (B) wealthy
    (C) selfish
    (D) helpful
    (E) musical

14. USURP:
    (A) seize from
    (B) corroborate with
    (C) emigrate from
    (D) yield to
    (E) deceive

15. QUARANTINE:
    (A) search
    (B) isolate
    (C) delude
    (D) display
    (E) appease

16. INTERMITTENT:
    (A) territorial
    (B) inconvenient
    (C) surly
    (D) fair
    (E) irregular

17. REPARATION:
    (A) amends
    (B) pretension
    (C) alliteration
    (D) mistakes
    (E) dedication

18. EMBARGO:
    (A) glorify
    (B) negotiate
    (C) shriek
    (D) restrict
    (E) permit

19. REPRIEVE:
    (A) prejudice
    (B) rest
    (C) encore
    (D) recurrence
    (E) generosity

20. ERRATIC:
    (A) arcane
    (B) ineligible
    (C) fitful
    (D) predictable
    (E) treachery

21. ANATHEMA:
    (A) musical lyric
    (B) powerful blessing
    (C) unreasonable question
    (D) sarcastic response
    (E) offensive word

22. LAUDABLE:
    (A) pitiful
    (B) praiseworthy
    (C) lifelike
    (D) talented
    (E) perpetual

GO ON TO THE NEXT PAGE.

The Tutorverse

23. ASTUTE:
   (A) intelligent
   (B) deliberate
   (C) foolish
   (D) uncomfortable
   (E) accidental

24. BELIE:
   (A) contradict
   (B) renovate
   (C) comprise
   (D) signify
   (E) recline

25. DIFFIDENT:
   (A) reliable
   (B) unique
   (C) reserved
   (D) regal
   (E) negligible

26. FACETIOUS:
   (A) thoughtful
   (B) atrocious
   (C) flippant
   (D) prodigious
   (E) productive

27. REMUNERATION:
   (A) fair compensation
   (B) avoidable obsolescence
   (C) incessant repetition
   (D) undivided attention
   (E) high performance

28. BLATANT:
   (A) latent
   (B) obvious
   (C) similar
   (D) furtive
   (E) flaunted

29. BLITHE:
   (A) becoming
   (B) young
   (C) carefree
   (D) agile
   (E) gratifying

30. OBSTREPEROUS:
   (A) incomprehensible
   (B) absurd
   (C) disruptive
   (D) culpable
   (E) repugnant

GO ON TO THE NEXT PAGE.

The Tutorverse

Analogies

The questions that follow ask you to find relationships between words. For each question, select the answer choice that best completes the meaning of the sentence.

Sample Question:

Jump is to leap as:	●ⒷⒸⒹⒺ

(A) twirl is to spin
(B) dance is to dancer
(C) runner is to race
(D) hot is to cold
(E) happy is to sad

Choice (A) is the best answer because jump and leap are synonyms, just as twirl and spin are synonyms. This choice states a relationship that is most like the relationship between jump and leap.

---

31. Gaunt is to plump as
    (A) unhealthy is to body
    (B) abundant is to scarce
    (C) large is to huge
    (D) gauntlet is to run
    (E) skinny is to thin

32. Plastic is to wrap as
    (A) preserve is to persevere
    (B) anchor is to metal
    (C) hang is to hanger
    (D) damage is to destroy
    (E) glass is to ceiling

33. Spark is to inferno as
    (A) ash is to smolder
    (B) extinguisher is to firefighter
    (C) engine is to ladder
    (D) boat is to wake
    (E) ship is to sail

34. Innovate is to copy as
    (A) approach is to crouch
    (B) author is to transcribe
    (C) inventor is to invention
    (D) refuse is to thank
    (E) refute is to confirm

35. Illness is to virus as
    (A) breeze is to fan
    (B) mug is to coffee
    (C) bowl is to cereal
    (D) bottle is to soda
    (E) plate is to food

36. Student is to lesson as
    (A) dog is to trick
    (B) instructor is to textbook
    (C) pet is to leash
    (D) child is to play
    (E) classmate is to principal

37. Doctor is to scalpel as
    (A) lumberjack is to chainsaw
    (B) nurse is to phlebotomist
    (C) typographer is to quill
    (D) cleaner is to household
    (E) professor is to grade

38. Furious is to angry as
    (A) child is to adult
    (B) man is to woman
    (C) capable is to able
    (D) worried is to annoyed
    (E) elated is to happy

GO ON TO THE NEXT PAGE.

The Tutorverse

39. Forth is to back as
   (A) fro is to to
   (B) bird is to dog
   (C) water is to cat
   (D) employ is to work
   (E) cook is to eat

40. Murder is to genocide as
   (A) birth is to death
   (B) remove is to obliterate
   (C) behead is to guillotine
   (D) flee is to escape
   (E) destroy is to befall

41. Balloon is to float as
   (A) vehicle is to transport
   (B) despot is to tyranny
   (C) sailboat is to sailor
   (D) police is to crime
   (E) truck is to trucker

42. Accountant is to calculator as
   (A) telemarketer is to phone
   (B) salesman is to door
   (C) banker is to teller
   (D) headmaster is to school
   (E) pirate is to parrot

43. Bed is to sleep as
   (A) engine is to parts
   (B) electrician is to electricity
   (C) read is to book
   (D) newspaper is to inform
   (E) entertain is to magazine

44. Grow is to beard as
   (A) buoy is to float
   (B) scroll is to read
   (C) draw is to picture
   (D) imagine is to memo
   (E) docking is to dock

45. Usher is to ticket as
   (A) driver is to garage
   (B) pilot is to airplane
   (C) secretary is to office
   (D) clerk is to folder
   (E) cashier is to money

46. Orator is to speak as
   (A) mime is to enunciate
   (B) burglar is to apprehend
   (C) maligner is to slander
   (D) taxidermist is to sequester
   (E) ally is to enemy

47. Forgotten is to forget as
   (A) ride is to ridden
   (B) buy is to bought
   (C) come is to came
   (D) drink is to drunk
   (E) given is to give

48. Roof is to shingle as
   (A) scoop is to bowl
   (B) series is to episode
   (C) lid is to jar
   (D) gutter is to siding
   (E) sound is to noise

49. Lettuce is to salad as
   (A) macaroni is to cheese
   (B) dressing is to vinegar
   (C) bread is to sliced
   (D) crumb is to loaf
   (E) banana is to peel

50. Wrench is to pipe as
   (A) plunger is to unclog
   (B) typewriter is to printer
   (C) quill is to parchment
   (D) tool is to toolbox
   (E) scroll is to ancient

51. Equation is to number as
   (A) variable is to decimal
   (B) numerator is to denominator
   (C) divide is to multiply
   (D) decimal is to integer
   (E) fraction is to numerator

52. Palpable is to apparent as
   (A) irreverent is to decent
   (B) vestigial is to functional
   (C) dubious is to doubtful
   (D) imperious is to emperor
   (E) fluent is to orator

GO ON TO THE NEXT PAGE.

53. Locomotive is to vehicle as influenza is to
    (A) treatment
    (B) ache
    (C) plasma
    (D) malady
    (E) respiration

54. Shampoo is to hair as
    (A) soap is to body
    (B) bathroom is to bathtub
    (C) shower is to vapor
    (D) blender is to kitchen
    (E) towel is to robe

55. Translucent is to opaque as unconscionable is to
    (A) appalling
    (B) horrendous
    (C) clear
    (D) wonderful
    (E) murky

56. Undertaker is to casket as executioner is to
    (A) verdict
    (B) eviscerate
    (C) guillotine
    (D) talisman
    (E) abhorrence

57. Protract is to extend as succumb is to
    (A) shorten
    (B) decrease
    (C) grovel
    (D) surrender
    (E) fight

58. Crop is to bumper as bun is to
    (A) ketchup
    (B) mustard
    (C) sauerkraut
    (D) hotdog
    (E) barbeque

59. Thread is to cloth as
    (A) mind is to matter
    (B) coat is to hot
    (C) cell is to organ
    (D) weave is to pattern
    (E) magazine is to page

60. Obey is to obeys as
    (A) sick is to sickly
    (B) invent is to invented
    (C) invent is to invents
    (D) help is to helping
    (E) help is to helpless

STOP
IF YOU FINISH BEFORE TIME IS UP,
CHECK YOUR WORK IN THIS SECTION ONLY.
YOU MAY NOT TURN TO ANY OTHER SECTION.

The Tutorverse

SECTION 4
25 Questions

There are five suggested answers after each problem in this section. Solve each problem in your head or in the space provided to the right of the problem. Then look at the suggested answers and pick the best one.

<u>Note</u>: Any figures or shapes that accompany problems in Section 1 are drawn as accurately as possible EXCEPT when it is stated that the figure is NOT drawn to scale.

Sample Question:

```
4 ÷ 2 =                    ●ⒷⒸⒹⒺ

              (A) 2
              (B) 4
              (C) 6
              (D) 8
              (E) 10
```

DO WORK IN THIS SPACE

1. A store put a pair of pants on sale for 30% off. When it didn't sell, the store further discounted the price 30% off the sale price. What percent of the original price does the pair of pants cost now?
   (A) 40%
   (B) 45%
   (C) 49%
   (D) 51%
   (E) 62%

2. Lori threw a baseball in the air. The baseball's height, y, in meters, with respect to time, x, in seconds, can be modeled by the function $y = -3x^2 + 6x + 18$. How long after Lori threw the ball, in seconds, did the baseball reach its maximum height?
   (A) 1
   (B) 2
   (C) 6
   (D) 18
   (E) 21

3. What is the circumference, in terms of π, of a circle with area 16π meters?
   (A) 4π meters
   (B) 8π meters
   (C) 16π meters
   (D) 32π meters
   (E) 64π meters

GO ON TO THE NEXT PAGE.

The Tutorverse

DO WORK IN THIS SPACE

4. $(-64) + (-18) - 80 =$
   (A) -2
   (B) -46
   (C) -82
   (D) -126
   (E) -162

5. What is the greatest common factor of $48m^4$, $24m^8$, and $30m^6$?
   (A) $6m^4$
   (B) $6m^8$
   (C) $12m^4$
   (D) $12m^8$
   (E) $24m^8$

6. What is the hundreds digit in the largest odd, 5-digit number that can be formed from the digits 7, 0, 8, 2, 6, where each digit is used only once?
   (A) 8
   (B) 7
   (C) 6
   (D) 2
   (E) 0

7. A certain type of bacteria has an initial population of 10^3. Each hour, each bacterium grows into 10^2 bacteria. How many bacteria are there after 3 hours?
   (A) 10^5
   (B) 10^9
   (C) 10^{15}
   (D) 10^{18}
   (E) 10^{24}

8. Ali received a raise in hourly pay from \$10 to \$15 at his part-time job. In how many fewer hours can he earn \$300 as a result of the raise?
   (A) 10
   (B) 12
   (C) 15
   (D) 18
   (E) 20

GO ON TO THE NEXT PAGE.

The Tutorverse

DO WORK IN THIS SPACE

9. What is the equation of the function displayed in the table below?
   (A) $y = -x + 4$
   (B) $y = -\frac{1}{3}x + 1$
   (C) $y = \frac{1}{3}x + 4$
   (D) $y = 3x + 1$
   (E) $y = -3x + 1$

x	y
-1	4
1	-2
3	-8
5	-14

10. If $a + b$ is divisible by 2, which of the following must also be divisible by 2?
    (A) $(a \times b) + 2$
    (B) $a + 2b$
    (C) $2a + b$
    (D) $2a + 2b$
    (E) $\frac{(a+b)}{2}$

11. Jill threw a baseball. The ball's height, y, in feet, with respect to time, x, in seconds, can be modeled by the function $y = -x^2 + 5x + 6$. How many seconds does it take the ball to hit the ground after it was thrown?
    (A) −6
    (B) −1
    (C) 1
    (D) 5
    (E) 6

12. Eight bins hold basketballs, and no bins are empty. If two bins hold the same number of basketballs, and the rest hold different numbers, what is the minimum number of basketballs in all eight bins?
    (A) 28
    (B) 29
    (C) 30
    (D) 31
    (E) 32

13. The average weight of 5 cats is 9 ounces and the average weight of 3 dogs is 25 ounces. What is the average weight, in ounces, of all 8 animals?
    (A) 15
    (B) 16
    (C) 17
    (D) 18
    (E) 60

GO ON TO THE NEXT PAGE.

The Tutorverse

DO WORK IN THIS SPACE

14. The formula for an arithmetic sequence is $a_n = a_1 + (n-1)d$. Which equation is the result of solving for n?

    (A) $n = d(a_n - a_1)$

    (B) $n = \dfrac{a_n}{d - a_1}$

    (C) $n = \dfrac{a_n - a_1 + d}{d}$

    (D) $n = (d-1)(a_n + a_1)$

    (E) $n = \dfrac{a_n}{a_1} + d$

15. In the figure shown, the triangle is isosceles. What is the value of x?

    (A) 36

    (B) 46

    (C) 72

    (D) 88

    (E) 92

    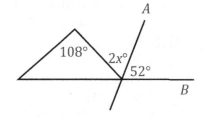

16. Which expression is equivalent to $\sqrt{\sqrt{x^{16}}}$?

    (A) x^2

    (B) x^4

    (C) x^8

    (D) x

    (E) $x^{\frac{1}{2}}$

17. Point P is at an unknown point in the xy-plane. It is translated 5 units left and 4 units up onto point P', which is located at $(0, 0)$. What were the coordinates of point P?

    (A) $(4, 5)$

    (B) $(5, 4)$

    (C) $(-5, 4)$

    (D) $(5, -4)$

    (E) $(-5, -4)$

18. Maria makes scarves and sells them for $12 each. Materials to make each scarf cost $8. How many scarves does Maria need to make to earn $500?

    (A) 25

    (B) 34

    (C) 42

    (D) 63

    (E) 125

GO ON TO THE NEXT PAGE.

The Tutorverse

DO WORK IN THIS SPACE

19. For the inequality $nx + 8 \le -12$, which value of n will result in the solution $4 \le x$?
    - (A) -5
    - (B) -4
    - (C) 0
    - (D) 4
    - (E) 5

20. What is the intersection of Set C, Set D, and Set E?

    Set C = {4, 6, 9, 15, 21}
    Set D = {6, 9, 15, 18, 20, 21}
    Set E = {6, 9, 15, 20, 21, 23}

    - (A) {6, 9}
    - (B) {6, 9, 15}
    - (C) {9, 15, 21}
    - (D) {6, 9, 15, 21}
    - (E) {4, 6, 9, 15, 18, 20, 21, 23}

21. Which of the following must be true if a rectangle with side lengths of L and W has an area of 48 and W is less than L?
    - (A) $2L + 2W = 48$
    - (B) $L^2 + W^2 = 48$
    - (C) $W < L + 48$
    - (D) $L \times W = 48$
    - (E) $W = 4$

22. A tree casts a shadow 35 feet long. If a 5'6" woman nearby casts an 11-foot shadow, how tall, in feet, is the tree?
    - (A) $17\frac{1}{2}$
    - (B) $17\frac{9}{11}$
    - (C) $29\frac{1}{2}$
    - (D) $68\frac{3}{4}$
    - (E) 70

23. Tom can assemble 3 toy cars in an hour while Bette can assemble 5 toy cars in an hour. If they both work together, how long will it take them to assemble 30 toy cars?
    - (A) 10 hours and 6 minutes
    - (B) 6 hours and 10 minutes
    - (C) 4 hours
    - (D) 3 hours and 45 minutes
    - (E) 3 hours

GO ON TO THE NEXT PAGE.

The Tutorverse

DO WORK IN THIS SPACE

24. The ages of the first ten people to enter an amusement park one day
    were 8, 38, 36, 5, 3, 65, 62, 37, 31, and 5. What was the mode of their
    ages?
    (A) 3
    (B) 5
    (C) 8
    (D) 61
    (E) 62

25. An airplane travels at a steady velocity in non-windy conditions. It takes
    4 hours to travel 2,000 miles directly against the wind current and 6
    hours to travel 3,600 miles in the same direction as the wind current.
    Which system of equations can be solved to find the airplane's velocity in
    non-windy conditions, v, and the wind's velocity, w? (*Note: distance =
    velocity × time*)
    (A) $v - w = 2{,}000$
         $v + w = 3{,}600$
    (B) $v - w = 600$
         $v + w = 500$
    (C) $v - w = 500$
         $v + w = 600$
    (D) $v - w = 3{,}600$
         $v + w = 2{,}000$
    (E) $v - w = 4$
         $v + w = 6$

STOP
**IF YOU FINISH BEFORE TIME IS UP,
CHECK YOUR WORK IN THIS SECTION ONLY.
YOU MAY NOT TURN TO ANY OTHER SECTION.**

The Tutorverse

SECTION 5
16 Questions

Those who came before us made certain that this country rode the first waves of the industrial revolutions, the first waves of modern invention, and the first wave of nuclear power, and this generation does not intend to founder in the backwash of the coming age of space. We mean to be a part of it – we mean to lead it. For the eyes of the world now look into space, to the moon and to the planets beyond, and we have vowed that we shall not see it governed by a hostile flag of conquest, but by a banner of freedom and peace. We have vowed that we shall not see space filled with weapons of mass destruction, but with instruments of knowledge and understanding.

Yet the vows of this Nation can only be fulfilled if we in this Nation are first, and, therefore, we intend to be first. In short, our leadership in science and in industry, our hopes for peace and security, our obligations to ourselves as well as others, all require us to make this effort, to solve these mysteries, to solve them for the good of all men, and to become the world's leading space-faring nation.

We set sail on this new sea because there is new knowledge to be gained, and new rights to be won, and they must be won and used for the progress of all people. For space science, like nuclear science and all technology, has no conscience of its own. Whether it will become a force for good or ill depends on man, and only if the United States occupies a position of pre-eminence can we help decide whether this new ocean will be a sea of peace or a new terrifying theater of war. I do not say that we should or will go unprotected against the hostile misuse of space any more than we go unprotected against the hostile use of land or sea, but I do say that space can be explored and mastered without feeding the fires of war, without repeating the mistakes that man has made in extending his writ around this globe of ours.

There is no strife, no prejudice, no national conflict in outer space as yet. Its hazards are hostile to us all. Its conquest deserves the best of all mankind, and its opportunity for peaceful cooperation many never come again.

We choose to go to the moon. We choose to go to the moon in this decade and do the other things, not because they are easy, but because they are hard, because that goal will serve to organize and measure the best of our energies and skills, because that challenge is one that we are willing to accept, one we are unwilling to postpone, and one which we intend to win, and the others, too.

1. The "new sea" (line 14) refers to
    (A) the new frontier of space
    (B) a newly discovered body of water
    (C) the hazards of any new exploration
    (D) the amount of knowledge to be gained
    (E) a possible location of a violent conflict

2. As used in line 19, "theater" most nearly means
    (A) cinema
    (B) dramatic
    (C) hall
    (D) realm
    (E) ocean

3. Based on the passage, the author would most likely recommend which of the following?
    (A) attempting to sail around the world without a plan
    (B) using a newly developed technology to conquer other countries
    (C) avoiding risks associated with a particularly difficult challenge
    (D) sharing the information learned from the exploration of a new land
    (E) keeping secret the knowledge gained from exploring a newly discovered planet

GO ON TO THE NEXT PAGE.

The Tutorverse

4. The author suggests that all of the following are reasons to explore space EXCEPT
   (A) to satisfy curiosity
   (B) the increase of knowledge and technology
   (C) to gain an advantage in future conflicts or wars
   (D) it will require people to join together and do their best
   (E) some challenges are worth attempting just for the sake of it

5. The author's tone in the last paragraph (lines 27-31) is best described as
   (A) belligerent
   (B) cautionary
   (C) flippant
   (D) impassioned
   (E) pessimistic

6. LIKELY:
   (A) adorable
   (B) unwieldy
   (C) loathsome
   (D) highly probable
   (E) completely unimaginable

7. BOLSTER:
   (A) build up
   (B) inhibit from
   (C) confine in
   (D) partition
   (E) provide to

8. MALIGNANT:
   (A) quick
   (B) beneficial
   (C) hurtful
   (D) ubiquitous
   (E) foreign

9. Insensitive is to numb as
   (A) unwavering is to constant
   (B) secure is to uncertain
   (C) mean is to nice
   (D) rude is to polite
   (E) bankrupt is to banker

10. Orderly is to cluttered as empathetic is to
    (A) pathetic
    (B) tragic
    (C) callous
    (D) telepathy
    (E) hopeless

11. Mammal is to mouse as snake is to
    (A) bird
    (B) chicken
    (C) amphibian
    (D) slither
    (E) reptile

12. Calories is to energy as
    (A) letter is to stamp
    (B) word is to song
    (C) handle is to hot
    (D) map is to globe
    (E) textbook is to knowledge

13. What is 20% of 20% of 200?
    (A) 4
    (B) 8
    (C) 40
    (D) 80
    (E) 128

14. What is the value of $(0.25 - 0.75)^3$?
    (A) −1.5
    (B) −0.125
    (C) 0
    (D) 0.125
    (E) 1.5

15. The diameter of a circle with area 36π is
    (A) 6
    (B) 12
    (C) 18
    (D) 36
    (E) 72

16. The line $-x + 2y = 6$ crosses the y-axis at
    (A) −1
    (B) 1
    (C) 2
    (D) 3
    (E) 6

The Tutorverse

Scoring the Diagnostic Practice Test (Form A)

Writing Sample – Unscored

Have a parent or trusted educator review the essay or story written for the writing sample. Important areas to focus on include organization, clarity of ideas, originality, and technical precision (spelling, grammar, etc.).

Sections 1-4 – Scored

Score the test using the answer sheet and referring to the answer key at the back of the book.

Step 1: For each section, record the number of questions answered correctly.

Step 2: For each section, record the number of questions answered incorrectly. Then, multiply that number by ¼ to calculate the penalty.

Section	Questions Correct
Quantitative *Section 1 + Section 4*	————
Reading *Section 2*	————
Verbal *Section 3*	————

Section	Questions Incorrect	Penalty
Quantitative *Section 1 + Section 4*	————	x 1/4 = ————
Reading *Section 2*	————	x 1/4 = ————
Verbal *Section 3*	————	x 1/4 = ————

Step 3: For each section, subtract the Penalty in *Step 2* from the Questions Correct in *Step 1*. This is the raw score. Note that the actual test will convert the raw score to a scaled score by comparing the student's performance with all other students in the same grade who took the test.

Section	Raw Score
Quantitative *Section 1 + Section 4*	————
Reading *Section 2*	————
Verbal *Section 3*	————

> **Consider**: How certain were you on the questions you guessed on? Should you have left those questions blank, instead? How should you change the way you guess and leave questions blank?

Carefully consider the results from the diagnostic practice test when forming a study plan. Remember, the Upper Level SSAT is given to students in grades 8-11. Unless the student has finished 11th grade, chances are that there is material on this test that he or she has not yet been taught. If this is the case, and the student would like to improve beyond what is expected of his or her grade, consider working with a tutor or teacher, who can help learn more about new topics.

Section 5 – Unscored

On the real test, the Experimental section will NOT be scored. Consider the student's performance on this section for practice purposes only. Did he or she do better on one section than other? Use this information along with the information from Sections 1-4 to form the study plan.

The Tutorverse

Quantitative

Overview

The Quantitative sections assess a student's command over various mathematics topics, including algebra, geometry, probability, statistics, and number theory.

There are two Quantitative sections on the Upper Level SSAT, both of which are scored.

On the Actual Test

Each of the two quantitative sections contain 25 questions (for a total of 50 math questions on the entire scored test).

Students have 30 minutes each to complete the two sections (for a total of 60 minutes on the entire scored test).

Every question in the Quantitative sections is multiple choice. There will be one question followed by five answer choices (A through E). Students are given blank space to the right of each question where they can do their work.

In This Practice Book

Below are the main content areas that are included in the Upper Level SSAT. A list of subtopics can be found in the table of contents.

- 🐢 Numbers Concepts & Operations
- 🐢 Algebra
- 🐢 Geometry & Measurements
- 🐢 Data Analysis & Probability

Considering the results of your diagnostic practice test, we recommend that students focus on the topics that are most challenging to them. Since there may be material in this workbook that they have not yet learned in school, we also encourage students to seek additional help from a trusted teacher or tutor to enhance their knowledge of those subjects.

Treat each question as you would questions on the real test. This means practicing whether or not to answer the question or leave it unanswered. **Remember**, on the actual test, answering a question correctly earns you 1 point, but answering a question incorrectly means you lose ¼ of a point. Therefore, attempt every question for the sake of practice (and read the online answer explanations), but try practicing leaving questions unanswered. Then, see whether or not you would have answered the question correctly.

The questions in each section are progressive, which means they start out easier, and become more and more difficult as they build on the concepts related to that topic. If students find that some questions are tricky, they should consider asking an educator for help. Don't be discouraged!

Tutorverse Tips!

You won't be able to use a calculator on the test. If, as you are answering a question, things start to get more and more complicated, take a step back and think about what the question is asking you to do. If necessary, use the answer choices themselves to help you arrive at the correct answer by plugging them into formulas or expressions.

The Tutorverse

You do **not** have to memorize customary unit conversion tables (for instance, the number of feet in a mile), as any such information will be provided. However, metric unit conversions will **not** be provided (i.e. the number of milliliters in a liter).

Guessing

Knowing whether or not to guess can be tricky. The Upper Level SSAT gives you 1 point for each question that is answered correctly. However, if you answer a question incorrectly, ¼ of a point will be deducted from your total score (see example below).

The formula for determining the raw score is:
(Number of Questions Answered Correctly × 1) – (Number of Questions Answered Incorrectly × ¼)

No points will be awarded or deducted for questions that are left unanswered. Therefore, answer easy questions first, and come back to tougher questions later.

<u>How Guessing Impacts A Score</u>

Since there are 150 scored questions (167 total questions – 1 writing prompt – 16 experimental questions), the highest possible raw score is 150 points. This would be awarded to students who answer all 150 questions correctly.

If a student answers 110 questions correctly **but answers 40 questions incorrectly**, he or she will have earned (110 × 1) – (40 × ¼), or 110 – 10 = 100 points.

If a student answers 110 questions correctly **but leaves 40 questions unanswered**, he or she will have earned (110 × 1) – (40 × 0), or 110 – 0 = 110 points.

Therefore, it is important to refrain from making wild guesses. Instead, try to use process of elimination to make an educated guess.

Number Concepts & Operations

Integers

1. What is the value of –27 + 39 – 12 + 45?
   (A) 99
   (B) 90
   (C) 84
   (D) 45
   (E) –45

2. Evaluate: (–25) + (–50) + 82 =
   (A) –75
   (B) –7
   (C) 7
   (D) 57
   (E) 107

3. Evaluate: (–44) + (–76) + 100 =
   (A) –120
   (B) –20
   (C) 32
   (D) 42
   (E) 68

4. Evaluate: (–35) – (–40) + 20 =
   (A) –55
   (B) –25
   (C) 15
   (D) 25
   (E) 55

5. Evaluate: –70 × –125 =
   (A) –8,750
   (B) –875
   (C) 170
   (D) 675
   (E) 8,750

6. Evaluate: 125 ÷ –5 =
   (A) –25
   (B) –5
   (C) 5
   (D) 12
   (E) 25

7. Evaluate: –16 × 15 × –14 =
   (A) –3,360
   (B) –3,375
   (C) –3,125
   (D) 3,375
   (E) 3,360

8. Evaluate: 5,000 ÷ –250 × 10 =
   (A) –250
   (B) –200
   (C) –20
   (D) 20
   (E) 200

Decimals

1. 0.2 × 50 =
   (A) 0.01
   (B) 0.1
   (C) 1
   (D) 10
   (E) 100

2. 0.5 × 0.4 =
   (A) 0.02
   (B) 0.2
   (C) 0.7
   (D) 2
   (E) 20

3. 0.09 × 1000 =
   (A) 0.009
   (B) 0.09
   (C) 9
   (D) 90
   (E) 900

4. What is the quotient of 7.2 and 0.3?
   (A) 0.24
   (B) 2.16
   (C) 2.4
   (D) 24
   (E) 240

The Tutorverse

5. What is the quotient of 5.12 and 0.2?
   (A) 256
   (B) 25.6
   (C) 10.24
   (D) 1.024
   (E) 0.256

6. What is the value of $(0.6 \times 0.4)^2$?
   (A) 0.0576
   (B) 0.24
   (C) 0.48
   (D) 0.576
   (E) 0.8

7. What is the value of $(0.75 - 0.2)^2$?
   (A) 71
   (B) 30.25
   (C) 0.71
   (D) 0.5329
   (E) 0.3025

8. What is the value of $(0.25 - 0.09)^2$?
   (A) 0.32
   (B) 0.256
   (C) 0.16
   (D) 0.0256
   (E) 0.016

9. Stephen purchased a baseball card at a yard sale for $5. When he looked up the value of the card online, he learned that the value was worth 0.45 times more than what he paid for it. What is the value of Stephen's baseball card?
   (A) $2.25
   (B) $2.75
   (C) $5.45
   (D) $7.25
   (E) $7.75

10. John finished a foot race in 11.56 seconds. This is 0.15 times less than his previous race time. What was his previous race time, in seconds?
   (A) 77
   (B) 65.4
   (C) 32.5
   (D) 14.4
   (E) 13.6

Fractions

1. All of the following products are equal EXCEPT
   (A) $4 \times \frac{1}{2}$
   (B) $6 \times \frac{1}{3}$
   (C) $8 \times \frac{1}{4}$
   (D) $10 \times \frac{3}{5}$
   (E) $20 \times \frac{1}{10}$

2. Eddie ran for $2\frac{2}{3}$ hours on Monday, $1\frac{1}{2}$ hours on Tuesday, and $1\frac{3}{4}$ hours on Wednesday. How many hours did Eddie run altogether?
   (A) $4\frac{1}{4}$
   (B) $4\frac{4}{5}$
   (C) $5\frac{1}{2}$
   (D) $5\frac{7}{12}$
   (E) $5\frac{11}{12}$

3. Which fraction is equivalent to $\left(\frac{5}{8}\right)^2 \div \frac{1}{4}$?
   (A) $\frac{25}{256}$
   (B) $\frac{25}{64}$
   (C) $\frac{16}{25}$
   (D) $\frac{25}{16}$
   (E) $\frac{64}{25}$

4. Which fraction is equivalent to $\left(\frac{2}{3}\right)^3 + \frac{2}{9}$?
   (A) $\frac{8}{9}$
   (B) $\frac{5}{9}$
   (C) $\frac{14}{27}$
   (D) $\frac{11}{27}$
   (E) $\frac{1}{3}$

The Tutorverse

5. Linda is making cookies in 3 different flavors. The amount of sugar, in cups, required for one batch of each recipe is shown below.

Chocolate Chip	Oatmeal Raisin	Peanut Butter
$1\frac{2}{3}$	$2\frac{5}{6}$	$3\frac{2}{9}$

What is the total amount of sugar, in cups, needed to make one batch each of all 3 flavors of cookies?

(A) $7\frac{13}{18}$

(B) $7\frac{1}{2}$

(C) 7

(D) $6\frac{13}{18}$

(E) $6\frac{1}{2}$

6. Joe bought a bag containing 10 cups of dog food. During the day, he poured out $3\frac{1}{2}$, $2\frac{1}{5}$, and $\frac{1}{10}$ cups of food. At the end of the day, how much food, in cups, is left in the bag?

(A) $5\frac{3}{17}$

(B) $5\frac{4}{5}$

(C) $4\frac{1}{8}$

(D) $4\frac{1}{5}$

(E) $4\frac{14}{17}$

7. What is the value of $\frac{1}{3}\times\frac{3}{5}\div\frac{5}{6}$?

(A) $\frac{5}{24}$

(B) $\frac{6}{25}$

(C) $\frac{3}{10}$

(D) $\frac{5}{12}$

(E) $\frac{17}{30}$

8. Tiffany ran for $\frac{3}{4}$ hour on Monday. On Friday, she ran for $\frac{3}{8}$ of that time. What fraction of an hour did Tiffany run on Friday?

(A) $\frac{9}{8}$

(B) $\frac{3}{8}$

(C) $\frac{9}{32}$

(D) $\frac{1}{2}$

(E) $\frac{6}{32}$

9. Use the chart below to answer the following question.

How the Millers Spend Their Monthly Income

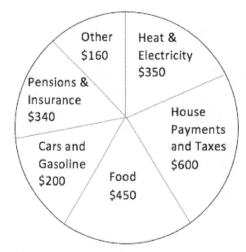

What fraction of the Miller's income is spent on house payments and taxes?

(A) $\frac{1}{6}$

(B) $\frac{1}{5}$

(C) $\frac{2}{7}$

(D) $\frac{7}{20}$

(E) $\frac{3}{5}$

10. The table below displays the total number of times Roger attempted to hit a baseball, as well as the number of actual hits.

Day	Attempts	Hits
1	37	6
2	28	8
3	24	4
4	36	9
5	40	3

What fraction of the attempts did Roger miss on Day 4 if every attempt resulted in a hit or a miss?

(A) $\frac{3}{4}$

(B) $\frac{1}{2}$

(C) $\frac{1}{4}$

(D) $\frac{1}{5}$

(E) $\frac{1}{6}$

11. If $\frac{5}{8}$ of m is 15, what is $\frac{3}{8}$ of $4m$?

(A) 24
(B) 32
(C) 36
(D) 40
(E) 96

12. An electronics store sold $\frac{3}{5}$ of its inventory of video games one week. If there are still 180 games in stock at the end of the week, how many games were there at the beginning of the week?

(A) 160
(B) 225
(C) 300
(D) 450
(E) 900

13. The stock market dropped by 25% on Monday but rebounded back to its original level on Tuesday. By what fraction of the Monday price did the stock market increase on Tuesday?

(A) $\frac{1}{4}$
(B) $\frac{1}{3}$
(C) $\frac{2}{5}$
(D) $\frac{3}{4}$
(E) 1

Percents

1. The owner of a horse ranch sold 30% of his property to his neighbor. Later that year, he sold 15% of the remainder of his property to another neighbor. What percent of the original property does he now have?

(A) 40.5%
(B) 45.0%
(C) 45.5%
(D) 55.0%
(E) 59.5%

2. A store offers a 20% discount on all tee-shirts. If a tee-shirt has an original price of $25.50, which of the following is the closest price after the discount is taken?

(A) $5.10
(B) $19.10
(C) $19.60
(D) $20.40
(E) $21.40

3. Mika purchased a television for $650. After two years, the value of the television had decreased 40%. What is the value of Mika's television two years after her purchase?

(A) $390
(B) $340
(C) $300
(D) $280
(E) $260

4. The table below displays the total number of times Roger attempted to hit a baseball, as well as the number of actual hits.

Day	Attempts	Hits
1	37	6
2	28	8
3	24	4
4	36	9
5	40	3

Which of the following is closest to the percent of total attempts Roger hit over the 5 days if every attempt resulted in a hit or a miss?

(A) 6%
(B) 10%
(C) 18%
(D) 20%
(E) 30%

5. James bought 3 shirts for $16.00 each and 4 pairs of socks for $3.50 each. There is an 8% sales tax added to James's purchase. What is the cost of James's purchase after tax?

(A) $49.50
(B) $60.95
(C) $62.00
(D) $66.96
(E) $72.50

The Tutorverse

6. Use the chart below to answer the following question.

How the Millers Spend Their Monthly Income

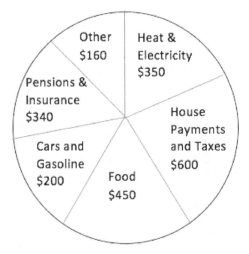

The amount the Millers spend on food is what percent of the amount they spend on house payments and taxes?
(A) 25%
(B) 30%
(C) 50%
(D) 75%
(E) 80%

7. What percent of 5 hours is 5 minutes and 15 seconds?
(A) 0.25%
(B) 1.03%
(C) 1.5%
(D) 1.72%
(E) 1.75%

8. What is 15% of 30% of 840?
(A) 3.78
(B) 37.8
(C) 38.6
(D) 137.8
(E) 378

9. 22 is 5% of
(A) 4.4
(B) 22
(C) 44
(D) 220
(E) 440

10. A store held a 40% off sale. If a game console has a sale price of $150, what was the original price?
(A) $250
(B) $300
(C) $375
(D) $400
(E) $450

11. Approximately what percent of 8 yards is 4 feet and 3 inches?
(A) 18%
(B) 28%
(C) 32%
(D) 53%
(E) 54%

12. What is 16% of 24% of 460?
(A) 17.664
(B) 28.675
(C) 36.5
(D) 124.6
(E) 184

13. After a 7% sales tax is applied, a shirt costs $27.82. What is the price of the shirt before tax?
(A) $20.82
(B) $25.75
(C) $25.87
(D) $26.00
(E) $30.12

14. A jacket costs $42.50 plus 6.5% sales tax. What is the cost of the jacket after tax, rounded to the nearest cent?
(A) $38.52
(B) $39.74
(C) $42.57
(D) $45.26
(E) $46.50

15. A furniture store is having a sale for 40% off everything in the store. A chair is marked down an additional 20% off the sale price. If the original price of the chair is $45.00, what is the final sale price of the chair?
(A) $3.60
(B) $17.60
(C) $18.00
(D) $21.60
(E) $27.00

The Tutorverse

Order of Operations

1. Which is the value of the expression
    $2^2 + [7 \div (4 + 3)]$?
    (A) 3
    (B) 5
    (C) 6
    (D) 7
    (E) $8\frac{3}{4}$

2. Which is the value of the expression
    $(4 + 3^2) - 7 \times \frac{1}{2}$?
    (A) $45\frac{1}{2}$
    (B) 21
    (C) $9\frac{1}{2}$
    (D) $3\frac{1}{2}$
    (E) 3

3. Which is the value of the expression
    $100 \div (2^3 - 3) \times 2$?
    (A) 50
    (B) 40
    (C) $16\frac{2}{3}$
    (D) $12\frac{1}{2}$
    (E) 10

4. Which is the value of the expression
    $4^3 \div 4^2 + 8 \times 9$?
    (A) 64
    (B) 72
    (C) 76
    (D) 88
    (E) 108

5. Which is the value of the expression
    $80 \div 4^2 + (10 - 6)$?
    (A) 4
    (B) 9
    (C) 15
    (D) 16
    (E) 19

6. Which is the value of the expression
    $(20 + 6) \times (20 - 6)$?
    (A) 514
    (B) 400
    (C) 364
    (D) 356
    (E) 134

7. Which is the value of the expression
    $10 \times 4^2 - (9 + 2)$?
    (A) 50
    (B) 149
    (C) 153
    (D) 275
    (E) 1,589

8. Which is the value of the expression
    $8 \times (9 + 7) - 3^3$?
    (A) 52
    (B) 70
    (C) 72
    (D) 101
    (E) 119

9. Which is the value of the expression
    $11 - \left(\frac{1}{5} + \frac{3}{10}\right) \div 6$?
    (A) $1\frac{3}{4}$
    (B) $10\frac{1}{2}$
    (C) $10\frac{11}{12}$
    (D) $10\frac{14}{15}$
    (E) $11\frac{1}{2}$

10. Which is the value of the expression
    $20 \div 5 + 5^3 - 10$?
    (A) 119
    (B) 110
    (C) 99
    (D) 80
    (E) 19

The Tutorverse

Number Theory

1. If a number is divisible by 6 and 7, then it is also divisible by which of the following numbers?
   (A) 4
   (B) 12
   (C) 13
   (D) 21
   (E) 28

2. What is the least common multiple of 12 and 28?
   (A) 4
   (B) 42
   (C) 56
   (D) 84
   (E) 336

3. How many 2-digit factors does 105 have?
   (A) 1
   (B) 2
   (C) 3
   (D) 4
   (E) 5

4. If $x - y$ is divisible by 3, which of the following must also be divisible by 3?
   (A) $x - y + 3$
   (B) $3x - y$
   (C) $x - 3y$
   (D) $x + y$
   (E) $\frac{(x-y)}{3}$

5. If 6 is a factor of m, which of the following must also be factors of m?
   (A) 2 and 3
   (B) 5
   (C) 4 and 6
   (D) 2, 3, and 12
   (E) 12 and 18

6. If $\sqrt{a}$ is an irrational number, which of the following values must result in a rational number when multiplied by $\sqrt{a}$?
   (A) $\sqrt{\frac{1}{a}}$
   (B) $\sqrt{a^2}$
   (C) a
   (D) a^2
   (E) a^3

7. If c is an even integer and d is an odd integer, which of the following statements must be true?
   (A) $c \times d$ is greater than 0
   (B) $c \times d$ is an odd integer
   (C) $c + d$ is an even integer
   (D) $c - d$ is an odd integer
   (E) $\frac{c \cdot d}{2}$ is an even integer

8. Which of the following statements must be true if g, h, and i are consecutive integers and $g < h < i$?
   (A) $\frac{g + h + i}{3}$ is an integer
   (B) $\frac{g - h - i}{3}$ is an integer
   (C) $g + h + i$ is odd
   (D) $g + h + i$ is even
   (E) $g - h - i$ is less than zero

Rules of Divisibility

1. $567 \div 7 =$
   (A) $\frac{5}{7} + \frac{6}{7} + \frac{7}{7}$
   (B) $\frac{500}{700} + \frac{60}{70} + \frac{7}{7}$
   (C) $\frac{500}{7} + \frac{60}{7} + \frac{7}{7}$
   (D) $\frac{500}{7} \times \frac{60}{7} \times \frac{7}{7}$
   (E) $\frac{5}{7} \times \frac{6}{7} \times \frac{7}{7}$

2. $2x + y$ represents a positive number divisible by 11. Which of the following must also be divisible by 11?
   (A) $\frac{2}{11}(x + y)$
   (B) $\frac{1}{11}(2x + y)$
   (C) $22x + y$
   (D) $2x + 11y$
   (E) $(5)2x + (5)y$

The Tutorverse

3. If $2a + 3b$ represents a positive number divisible by 7, which of the following must also be divisible by 7?
(A) $3a + 4b$
(B) $4a + 3b$
(C) $\frac{2}{7}(a) + \frac{3}{7}(b)$
(D) $21a + 3b$
(E) $14a + 14b$

4. $123 \div 3 =$
(A) $\frac{1}{3} + \frac{2}{3} + \frac{3}{3}$
(B) $\frac{1}{3} \times \frac{2}{3} \times \frac{3}{3}$
(C) $\frac{1000}{30} + \frac{200}{30} + \frac{30}{30}$
(D) $\frac{1000}{3} + \frac{200}{3} + \frac{30}{3}$
(E) $\frac{100}{3} \times \frac{20}{3} \times \frac{3}{3}$

5. If a is a number divisible by 7, what is the remainder of $3a$ divided by 4?
(A) 0
(B) 1
(C) 2
(D) 3
(E) It cannot be determined from the given information.

6. If a and b are distinct positive whole numbers, which of the following is true?
(A) The difference of a and b is negative.
(B) The difference of b and a is negative.
(C) The difference of a and b divided by their sum is negative.
(D) The difference of a and b divided by their sum is less than 1.
(E) The product of a and b divided by their sum is greater than 1.

7. If f and g are two positive whole numbers, and $f - g$ is a positive whole number, which of the following must be true?
(A) The number f divided by g is a positive whole number.
(B) The number g divided by f is a positive whole number.
(C) The product of f and g is divisible by the sum of f and g.
(D) The sum of f and g is divisible by both f and g.
(E) The product of f and g is divisible by both f and g.

8. If $W \div 5$ has a remainder of 4, what is the remainder of $3W \div 5$?
(A) 0
(B) 1
(C) 2
(D) 3
(E) 4

Place Value

1. What is the value of the underlined digit?
1,024.8<u>6</u>
(A) 6
(B) 6 ones
(C) 6 tenths
(D) 6 tens
(E) 6 hundredths

2. What is the value of the thousands digit in the standard form of 7.8416×10^5?
(A) 8 thousand
(B) 7 thousand
(C) 6 thousand
(D) 4 thousand
(E) 1 thousand

3. What is the value of the tens digit in the standard form of 4.9025×10^3?
(A) 0 tens
(B) 2 tens
(C) 4 tens
(D) 5 tens
(E) 9 tens

4. In the number 49,821.091, the 9 in the thousands place is how many times the value of the 9 in the hundredths place?
(A) 100,000
(B) 10,000
(C) 9,000
(D) 1,000
(E) 100

The Tutorverse

5. What is the value of the underlined digit?
921.68<u>7</u>
(A) 7 tenths
(B) 7 hundred
(C) 7 hundredths
(D) 7 thousand
(E) 7 thousandths

6. What is the value of the underlined digit?
<u>1</u>4,256.09
(A) 1 hundred
(B) 1 hundredth
(C) 1 thousand
(D) 10 thousand
(E) 10 thousandths

7. What is the value of the thousandths digit in the standard form of 92.8×10^{-4}?
(A) −4 thousandths
(B) 0
(C) 2 thousandths
(D) 8 thousandths
(E) 9 thousandths

8. In the number 47,561.206, the 6 in the tens place is how many times the value of the 6 in the thousandths place?
(A) 0.1
(B) 100
(C) 1,000
(D) 10,000
(E) 100,000

9. What is the value of the ones digit in the standard form of $7,562.18 \times 10^{-3}$?
(A) 2 ones
(B) 5 ones
(C) 6 ones
(D) 7 ones
(E) 8 ones

10. In the number 342,906.48, the 4 in the tenths place is how many times the value of the 4 in the ten-thousands place?
(A) 100,000
(B) 10,000
(C) 1,000
(D) 0.001
(E) 0.00001

Time/Money Concepts

1. At a bookstore, an ebook reader costs $62.50 and each ebook costs $4.75. If Dylan uses a $100 gift card to buy 1 ebook reader and 6 ebooks, and no taxes or shipping charges are applied, how much change will he receive?
(A) $9.00
(B) $13.75
(C) $23.25
(D) $32.75
(E) $37.50

2. Marshall's average time for each lap run around a track was 2 minutes and 36 seconds. How long does it take Marshall to run 4 laps around the track?
(A) 8 minutes and 38 seconds
(B) 9 minutes and 44 seconds
(C) 10 minutes and 24 seconds
(D) 10 minutes and 44 seconds
(E) 11 minutes and 36 seconds

3. A grocery store is offering a 10% discount on boxes of cereal. In addition, it is offering one box free with the purchase of three. A customer uses both offers to get 4 boxes with an original price of $3.40 each. How much does the customer save using both offers?
(A) $3.06
(B) $4.42
(C) $4.56
(D) $9.18
(E) $13.60

4. Bonnie bought a doll for 30% off the original price. She paid a 5% sales tax, which was $2.52. What was the original price before the discount?
(A) $15.12
(B) $35.28
(C) $50.40
(D) $56.00
(E) $72.00

5. A runner runs up a mountain and then the same distance down again, for a total of 26 miles. His average speed on the way up the mountain is 6 miles per hour. His speed on the way down is 10 miles per hour. In hours, how long does it take him to run to the top of the mountain and back down?
(A) 3 hours 25 minutes
(B) 3 hours 15 minutes
(C) 3 hours 28 minutes
(D) 3 hours 46 minutes
(E) 6 hours 56 minutes

6. Jack spends a total of $2,000 on his credit card. The card has a 20% annual interest rate. How much will he owe after 2 years if he doesn't pay any of the amount owed?
(A) $2,400
(B) $2,420
(C) $2,800
(D) $2,880
(E) $3,000

7. A savings account has earned 10% interest for 3 years. If the account has a balance of $1,331, what was the principal (initial deposit) if there have been no additional deposits or withdrawals?
(A) $1.33
(B) $970.30
(C) $1,000.00
(D) $1,023.85
(E) $1,930.12

8. At a clothing store, a sweater was discounted twice. First, the price was discounted 10%, then an additional 20% was taken off the new price. The final discounted price was $36.00. What was the original price of the sweater?
(A) $45
(B) $50
(C) $72
(D) $85
(E) $90

Estimation

1. Estimate the quotient when 71,994 is divided by 243.
(A) 200
(B) 300
(C) 450
(D) 500
(E) 600

2. Estimate the sum of $\sqrt{50}$ and $\sqrt{80}$.
(A) 12
(B) 13
(C) 14
(D) 15
(E) 16

3. What percent of 5,037 is closest to 756?
(A) 10%
(B) 15%
(C) 20%
(D) 25%
(E) 30%

4. Estimate the value of $\frac{103}{1013} + \frac{246}{1246}$.
(A) 0.12
(B) 0.15
(C) 0.2
(D) 0.3
(E) 0.35

5. Estimate the value of $\sqrt[3]{998}$ divided by $\sqrt[3]{126}$.
(A) 1
(B) 2
(C) 2.5
(D) 3
(E) 4

6. Which is closest to 24.9% of 7,989?
(A) 1,999
(B) 3,808
(C) 4,201
(D) 5,966
(E) 7,865

7. According to the table, about how much rain, in inches, fell in total from Monday to Sunday, inclusive?

Day	Rainfall
Monday	2.04"
Tuesday	2.07"
Wednesday	0.96"
Thursday	2.99"
Friday	1.98"
Saturday	2.01"
Sunday	0.97"

   (A) 10
   (B) 11
   (C) 12
   (D) 13
   (E) 14

8. Estimate the quotient of 98,765 and 432.
   (A) 100
   (B) 250
   (C) 400
   (D) 500
   (E) 1,000

9. Estimate what percent 797 is of 2,502.
   (A) 16%
   (B) 20%
   (C) 25%
   (D) 32%
   (E) 40%

10. On the first day, a safari expedition finds 4 black leopards and 15 spotted ones. The second day, 2 black leopards and 7 spotted ones are found. On the third day, 2 black leopards and 10 spotted leopards are found. What percentage of leopards found on this safari were black?
   (A) 10%
   (B) 20%
   (C) 25%
   (D) 30%
   (E) 40%

Unit Analysis

1. How many inches are there in 13 feet?
   (A) 56
   (B) 66
   (C) 156
   (D) 166
   (E) 210

2. How many liters are there in 2.6 kiloliters?
   (A) 26
   (B) 260
   (C) 2,600
   (D) 26,000
   (E) 260,000

3. How many kilometers are there in 150 meters?
   (A) 0.015
   (B) 0.15
   (C) 1,500
   (D) 15,000
   (E) 150,000

4. How many grams are there in 200 kilograms?
   (A) 0.2
   (B) 2
   (C) 20
   (D) 20,000
   (E) 200,000

5. How many inches are there in 1.5 miles?
   (*Note: 5,280 feet = 1 mile*)
   (A) 18
   (B) 7,920
   (C) 31,680
   (D) 63,360
   (E) 95,040

6. The distance between two towns is 2.45 kilometers. How many millimeters apart are the two cities?
   (A) 0.00000245
   (B) 0.00245
   (C) 2,450
   (D) 245,000
   (E) 2,450,000

The Tutorverse

7. A sheet of paper weighs 2.3 milligrams. A pad of paper has 150 sheets of paper. How many kilograms does the pad weigh?
   (A) 0.000345
   (B) 0.00345
   (C) 3,450
   (D) 3,450,000
   (E) 345,000,000

8. A supermarket has 68 bags of potatoes for sale. Each bag weighs 3 pounds. How many tons of potatoes does the supermarket have for sale? *(1 ton = 2,000 pounds)*
   (A) 0.0102
   (B) 0.0204
   (C) 0.102
   (D) 0.204
   (E) 408,000

Computational Clue Problems

1. Two numbers whose difference is 7 add to 57. What is the larger number?
   (A) 25
   (B) 32
   (C) 42
   (D) 50
   (E) 64

2. Amy has $720 in the bank. If she takes out 35% of her money, how much money does she have left in the bank?
   (A) $252
   (B) $458
   (C) $468
   (D) $655
   (E) $685

3. Six more than twice the cube root of a number is 12. What is the number?
   (A) $\sqrt[3]{3}$
   (B) $\sqrt[3]{12}$
   (C) 27
   (D) 216
   (E) 729

4. Arnold saved $600 this summer, which is 80% of what he saved last summer. How much money did Arnold save last summer?
   (A) $480
   (B) $500
   (C) $720
   (D) $750
   (E) $760

5. What is the product of the square roots of two consecutive perfect squares whose difference is 23?
   (A) 72
   (B) 90
   (C) 110
   (D) 132
   (E) 156

6. The quotient of 4 less than a number and 3 is 3. What is the number?
   (A) 5
   (B) 6
   (C) 12
   (D) 13
   (E) 21

7. Of three consecutive odd integers, the difference between twice the greatest and the least is 11. What is the greatest of the three?
   (A) 5
   (B) 7
   (C) 8
   (D) 9
   (E) 11

8. Shawn has $60. He spends 20% of his money on clothes, and then 25% of what he has left on food. How much money does Shawn have left after both purchases?
   (A) $3
   (B) $15
   (C) $27
   (D) $33
   (E) $36

The Tutorverse

Sequences, Patterns, Logic

1. Find the seventh number in the sequence:
   –3, 8, 19, 30,...
   (A) 61
   (B) 62
   (C) 63
   (D) 64
   (E) 65

2. 0, 1, 4, 9, 16, 25 ...
   If the pattern above were to continue, what is the tenth number in the sequence?
   (A) 10
   (B) 35
   (C) 81
   (D) 100
   (E) 385

3. The first term of a sequence is 3. Each successive term is 3 times the previous one. Out of the first 20 terms, what fraction are perfect squares?
   (A) $\frac{1}{5}$
   (B) $\frac{1}{4}$
   (C) $\frac{1}{2}$
   (D) $\frac{3}{4}$
   (E) $\frac{4}{5}$

4. Let statement X be "All cats have claws." Let statement Y be "Lynxes are cats." Let statement Z be "An animal is a predator if and only if it has claws." If statements X, Y, and Z are all true, which statement is not necessarily true?
   (A) Lynxes have claws.
   (B) Lynxes are predators.
   (C) All cats are predators.
   (D) If a certain animal is not a cat, it is not a predator.
   (E) If an animal does not have claws, then it is not a lynx.

5. Daniel plans to read a book in March. He plans to read one page on March 1, two pages on March 2, three pages on March 3, and so on. If the book contains 1,000 pages, how many pages will Daniel have left to read after March 31?
   (A) 907
   (B) 504
   (C) 496
   (D) 93
   (E) 8

6. The first 10 powers of two are 2, 4, 8, 16, 32, 64, 128, 256, 512, and 1,024. Find the units (ones) digit of 2^{100}.
   (A) 0
   (B) 2
   (C) 4
   (D) 6
   (E) 8

7. On an 8 by 8 checkerboard, all the perimeter squares are painted. How many squares are painted?
   (A) 20
   (B) 24
   (C) 28
   (D) 32
   (E) 36

8. If the statement "If lobster was ordered, the meal was expensive" is true, which statement is also always true?
   (A) If the meal was not expensive, then lobster was not ordered.
   (B) If lobster was not ordered, then the meal was expensive.
   (C) If the meal wasn't expensive, then lobster was ordered.
   (D) Lobster is expensive at every restaurant.
   (E) If the meal was expensive, lobster must have been ordered.

The Tutorverse

9. Alex is older than Brady, who is in turn older than Curtis. Dennis is older than Ebu. When Ebu was born, Brady was 4 years old. When Dennis was born, Brady had not yet been born. Which statement is necessarily true?
   (A) Curtis is the youngest.
   (B) Alex is the oldest.
   (C) Dennis is older than Curtis.
   (D) Alex is older than Dennis.
   (E) Ebu is older than Curtis.

10. Find the sum of the first 10 positive multiples of 3.
   (A) 30
   (B) 66
   (C) 99
   (D) 165
   (E) 330

11. Find the product of $\left(\frac{1}{2}\right)\left(\frac{2}{3}\right)\left(\frac{3}{4}\right)\left(\frac{4}{5}\right)\cdots\left(\frac{98}{99}\right)\left(\frac{99}{100}\right)$.
   (A) 100
   (B) 1
   (C) 0.1
   (D) 0.01
   (E) 0.001

12. In the series 1, 3, 4, 7, 11, 18, 29... , what is the tenth term?
   (A) 47
   (B) 62
   (C) 76
   (D) 123
   (E) 199

Algebra

Common Factor

1. What is the greatest common factor of $12b^2$ and 16?
   (A) 4
   (B) $4b$
   (C) $12b$
   (D) 48
   (E) $48b^2$

2. What is the greatest common factor of $6a^3$ and $15a^4$?
   (A) $3a$
   (B) $3a^3$
   (C) $6a^3$
   (D) $9a^4$
   (E) $15a^4$

3. What is the greatest common factor of $32p^4$, p^8, and 16?
   (A) $32p^8$
   (B) $16p$
   (C) $8p$
   (D) p^4
   (E) 1

4. What is the greatest common factor of $9ab^2c$ and a^2b?
   (A) ab
   (B) ab^2
   (C) $3ab$
   (D) $9abc$
   (E) $9a^2b^2$

5. What is the greatest common factor of $40b^2$ and $25a^2b$?
   (A) $5b$
   (B) $5b^2$
   (C) $15b$
   (D) $15b^2$
   (E) $5ab^2$

6. What is the greatest common factor of $72c^5d^3$, $56c^3d^8$, and $40c^4d^2$?
   (A) $24c^5d^8$
   (B) $24c^3d^2$
   (C) $16c^3d^2$
   (D) $8c^4d^3$
   (E) $8c^3d^2$

7. What is the greatest common factor of $2x^2y^4$, $6y^2z^4$, and x^2z^4?
   (A) $2x^2z^4$
   (B) $2x^2y^2$
   (C) x^2yz
   (D) x^2yz^4
   (E) 1

8. If z is a prime number, what is the least common multiple of $10z^6$, $12z$, and $6z^3$?
   (A) $24z$
   (B) $24z^6$
   (C) $60z$
   (D) $60z^6$
   (E) $60z^3$

9. If x and y are prime numbers, what is the least common multiple of $12x^2y^3$ and $16x^3y$?
   (A) $48x^3y^3$
   (B) $48x^2y$
   (C) $4x^3y^3$
   (D) $4x^2y$
   (E) $4xy$

10. If a and b are prime numbers, what is the least common multiple of $40a^5$ and $24a^4b^2$?
    (A) $120a^5b^2$
    (B) $120a^4b$
    (C) $80a^5b^2$
    (D) $80a^4$
    (E) $8a^5b^2$

11. If c and d are prime numbers, what is the least common multiple of $6c^2$, $8cd$, and $4d^3$?
    (A) $24cd$
    (B) $24c^2d$
    (C) $24c^2d^3$
    (D) $48cd$
    (E) $48c^2d^3$

12. If p and q are prime numbers, what is the least common multiple of 28, $14pq$, and $7p^7$?
    (A) $28p^7$
    (B) $28pq$
    (C) $28p^7q$
    (D) $56pq$
    (E) $56p^7q$

13. What is the greatest common factor of $x^2 + 8x + 15$ and $x^2 + 7x + 12$?
    (A) $x + 1$
    (B) $x + 2$
    (C) $x + 3$
    (D) $x + 4$
    (E) $x + 5$

14. What is the greatest common factor of $9x^2 - 1$ and $9x^2 - 6x + 1$?
    (A) 1
    (B) $3x$
    (C) $9x^2$
    (D) $3x + 1$
    (E) $3x - 1$

15. What is the least common multiple of $4x + 8$ and $6x + 6$, if x is a prime number?
    (A) 2
    (B) $2x + 2$
    (C) $12x + 24$
    (D) $12x^2 + 36x + 24$
    (E) $24x^2 + 72x + 48$

16. What is the greatest common factor of $6(x^2 - 9)$ and $8(x^2 + 9)$?
    (A) 2
    (B) $2x + 6$
    (C) $x + 3$
    (D) $x - 3$
    (E) $2x - 6$

Factoring

1. Which expression is equivalent to $-x^2 + x + 20$?
   (A) $(x + 4)(x - 5)$
   (B) $(x - 4)(x - 5)$
   (C) $-(x + 4)(x - 5)$
   (D) $-(x - 4)(x + 5)$
   (E) $-(x - 2)(x + 10)$

2. Which expression is equivalent to $3x^2 + 13x + 4$?
   (A) $(3x + 1)(x + 4)$
   (B) $(3x - 1)(3x - 4)$
   (C) $(3x - 1)(x - 4)$
   (D) $3(x + 1)(x + 4)$
   (E) $3(x + 1)(x + 12)$

3. Which expression is equivalent to
$15m^2 + 35m + 10$?
(A) $(15m + 1)(m + 2)$
(B) $15(m + 7)(m + 2)$
(C) $5(m + 7)(m + 2)$
(D) $5(3m + 1)(m + 2)$
(E) $5(3m + 1)(m + 5)$

4. Which expression is equivalent to
$2m^2 + 24m + 40$?
(A) $(2m + 8)(m + 5)$
(B) $2(m + 10)(m + 2)$
(C) $2(m + 8)(m + 5)$
(D) $2(m + 4)(m + 5)$
(E) $2(m - 10)(m - 2)$

5. Which expression is equivalent to
$2k^2 + 10k + 12$?
(A) $2(k + 2)(k + 3)$
(B) $2(k + 1)(k + 5)$
(C) $2(k + 5)(k + 2)$
(D) $(2k + 1)(k + 2)$
(E) $(2k + 1)(k + 5)$

6. Which expression is equivalent to
$3x^2 + 9x - 30$?
(A) $(3x + 3)(x - 6)$
(B) $(3x + 1)(x - 3)$
(C) $3(x - 5)(x + 6)$
(D) $3(x - 5)(x + 2)$
(E) $3(x + 5)(x - 2)$

7. Which expression is equivalent to
$-2x^2 - 6x - 4$?
(A) $-(x + 1)(x + 2)$
(B) $(2x + 1)(x + 2)$
(C) $-2(x + 1)(x + 2)$
(D) $2(x - 1)(x - 2)$
(E) $-2(x + 2)(x + 2)$

8. Which expression is equivalent to
$4x^2 + 8x - 60$?
(A) $4(x + 5)(x - 3)$
(B) $(4x + 2)(x + 5)$
(C) $4(x + 5)(x + 3)$
(D) $4(x - 5)(x - 3)$
(E) $(4x - 2)(x + 5)$

9. Which expression is equivalent to
$x^3 - x^2 - 12x$?
(A) $(x^2 + 3)(x - 4)$
(B) $x(x + 3)(x - 4)$
(C) $x(x - 3)(x - 4)$
(D) $x(x + 2)(x - 6)$
(E) $(x^2 + 2)(x - 6)$

10. Which expression is equivalent to
$3x^2 - x - 2$?
(A) $3(x + 2)(x - 1)$
(B) $3(x - 2)(x - 1)$
(C) $(3x + 2)(x - 1)$
(D) $(3x - 2)(x - 1)$
(E) $(3x + 1)(3x - 1)$

Ratio and Proportions

1. If 6 bottles of iced tea cost $7.50, how much
would 4 bottles cost at this rate?
(A) $1.25
(B) $3.75
(C) $5.00
(D) $5.50
(E) $11.25

2. Jared's garage door needed to be repainted. If
he spent $35.00 on paint and the door
measures 10 feet by 7 feet, how much did he
spend per square foot?
(A) $0.02
(B) $0.05
(C) $0.20
(D) $0.50
(E) $2.00

3. What percent of the figure shown is shaded?

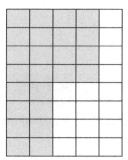

(A) 16%
(B) 24%
(C) 40%
(D) 60%
(E) $66\frac{2}{3}$%

The Tutorverse

4. Amelia earns $15 per hour at her job. However, if she works more than 40 hours in a week, she earns $22 per hour for each additional hour after the first 40 hours. If Amelia worked 46 hours last week, how much money did she earn?
   (A) $690
   (B) $732
   (C) $851
   (D) $880
   (E) $1,012

5. Ms. Lee paid $135,000 for a rectangular lot 500 feet wide by 750 feet long. What was the cost she paid per square foot?
   (A) $0.03
   (B) $0.04
   (C) $0.11
   (D) $0.36
   (E) $0.40

6. A survey asked students if they preferred chocolate or vanilla ice cream. The ratio of the number of students who prefer chocolate to the number of student who prefer vanilla is 3:2. How many students were surveyed if 140 students prefer vanilla?
   (A) 210
   (B) 280
   (C) 350
   (D) 420
   (E) 700

7. At Mountainview High School, the ratio of teachers to students is 2 to 15. Which equation represents the relationship between the number of teachers, T, and the number of students, S?
   (A) $T = 2S$
   (B) $T = 15S$
   (C) $T = \frac{1}{15}S$
   (D) $T = \frac{2}{15}S$
   (E) $T = \frac{15}{2}S$

8. In a jar containing dry beans, the ratio of white beans to kidney beans is 5:4. If 30 white beans were replaced with 30 kidney beans, the ratio would be 1:1. How many more white beans are there than kidney beans?
   (A) 540
   (B) 240
   (C) 192
   (D) 60
   (E) 48

9. On a recent road trip, Tim drove 90 miles in 1 hour 30 minutes. She then stopped for 30 minutes to get a snack and put gas in her car. Then she drove 130 miles in 2 hours. What is Tim's average speed, in miles per hour, during her entre trip?
   (A) 55
   (B) 57.5
   (C) 60
   (D) 62.5
   (E) 65

10. Julio's office is 28 miles away from his house. Depending on traffic, his average speed is between 35 and 40 miles per hour. The amount of time, in minutes, it takes Julio to drive to work must be between
    (A) 7 and 8
    (B) 35 and 40
    (C) 42 and 48
    (D) 70 and 80
    (E) 75 and 86

11. If a number is decreased by 25% of its value and then increased by 40% of its new value, what will be the percent change from the original number?
    (A) 5% increase
    (B) 10% increase
    (C) 15% increase
    (D) 15% decrease
    (E) 25% decrease

The Tutorverse

12. A sweater is on sale for 35% off. What is the ratio of the discounted price to the original price?
   (A) $\frac{7}{20}$
   (B) $\frac{7}{13}$
   (C) $\frac{13}{20}$
   (D) $\frac{20}{13}$
   (E) $\frac{13}{7}$

13. On a map, a scale indicates that 2 inches = 23 miles. If two cities are 40.25 miles apart, how far apart would they be on the map?

   (A) 4 miles
   (B) 3.5 miles
   (C) 16.25 inches
   (D) 4 inches
   (E) 3.5 inches

Word Problems

1. Lara has $600 in her bank account. She deposits $20 every week. After how many weeks will Lara have $1,000 in her bank account if she does **not** spend any money?
   (A) 18
   (B) 20
   (C) 24
   (D) 30
   (E) 40

2. A swimming pool that has a capacity of 2,800 gallons of water has 1,200 gallons of water in it. Jill plans to fill up the pool with a pump that pumps 50 gallons of water per minute. Which set represents a list of some of the possible numbers of minutes Jill can run the pump for without overflowing the pool?
   (A) {18, 21, 31, 33}
   (B) {22, 25, 29, 34}
   (C) {26, 29, 30, 31}
   (D) {31, 33, 34, 36}
   (E) {22, 26, 29, 34}

3. Two numbers have a sum of 84. One is twice the other. What is the larger number?
   (A) 21
   (B) 24
   (C) 28
   (D) 42
   (E) 56

4. A rectangular garden has a perimeter of 20 feet. One side is two feet longer than the other. How long is the shorter side?
   (A) 3 ft
   (B) 4 ft
   (C) 6 ft
   (D) 9 ft
   (E) 11 ft

5. Phoebe has $400. After how many weeks will she have exactly $100 if she spends $10 each week and does **not** earn additional money?
   (A) 10
   (B) 15
   (C) 30
   (D) 40
   (E) 200

6. Casey can assemble 8 toy trucks in 3 hours while Jessie can assemble 10 toy trucks in 4 hours. What is the rate, in toy trucks per hour, at which they can work together?
   (A) $\frac{6}{31}$
   (B) $\frac{4}{17}$
   (C) $\frac{4}{3}$
   (D) $\frac{17}{4}$
   (E) $\frac{31}{6}$

7. Phil can assemble 9 toy trucks in 3 hours. Mark can assemble 11 toy trucks in 4 hours. How many trucks can they assemble together in 36 hours?
   (A) 90
   (B) 99
   (C) 108
   (D) 186
   (E) 207

8. Pete stuffs 5 gift bags every 6 minutes. Hannah stuffs 3 gift bags every 5 minutes. How many gift bags can they stuff together in an hour?
   (A) 28
   (B) 36
   (C) 50
   (D) 72
   (E) 86

The Tutorverse

9. At a museum, 3 adults and 5 children paid a total of $81 admission, whereas 1 adult and 3 children paid a total of $39. What is the entrance fee for one adult and one child?
   (A) $9
   (B) $12
   (C) $21
   (D) $24
   (E) $36

10. At a store, 1 carton of milk and 2 loaves of bread cost $5.60, whereas 3 cartons of milk and 2 loaves of bread cost $10.80. What is the cost of 1 loaf of bread?
    (A) $0.75
    (B) $1.50
    (C) $2.00
    (D) $2.50
    (E) $3.00

11. A restaurant serves hamburgers for $7 and drinks for $3. During the lunch rush, 61 items were sold for $323. If all 61 items were hamburgers and drinks, how many hamburgers were sold in all?
    (A) 26
    (B) 35
    (C) 38
    (D) 46
    (E) 107

12. At the store, chicken feed sells for $3.50 per pound and cow feed sells for $4.25 per pound. Using the same rates per pound, the warehouse sells a 20-pound mix of chicken and cow feed for $3.80 per pound. Which system of equations can be used to determine the number of pounds of chicken feed, x, and the number of pounds of cow feed, y, in the mixture that sells for $3.80 per pound?
    (A) $x + y = 20$
        $3.5x + 4.25y = 76$
    (B) $x + y = 76$
        $3.5x + 4.25y = 20$
    (C) $x + y = 20$
        $3.5x + 4.25y = 3.8$
    (D) $x + y = 3.8$
        $3.5x + 4.25y = 76$
    (E) $x + y = 76$
        $3.5x + 4.25y = 3.8$

13. A pet food store pays the pet food company $3.50 per pound for chicken cat food and $4.25 per pound for beef cat food. The store pays $3.80 for a 20-pound mixture of chicken and beef cat food. At these rates, how many pounds of chicken food, x, and how many pounds of beef food, y, are in the mixture?
    (A) $x = 10, y = 10$
    (B) $x = 6, y = 14$
    (C) $x = 8, y = 12$
    (D) $x = 14, y = 6$
    (E) $x = 12, y = 8$

14. The cost of an adult ticket at a movie theater is $12.50. The cost of a children's ticket is $8.00. A family spent $99.00 on 9 movie tickets. Which system of equations can help you find the number of adult tickets, x, and children's tickets, y, the family bought?
    (A) $x + y = 99$
        $12.5x + 8y = 20.5$
    (B) $x + y = 20.5$
        $12.5x + 8y = 99$
    (C) $x + y = 9$
        $12.5x + 8y = 20.5$
    (D) $x + y = 20.5$
        $12.5x + 8y = 9$
    (E) $x + y = 9$
        $12.5x + 8y = 99$

15. A certain number of liters of 20% sugar solution is to be mixed with a certain number of liters of 15% sugar solution to make 12 liters of 18% sugar solution. How many liters of the 20% solution, x, and how many liters of the 15% solution, y, are needed to make 12 liters of 18% solution?
    (A) $x = 7, y = 5$
    (B) $x = 6, y = 6$
    (C) $x = 7.2, y = 4.8$
    (D) $x = 4.8, y = 7.2$
    (E) $x = 2.4, y = 9.6$

16. A mixture containing 8% sodium chloride is to be mixed with 2 quarts of a mixture that is 12% sodium chloride in order to obtain a solution that is 9% sodium chloride. How much of the 8% solution must be used?
    (A) 1 quart
    (B) 2 quarts
    (C) 4 quarts
    (D) 6 quarts
    (E) 8 quarts

17. The instructions on a can of instant iced tea mix say to mix 2 cups of mix with 1 pint of water. How much of the mix should be used with 2 gallons of water? (*Note: 1 gallon = 8 pints = 16 cups*)
    (A) 16 cups
    (B) 18 cups
    (C) 24 cups
    (D) 32 cups
    (E) 36 cups

18. A certain number of pounds of mixed nuts containing 25% peanuts is mixed with a certain number of pounds of mixed nuts containing 11% peanuts to make 20 pounds of mixed nuts containing 18% peanuts. How many pounds of 25% mixture, x, and how many pounds of 11% mixture, y are needed to make 20 pounds containing 18% peanuts? *(Round to the nearest hundredth.)*
    (A) $x = 9.33, y = 10.66$
    (B) $x = 10, y = 10$
    (C) $x = 12, y = 8$
    (D) $x = 8, y = 12$
    (E) $x = 3.6, y = 16.4$

19. A boat travels at a steady velocity on a track. While traveling at this velocity, it takes 3 hours to travel 135 miles against a current and 2 hours to travel 104 miles with the current. What is the car's velocity, in miles per hour, on the track? (*Note: distance = velocity × time*)
    (A) 45
    (B) 46.5
    (C) 48.5
    (D) 50
    (E) 52

20. A red car is traveling at a velocity of 55 miles per hour when it is passed by a green car traveling 70 miles per hour. How long will it take for the car that passed to be one mile ahead of the slower car? (*Note: distance = velocity × time*)
    (A) 2 minutes
    (B) 4 minutes
    (C) 6 minutes
    (D) 15 minutes
    (E) 45 minutes

21. Cindy throws a rock in the air. The rock's height, y, in feet, with respect to time, x, in seconds, can be modeled by the function $y = -2x^2 + 10x + 28$. When does the rock hit the ground, in seconds?
    (A) −2
    (B) 2
    (C) 5
    (D) 6
    (E) 7

22. A toy rocket is launched in the air. The rocket's height, y, in feet, with respect to horizontal distance, x, in feet can be modeled by the function $y = -2x^2 + 10x + 12$. How far from the starting point did the rocket land, in feet?
    (A) 1
    (B) 5
    (C) 6
    (D) 7
    (E) 9

Interpreting Variables

1. The original price, p, of a shirt is reduced by 35%. Which expression represents the new price?
   (A) $1.35p$
   (B) $p(1 - 0.65)$
   (C) $\frac{35p}{100}$
   (D) $p(1 - 0.35)$
   (E) $0.35p$

2. Gene bought a 1,200-page paperback novel and reads 30 pages per day. Which expression represents the number of pages Gene has left to read after d days?
   (A) $1,200 - 30d$
   (B) $d(1,200 - 30)$
   (C) $1,200 + 30d$
   (D) $3,600d$
   (E) $1,170d$

The Tutorverse

3. The expression $250 + 600w$ represents the total amount of money Tabitha has in her bank account w weeks after starting her new job. Which scenario is best described by the expression?
   (A) She started with $600 in her account, and earns $250 per week.
   (B) She earns $600 plus a $250 bonus each week.
   (C) She pays a $250 fee, and earns $600 per week.
   (D) She earns $600 per week, and is taxed $250 per week.
   (E) She started with $250 in her account, and earns $600 per week.

4. Which of the following gives the number of dollars in a nickels, b dimes, and 4 quarters?
   (A) $5a + 10b + 4(25)$
   (B) $5a + 10b + 1$
   (C) $0.05a + 0.1b + 1$
   (D) $4(0.05a + 0.1b)$
   (E) $0.25(0.5a + 0.1b)$

5. Which of the following must be true if a rectangle with side lengths of B and H has a perimeter of 60 and H is less than B?
   (A) $2B + 2H = 60$
   (B) $2B + 2H \le 60$
   (C) $H > 2B$
   (D) $H \times B = 60$
   (E) $H + 30 < B$

6. Choose the inequality represented by the statement: "The product of sixty times a number and fourteen times another number is less than sixty-two."
   (A) $60x + 14y < 62$
   (B) $60x + 14y > 62$
   (C) $74(x + y) < 62$
   (D) $60x \times 14y < 62$
   (E) $60xy < 62 + 14$

7. A car salesperson earns a base salary of $30,000 plus a commission of $800 for every car she sells. Which equation shows the total amount of income the salesperson earns, if she sells c cars in a month?
   (A) $30,000 - 800c$
   (B) $30,800 + c$
   (C) $29,200 + 800c$
   (D) $30,000 + c^2$
   (E) $30,000 + 800c$

8. A cell phone plan costs $40 per month for unlimited calling plus $0.15 per text message. Which of the following expressions represents the total cost of the phone plan after t text messages?
   (A) $40.15t$
   (B) $40 + 0.15t$
   (C) $40 - 0.15t$
   (D) $40 + 0.15t^2$
   (E) $t(40 + 0.15)$

9. The expression $15 + 5c$ represents the height, in inches, of Oscar's bamboo plant. Which scenario is best described by the expression?
   (A) The plant grows 15 inches per month.
   (B) The plant started at 15 inches and grows c inches per month.
   (C) The plant started at 15 inches, and Oscar cuts c inches per month.
   (D) The plant started at 15 inches, and grows 5 inches per month.
   (E) Oscar moves the plant 15 inches higher on a shelf c times per month.

10. The expression $2.5c - 20$ represents the total profit Sebastian earns from selling lemonade that he makes himself. Which scenario is best described by the expression?
    (A) Sebastian spent $2.50 on ingredients and sells the lemonade for 20 cents per cup.
    (B) Sebastian sells lemonade for $2.50 per cup with a 20 cent discount.
    (C) Sebastian lost $22.50 selling lemonade.
    (D) Sebastian sells lemonade for $2.50 per cup and spent $20 on ingredients.
    (E) Sebastian sells lemonade for $2.50 per cup, and receives $20 in tips.

11. Laura has p more apples than Billy. Billy has 12 apples. How many apples does Laura have?
    (A) $\frac{12}{p}$
    (B) $p - 12$
    (C) $12p$
    (D) $12 + p$
    (E) $12 - p$

The Tutorverse

12. Choose the inequality represented by the statement, "The product of two times a number and 3 times another number is less than or equal to 99."
    (A) $2a \times 3y \le 99$
    (B) $2a \times 3y \ge 99$
    (C) $2a + 3y \le 99$
    (D) $a^2 + y^2 \le 99$
    (E) $2a \times 3y = 99$

13. What is the value of $|4x + 6|$ when $x = -5$?
    (A) –26
    (B) –14
    (C) 11
    (D) 14
    (E) 26

14. The expression $100(1 + 0.01)^y$ represents the total amount of money in Matthew's savings account. Which scenario is best represented by this expression?
    (A) He accrues $100 per year.
    (B) He accrues 100 per year and pays $0.01 in fees.
    (C) He started with $100 and accrues $1.01 in interest per year.
    (D) He started with $100 and accrues $0.01 in interest per year.
    (E) He started with $0.01 and accrues $100 per year.

15. The expression $120x - 50$ represents the amount of income Fernanda earns each week after expenses are subtracted. What does x represent in this expression?
    (A) the amount of her paycheck
    (B) the amount of her bonus
    (C) the amount of money she spent
    (D) the number of checks she received
    (E) the number of hours she worked

16. The expression $20x + 5$ represents the total amount of money that Arthur saved over x weeks. Which number or expression represents the total amount of money he saved at week 4?
    (A) 85
    (B) 29
    (C) $4x$
    (D) $20x + 4$
    (E) 80

17. Jose receives $800 for his birthday, and spends $10 per week. Which expression represents the amount of money Jose has after x weeks?
    (A) $800 + 10x$
    (B) $800x + 10$
    (C) $810 + x$
    (D) $800 - 10x$
    (E) $800(10x)$

Equations Based on Word Problems

1. The area of a triangle can be found using the equation $A = \frac{1}{2}bh$. Which equation is the result of solving for h?
    (A) $h = \frac{2A}{b}$
    (B) $h = \frac{b}{2A}$
    (C) $h = \frac{b}{A}$
    (D) $h = \frac{A}{b}$
    (E) $h = \frac{1}{2}bA$

2. The area of a parallelogram can be found using the equation $A = bh$. Which equation is the result of solving for b?
    (A) $b = 2hA$
    (B) $b = \frac{h}{A}$
    (C) $b = \frac{A}{2}$
    (D) $b = hA$
    (E) $b = \frac{A}{h}$

3. The circumference of a circle can be found using the equation $C = 2\pi r$. Which equation is the result of solving for π?
    (A) $\pi = 2Cr$
    (B) $\pi = \frac{Cr}{2}$
    (C) $\pi = 2\frac{C}{r}$
    (D) $\pi = \frac{C}{r}$
    (E) $\pi = \frac{C}{2r}$

The Tutorverse

4. The volume of a cylinder can be found using the equation $V = \pi r^2 h$. Which equation is the result of solving for r?

(A) $r = \dfrac{V}{\pi h}$

(B) $r = \pm\sqrt{\dfrac{V}{\pi h}}$

(C) $r = \sqrt{\dfrac{V}{\pi h}}$

(D) $r = \dfrac{1}{2}V\pi h$

(E) $r = \sqrt{\dfrac{\pi}{Vh}}$

5. The volume of a sphere can be found using the equation $V = \dfrac{4}{3}\pi r^3$. Which equation is the result of solving for π?

(A) $\pi = \sqrt[3]{\dfrac{V}{r}}$

(B) $\pi = \dfrac{3V}{4r^3}$

(C) $\pi = \dfrac{3}{4}Vr$

(D) $\pi = \sqrt[3]{\dfrac{3V}{4r}}$

(E) $\pi = \dfrac{4V}{3r^3}$

6. The volume of a cone can be found using the equation $V = \dfrac{1}{3}\pi r^2 h$. Which equation is the result of solving for r?

(A) $r = \pm\sqrt{\dfrac{3V}{\pi h}}$

(B) $r = \sqrt[3]{\pi h V}$

(C) $r = \sqrt[3]{\dfrac{3V}{\pi h}}$

(D) $r = \sqrt{\dfrac{3V}{\pi h}}$

(E) $r = \dfrac{1}{3}\sqrt{\pi V h}$

7. The volume of a pyramid can be found using the equation $V = \dfrac{1}{3}Bh$. Which equation is the result of solving for B?

(A) $B = \dfrac{Vh}{3}$

(B) $B = 3Vh$

(C) $B = \dfrac{V}{3h}$

(D) $B = \dfrac{V}{h}$

(E) $B = \dfrac{3V}{h}$

8. The formula for finding the slope of a line is $y = mx + b$. Which equation is the result of solving for x?

(A) $x = \dfrac{y+b}{m}$

(B) $x = \dfrac{y-b}{m}$

(C) $x = \dfrac{m}{y-b}$

(D) $x = \dfrac{m}{yb}$

(E) $x = my + b$

9. The equation of the Pythagorean Theorem is $a^2 + b^2 = c^2$. Which equation is the result of solving for b?

(A) $b = \sqrt{c^2 - a^2}$

(B) $b = \sqrt{c - a}$

(C) $b = \sqrt{a^2 - c^2}$

(D) $b = \sqrt{c^2 + a^2}$

(E) $b = \sqrt{c + a}$

Equations Based on Illustrations

1. The distance $BC = 18$. If $AD = 3CD$ and $AB = \dfrac{4}{3}BC$, find the length of CD.

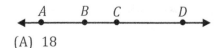

(A) 18
(B) 21
(C) 24
(D) 42
(E) 63

2. $AB = \dfrac{3}{8}$ of AC, and $AD = (CD)^2$. If $BC = 35$, find the length of AD.

(A) 8
(B) 21
(C) 56
(D) 64
(E) 72

The Tutorverse

3. In isosceles triangle *ABC*, *D* is the midpoint of base *BC*. The length of *BC* is 18. If the area of *ABC* is 108, find the length of *AC*.

(A) 6
(B) 9
(C) 12
(D) 15
(E) 18

4. In the figure below, the isosceles triangle *ABE* has a base length of 10. The rectangle *ABCD* and the triangle *ABE* have equal perimeters, and the area of the rectangle is 70. Find the length of side *AE*.

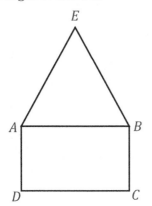

(A) 7
(B) 10
(C) 12
(D) 15
(E) 17

5. *AE* = 39, *BC* = 2*AB*, *CD* = 3*BC*, and *DE* = 4*AB*. Find *BD*.

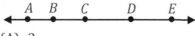

(A) 3
(B) 6
(C) 9
(D) 18
(E) 24

6. In the above isosceles trapezoid, the area is 240. If *AD* = 15 and *BC* = 25, find the length of one of the legs.

(A) 12
(B) 13
(C) 15
(D) 16
(E) 20

7. Consider square *ABCD*, and the semicircle with diameter *AB*. If the semicircle has area 18π, find the perimeter of the square.

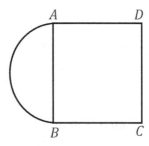

(A) 6
(B) 24
(C) 36
(D) 48
(E) 144

8. *A*, *B*, and *C* all represent positive perfect square integers on the number line. If *B* is the average (arithmetic mean) of *A* and *C*, and *C* < 50, find the value of *B*.

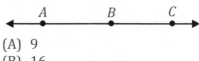

(A) 9
(B) 16
(C) 25
(D) 36
(E) 49

The Tutorverse

9. $AB = 8$. DE is twice as long as BC. $AE = 80$. If the length of CD is the average (arithmetic mean) of the lengths of BC and DE, find the length of AD.

(A) 16
(B) 24
(C) 32
(D) 40
(E) 48

10. C is the midpoint of AE. If $BC = 4$ and $AE = 28$, find BE.

$$A \quad\quad B\ C \quad\quad D \quad\quad E$$

(A) 4
(B) 6
(C) 14
(D) 18
(E) It cannot be determined from the given information.

Rational Expressions

1. Which expression is equivalent to $x + \dfrac{x-5}{2} - \dfrac{x-1}{2}$?
   (A) $x - 2$
   (B) $2x - 3$
   (C) $\dfrac{2x-3}{5}$
   (D) $\dfrac{x-2}{3}$
   (E) $x - 3$

2. Which expression is equivalent to $\left(\dfrac{5}{x+3}\right)\left(\dfrac{2}{x-7}\right)$?
   (A) $\dfrac{5x-35}{2x+6}$
   (B) $\dfrac{10}{x^2+8x+21}$
   (C) $\dfrac{10}{x^2-4x-21}$
   (D) $\dfrac{2x+6}{5x-35}$
   (E) $\dfrac{7}{2x-4}$

3. Which expression is equivalent to $\dfrac{5}{x} + \dfrac{3}{y}$?
   (A) $\dfrac{8}{xy}$
   (B) $\dfrac{5y+3x}{x+y}$
   (C) 8
   (D) $\dfrac{5y+3x}{xy}$
   (E) $\dfrac{3x-5y}{xy}$

4. If $\dfrac{x}{x+1} = 0.8$, what is the value of $\dfrac{x-3}{x-2}$?
   (A) 0.4
   (B) 0.5
   (C) 0.6
   (D) 0.7
   (E) 0.8

5. Which expression is equivalent to $\dfrac{x-1}{2} - \left(x+\dfrac{1}{2}\right)$?
   (A) $\dfrac{-x-2}{2}$
   (B) $\dfrac{3x+2}{2}$
   (C) $\dfrac{3x-2}{2}$
   (D) $-\dfrac{1}{2}$
   (E) $\dfrac{-x+2}{2}$

6. Which expression is equivalent to $\dfrac{x+2}{3} + 2\left(x+\dfrac{1}{3}\right)$?
   (A) $\dfrac{3x+3}{3}$
   (B) $\dfrac{x+3}{3} + 2x$
   (C) $\dfrac{7x+4}{3}$
   (D) $\dfrac{4x+4}{6x}$
   (E) $\dfrac{3x+4}{3x}$

7. If $\dfrac{x}{x+3} = 0.625$, what is the value of $\dfrac{x-4}{x-1}$?
   (A) 0.25
   (B) 0.375
   (C) 0.4
   (D) 0.6
   (E) 0.875

8. Which expression is equivalent to $\dfrac{2}{x+1} + \dfrac{6}{x-2}$?
   (A) $\dfrac{5}{(x+1)(x-2)}$
   (B) $\dfrac{8x+10}{(x+1)(x-2)}$
   (C) $\dfrac{5}{2x-1}$
   (D) $\dfrac{8x+2}{(x+1)(x-2)}$
   (E) $\dfrac{8x+2}{2x-1}$

The Tutorverse

9. Which expression is equivalent to

$$\frac{5}{x+1} - \frac{2}{x-1}?$$

(A) $\dfrac{3x-7}{x^2-1}$

(B) $\dfrac{7x-7}{x^2-1}$

(C) $\dfrac{3x-7}{x^2+1}$

(D) $\dfrac{3x-3}{x^2-1}$

(E) $\dfrac{3}{2x}$

10. Which expression is equivalent to

$$\left(\frac{4}{x+2}\right)\left(\frac{2}{x-6}\right)?$$

(A) $\dfrac{6}{x^2-5x-12}$

(B) $\dfrac{2x+4}{4x-24}$

(C) $\dfrac{8}{x^2-4x-12}$

(D) $\dfrac{4x-24}{2x+4}$

(E) $\dfrac{8}{x^2+8x+12}$

Exponential Expressions

1. For the expression N^3, which value of N yields the greatest result?

(A) $-\dfrac{1}{4}$

(B) $-\dfrac{1}{2}$

(C) -1

(D) -2

(E) -3

2. For the expression Q^4, which of the following values of Q yields the least result?

(A) -3

(B) $-\dfrac{3}{2}$

(C) 0

(D) $\dfrac{3}{2}$

(E) 3

3. Simplify the following expression: $(a^3 \times a^{-1})^2$

(A) a^6

(B) a^4

(C) a^{-1}

(D) a^{-4}

(E) a^{-6}

4. Simplify the following expression:
$5(3xy + 2xy)^2$

(A) $125x^2y^2$

(B) $625x^2y^2$

(C) $125x^4y^4$

(D) $625x^4y^4$

(E) $180x^2y^2$

5. Simplify the following expression:
$(x^2 + y^2)^2$

(A) x^4y^4

(B) $x^4 + y^4 + x^2y^2$

(C) $x^4 + y^4 + x^4y^4$

(D) $x^4 + y^4 + 2x^2y^2$

(E) $x^4 + y^4$

6. Simplify the following expression: $\left(\dfrac{x^2yz^3}{x^3y^3z}\right)^{-1}$

(A) $x^5y^3z^4$

(B) $\dfrac{1}{x^5y^3z^4}$

(C) $\dfrac{1}{xyz^2}$

(D) $\dfrac{z^2}{xy}$

(E) $\dfrac{xy^2}{z^2}$

7. Simplify the following expression: $(x+y)^{-2}$

(A) $x^{-2} + y^{-2}$

(B) $-x^2 - y^2$

(C) $\dfrac{1}{x^2 + 2xy + y^2}$

(D) $\dfrac{1}{x^2 + y^2}$

(E) $x^{-2} + 2x^{-1}y^{-1} + y^{-2}$

8. Since $i = \sqrt{-1}$, then $(i)^{45} =$

(A) 45

(B) 1

(C) -1

(D) $\sqrt{-1}$

(E) $-\sqrt{-1}$

9. When flipping a penny, what is the probability of landing on heads five times in a row?

(A) $\dfrac{1}{2}$

(B) $\dfrac{1}{5}$

(C) $\dfrac{1}{10}$

(D) $\dfrac{1}{16}$

(E) $\dfrac{1}{32}$

The Tutorverse

10. An object falls from a building. Its height in feet, H(t), t seconds after being dropped, is given by the following equation: H(t) = –10(t)^2 + 2t + 100. What is the object's height 2.5 seconds after being dropped?

   (A) 167.5 ft
   (B) 42.5 ft
   (C) 32.5 ft
   (D) 40 ft
   (E) 5 ft

11. Simplify the following expression:

$$\left(\frac{(x^2+3x+2)^2}{(x+1)^2}\right)^{-1}$$

   (A) $x^2 + 4x + 4$
   (B) $(x + 2)^2$
   (C) $x^2 + 2x + 1$
   (D) $-x^2 - 4x - 4$
   (E) $\frac{1}{(x+2)^2}$

Radical Expressions

1. Which expression is equivalent of $\sqrt{\frac{36}{49}}$?

   (A) $\sqrt{\frac{6}{7}}$
   (B) $\frac{6}{7}$
   (C) $\frac{6}{49}$
   (D) $\frac{36}{49}$
   (E) $\frac{72}{98}$

2. Which expression is equivalent to $\sqrt[3]{x^6}$?

   (A) $x^{\frac{1}{3}}$
   (B) $x^{\frac{1}{2}}$
   (C) x^2
   (D) x^6
   (E) x^{18}

3. Which expression is equivalent to $\sqrt[3]{\frac{216}{27}}$?

   (A) 8
   (B) 3
   (C) $\frac{8}{3}$
   (D) 2
   (E) $\frac{1}{2}$

4. Which expression is equivalent to $\sqrt{\frac{16}{36}x^2}$?

   (A) $\frac{2x}{3}$
   (B) $\frac{4}{9}x$
   (C) $\frac{4}{6}x^2$
   (D) $4x$
   (E) $6x^2$

5. Which fraction is equivalent to $\sqrt{\frac{4x}{64}}$ when $x = 4$?

   (A) $\frac{1}{4}$
   (B) $\frac{1}{8}$
   (C) $\frac{1}{2}$
   (D) $\frac{1}{16}$
   (E) $\frac{2}{1}$

6. Which expression is equivalent to $\frac{4}{\sqrt{2}}$?

   (A) 8
   (B) $8\sqrt{2}$
   (C) 4
   (D) $4\sqrt{2}$
   (E) $2\sqrt{2}$

7. Which expression is equivalent to $\frac{9}{\sqrt{3}}$?

   (A) 3
   (B) $\sqrt{9}$
   (C) 9
   (D) $3\sqrt{3}$
   (E) $9\sqrt{3}$

8. What is the value of the expression $\sqrt[3]{2^x}$ when $x = 6$?

   (A) 512
   (B) 72
   (C) 12
   (D) 6
   (E) 4

The Tutorverse

9. Which expression is equivalent to $\sqrt{\sqrt{\sqrt{x^{48}}}}$?

   (A) x^6

   (B) x^3

   (C) x^{12}

   (D) x^{24}

   (E) x^{16}

10. Which expression is equivalent to $\frac{5}{\sqrt{5}}$?

    (A) $\sqrt{5}$

    (B) $2\sqrt{5}$

    (C) 5

    (D) $5\sqrt{1}$

    (E) $5\sqrt{5}$

11. Which of the following is equivalent to $\sqrt[3]{54} + \sqrt[3]{16}$?

    (A) $3\sqrt[3]{6} + 4$

    (B) $3\sqrt[3]{3} + 2\sqrt[3]{2}$

    (C) 5

    (D) $5\sqrt[3]{2}$

    (E) 7

12. Which is equivalent to $\sqrt{\frac{5x}{25}}$ when $x = 20$?

    (A) 5

    (B) 4

    (C) 2

    (D) $\frac{1}{2}$

    (E) $\frac{1}{4}$

13. Which expression is equivalent to $\sqrt[3]{\sqrt[3]{\sqrt[3]{x^{72}}}}$?

    (A) x^{36}

    (B) x^{24}

    (C) x^{18}

    (D) x^8

    (E) x^4

14. Which expression is equivalent to $\frac{6}{\sqrt{2}}$?

    (A) $\sqrt{3}$

    (B) 3

    (C) $3\sqrt{2}$

    (D) 6

    (E) $6\sqrt{2}$

15. Which expression is equivalent to $\frac{36}{\sqrt{24}}$?

    (A) 6

    (B) $4\sqrt{8}$

    (C) 4

    (D) $3\sqrt{6}$

    (E) $2\sqrt{6}$

Polynomial Expressions

1. Which expression is equivalent to $(x + 4) - (x^2 - 3x + 6)$?

   (A) $x^2 + 4x + 10$

   (B) $-x^2 - 2x + 2$

   (C) $x^2 - 2x + 2$

   (D) $-x^2 + 4x - 2$

   (E) $-x^2 + 7x - 10$

2. Which expression is equivalent to $3a(4x - 3y)$?

   (A) $12ax - 9ay$

   (B) $12ax + 9ay$

   (C) $12ax - ay$

   (D) $4ax - y$

   (E) $4x^2 - 9y$

3. Which expression is equivalent to $(2x^2 - 3x + 5) + (3x^2 + x) - (7x - 9)$?

   (A) $5x^2 + 11x + 14$

   (B) $5x^2 + 5x - 4$

   (C) $5x^2 - 9x + 14$

   (D) $x^2 - 9x - 4$

   (E) $x^2 - 4x - 14$

4. Which expression is equivalent to $(x + 4)(x - 6)$?

   (A) $x^2 + 10x + 24$

   (B) $x^2 - 2x - 24$

   (C) $x^2 - 10x + 24$

   (D) $x^2 + 2x - 24$

   (E) $x^2 + 2x + 24$

The Tutorverse

5. Which expression is equivalent to
(3x – 2)(2x + 7)?
(A) $6x^2 + 25x – 14$
(B) $6x^2 + 17x + 14$
(C) $6x^2 + 17x – 14$
(D) $6x^2 – 25x – 14$
(E) $6x^2 – 17x – 14$

6. What is the coefficient of the term containing
xy when $3(x + y)^2$ is expanded and like terms
are combined?
(A) –6
(B) –3
(C) 1
(D) 3
(E) 6

7. Which expression is equivalent to
$(x^2 – x + 3)(x^2 + 2x – 3)$?
(A) $x^4 + 3x^3 + 8x^2 + 9x + 9$
(B) $x^4 + 3x^3 – 2x^2 – 9x – 9$
(C) $x^4 + x^3 + 2x^2 – 9x – 9$
(D) $x^4 – x^3 – 8x^2 + 9x + 9$
(E) $x^4 + x^3 – 2x^2 + 9x – 9$

8. Which expression is equivalent to
$(3x^2 + 2x – 2) + (3x^2 + x) – (3x + 2)$?
(A) $3x^2 – 2$
(B) $6x^2 – 4$
(C) $6x^2 – 6x$
(D) $6x^2 – 6x – 4$
(E) $6x^2 + 3x – 4$

9. Which expression is equivalent to
$(x^2 + 4x + 2) – (4x^2 – 6) + (7x – 8)$?
(A) $5x^2 + 5x – 6$
(B) $–3x^2 – 11x + 12$
(C) $5x^2 + 11x$
(D) $–3x^2 + 11x$
(E) $–3x^2 – 5x$

10. Which expression is equivalent to
$(5x^2 + 3y)(2x – 6y)$?
(A) $10x^2 – 24xy – 18y^2$
(B) $10x^3 + 30x^2y + 6xy + 18y^2$
(C) $10x^3 – 30x^2y + 6xy – 18y^2$
(D) $5x^3 – 15x^2y + 3xy – 9y^2$
(E) $5x^3 + 5x + 6y – 18y^2$

11. Which expression is equivalent to
$(x^2 + 5x – 6) – (4x^2 + 9x) – (x + 5)$?
(A) $5x^2 + 15x + 11$
(B) $–3x^2 – 5x – 11$
(C) $5x^2 + 15x – 1$
(D) $5x^2 – 5x – 1$
(E) $–3x^2 – 5x – 1$

12. Which expression is equivalent to
$(8x^2 + 7x + 9) – (3x^2 – 5x + 2)$?
(A) $11x^3 + 12x + 11$
(B) $5x^2 + 12x + 7$
(C) $5x^2 + 2x + 7$
(D) $11x^2 + 2x + 11$
(E) $5x^2 + 2x + 11$

13. Which expression is equivalent to
$(6x – 3)(2x – 5)$?
(A) $4x^2 + 12x + 5$
(B) $12x^2 – 24x + 15$
(C) $12x^2 – 36x – 15$
(D) $12x^2 + 24x – 15$
(E) $12x^2 – 36x + 15$

Solving Algebraic Equations for a Variable

1. If $–25 = x – 5$, what is the value of x?
(A) –30
(B) –20
(C) –5
(D) 5
(E) 20

2. What is the value of a if $18.5 – 2a = 10.5$?
(A) $–\frac{29}{2}$
(B) –4
(C) 4
(D) 8
(E) $\frac{29}{2}$

3. What is the value of b if $8b + 20 = 3b - 5$?
   (A) -5
   (B) -3
   (C) 1
   (D) 3
   (E) 5

4. If $9x - 1 = 7(x + 1) - 2x$, what is the value of x?
   (A) -2
   (B) $-\dfrac{4}{3}$
   (C) $\dfrac{4}{3}$
   (D) $\dfrac{3}{2}$
   (E) 2

5. What is the value of y if
   $3y - 4(y + 1) + 7 = 1 - 4y$?
   (A) $\dfrac{3}{2}$
   (B) $\dfrac{3}{7}$
   (C) $-\dfrac{2}{3}$
   (D) $-\dfrac{7}{3}$
   (E) It cannot be determined from the given information.

6. How many solutions does the equation $4(x - 1) - x = 3x - 4$ have?
   (A) 0
   (B) 1
   (C) 2
   (D) 3
   (E) There are infinitely many solutions.

7. Which equation represents the result of solving $6x = y$ for x?
   (A) $x = y - 6$
   (B) $x = y + 6$
   (C) $x = 6y$
   (D) $x = \dfrac{6}{y}$
   (E) $x = \dfrac{y}{6}$

8. Which equation represents the result of solving $A = LW$ for L?
   (A) $L = A - W$
   (B) $L = A + W$
   (C) $L = AW$
   (D) $L = \dfrac{A}{W}$
   (E) $L = \dfrac{W}{A}$

9. Which equation represents the result of solving $18 = \frac{1}{2}bh$ for b?
   (A) $b = \dfrac{36}{h}$
   (B) $b = \dfrac{9}{h}$
   (C) $b = 9h$
   (D) $b = 36h$
   (E) $b = \dfrac{h}{36}$

10. If $\dfrac{x}{y} = k$, what is x in terms of y and k?
    (A) ky
    (B) $\dfrac{k}{y}$
    (C) $\dfrac{y}{k}$
    (D) $k + y$
    (E) $k - y$

11. If $P = 2L + 2W$, which expression represents W?
    (A) $2(P + 2L)$
    (B) $2(P - 2L)$
    (C) $\dfrac{P - 2L}{2}$
    (D) $\dfrac{2P - L}{2}$
    (E) $\dfrac{P + 2L}{2}$

12. If $V = \pi r^2 h$, what is r in terms of V, π, and h?
    (A) $V - \pi h^2$
    (B) $\dfrac{V - \pi h}{2}$
    (C) $\dfrac{V}{\pi h^2}$
    (D) $\sqrt{\dfrac{V}{\pi h}}$
    (E) $\dfrac{\sqrt{V}}{\pi h}$

13. Which equation represents the result of solving $12 = ax + 3x$ for x?
    (A) $\dfrac{12}{3a}$
    (B) $\dfrac{9}{a}$
    (C) $12 - 3a$
    (D) $\dfrac{12}{a + 3}$
    (E) $\dfrac{12 - a}{3}$

14. Which equation represents the line graphed below?

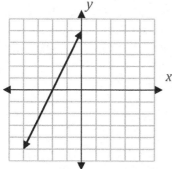

(A) $y = \frac{2}{5}x + 5$

(B) $y = -\frac{2}{5}x - 3$

(C) $y = \frac{5}{2}x + 5$

(D) $y = -\frac{5}{2}x + 5$

(E) $y = \frac{5}{2}x - 3$

15. What is the equation of the function displayed in the table below?

x	y
–4	–3
–2	0
0	3
2	6

(A) $y = \frac{2}{3}x + 3$

(B) $y = 3x - 2$

(C) $y = 3x + 3$

(D) $y = \frac{3}{2}x + 3$

(E) $y = \frac{3}{2}x - 2$

16. What is the equation of the line graphed on the coordinate plane below?

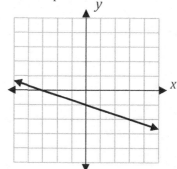

(A) $y = -3x - 1$

(B) $y = \frac{1}{3}x - 1$

(C) $y = \frac{1}{3}x - 3$

(D) $y = -\frac{1}{3}x - 3$

(E) $y = -\frac{1}{3}x - 1$

17. What is the equation of the function displayed in the table below?

x	y
–4	–3
–1	3
3	11
5	15

(A) $y = 3x$

(B) $y = -4x - 3$

(C) $y = 2x + 5$

(D) $y = -2x - 5$

(E) $y = \frac{1}{2}x - \frac{5}{2}$

Quadratic Equations

1. Which are the solutions to the equation $5x^2 + 6x + 1 = 0$?

(A) $-\frac{1}{5}, -1$

(B) $\frac{1}{5}, 1$

(C) $\frac{1}{2}, 1$

(D) $-\frac{1}{2}, -3$

(E) $\frac{1}{2}, 3$

2. Which are the solutions to the equation $x^2 - 12 = x$?

(A) –4, 3

(B) –3, 4

(C) 2. 6

(D) –2, 6

(E) 3, 4

The Tutorverse

3. Which are the solutions to the equation $(x - 3)^2 = 16$?
   (A) $-1, 7$
   (B) $3, \sqrt{13}$
   (C) $3, 4$
   (D) $1, -7$
   (E) $4, \sqrt{3}$

4. Which are the solutions to the equation $3x^2 - 24x + 36 = 0$?
   (A) $3, 12$
   (B) $6, 8$
   (C) $2, 6$
   (D) $-2, 6$
   (E) $-6, 6$

5. Dante throws a rock in the air. The rock's height, y, in feet, with respect to time, x, in seconds, can be modeled by the function $y = -3x^2 + 15x + 18$. How many seconds does it take the rock to hit the ground after it was thrown?
   (A) 1
   (B) 2
   (C) 3
   (D) 5
   (E) 6

6. Which are the solutions to the equation $x^2 + 10x = -16$?
   (A) $2, 5$
   (B) $4, 13$
   (C) $-4, 5$
   (D) $-8, -2$
   (E) $-2, 8$

7. Which are the solutions to the equation $x^2 - 30 = x$?
   (A) $5, 6$
   (B) $-5, 6$
   (C) $-6, 5$
   (D) $-2, 15$
   (E) $-2, -15$

8. Which are the solutions to the equation $x^2 - 8x = -12$?
   (A) $2, 6$
   (B) $3, 4$
   (C) $-4, 4$
   (D) $-4, 3$
   (E) $-6, 2$

9. Amar launches a model rocket. The rocket's height, y, in feet, with respect to time, x, in seconds, can be modeled by the function $y = -x^2 + 7x + 8$. How many seconds does it take the rocket to hit the ground after it was launched?
   (A) -1
   (B) 1
   (C) 4
   (D) 7
   (E) 8

10. Which are the solutions to the equation $2x^2 - 7x + 5 = 0$?
    (A) $2, 5$
    (B) $\frac{2}{5}, 7$
    (C) $-\frac{5}{2}, -1$
    (D) $5, 7$
    (E) $1, \frac{5}{2}$

11. Which are the solutions to the equation $x^2 - 8 = 7x$?
    (A) $-7, 8$
    (B) $-1, 8$
    (C) $1, -8$
    (D) $1, -7$
    (E) $1, 7$

12. Which are the solutions to the equation $x^2 - 27 = 6x$?
    (A) $3, 6$
    (B) $3, 9$
    (C) $-3, 6$
    (D) $-3, 9$
    (E) $-9, 3$

13. Which are the solutions to the equation $x^2 + 21 = -10x$?
    (A) $3, 7$
    (B) $2, 5$
    (C) $-3, 7$
    (D) $-3, -7$
    (E) $-2, 5$

14. Which are the solutions to the equation $x^2 - 14x = -13$?
    (A) $6, 7$
    (B) $1, 13$
    (C) $-6, 7$
    (D) $-1, 13$
    (E) $-13, -1$

15. Carlos kicked a kickball. The ball's height, y, in feet, with respect to time, x, in seconds, can be modeled by the function $y = -x^2 + x + 12$. How many seconds does it take the ball to hit the ground after it was kicked?
    (A) 1
    (B) 2
    (C) 3
    (D) 4
    (E) 6

16. Tommy threw a baseball from the roof of his parent's house. The ball's height, y, in feet, with respect to time, x, in seconds, can be modeled by the function $y = -2x^2 + 12x + 32$. How long after Tommy threw the ball, in seconds, did the baseball reach its maximum height?
    (A) 2
    (B) 3
    (C) 8
    (D) 12
    (E) 32

Inequalities

1. Which inequality represents the solution of $x + 4y - 2 > 5x + 6$ in terms of x?
   (A) $y > x + 2$
   (B) $y > \frac{3}{2}x + 1$
   (C) $y > 4x + 8$
   (D) $y > x + 8$
   (E) $y > 4x + 2$

2. If $\frac{3}{8} < x < \frac{2}{3}$, which fraction could be the value of x?
   (A) $\frac{5}{6}$
   (B) $\frac{3}{4}$
   (C) $\frac{7}{10}$
   (D) $\frac{1}{2}$
   (E) $\frac{1}{10}$

3. Which inequality represents all possible solutions of $4 < -3x - 2 < 13$?
   (A) $2 < x < 5$
   (B) $-2 < x < -5$
   (C) $x < -2$ and $x > -5$
   (D) $x > 2$ and $x < 5$
   (E) $x > -2$ and $x < -5$

4. Marsha makes earrings and sells them online. Materials cost $3 per pair, and she sells them for $12 per pair. Which inequality represents the number of pairs of earrings, e, Marsha needs to make and sell to earn at least $300?
   (A) $12e \geq \$300$
   (B) $3e \geq \$300$
   (C) $9e \geq \$300$
   (D) $300e \leq 12$
   (E) $12e - 3 \leq 300$

5. Which value of x is a solution to the inequality $3x + 5 < 4x - 9$?
   (A) -14
   (B) -7
   (C) 7
   (D) 14
   (E) 15

6. Which inequality represents all possible solutions of $2x - 5 \leq 4x + 5$?
   (A) $x \leq \frac{1}{10}$
   (B) $x \leq 5$
   (C) $x \leq -2$
   (D) $x \leq -5$
   (E) $x \geq -5$

7. Which inequality represents all possible solutions of $4 \leq -2x - 2$ or $3x + 3 \leq 12$?
   (A) $x \leq 2$ or $x \leq 4$
   (B) $1 \leq x \leq 6$
   (C) $-3 \leq x \leq 3$
   (D) $x \leq -3$ or $x \leq 3$
   (E) $x \leq 1$ or $x \geq 6$

8. Consider the inequality $mx + 5 > -15$. What value of m will result in the solution $x < 5$?
   (A) -5
   (B) -4
   (C) -2
   (D) 2
   (E) 4

9. Which number line represents the solution to the inequality $-3(x + 2) > x - 2$?

(A)

(B)

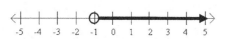

(C)

(D)

(E)

10. The drama club is selling tickets to the school play for $8 each. The drama club spent $200 on props and costumes for the play. They want to make at least $100 more in ticket sales than they spent. Which inequality represents the number of tickets, t, the drama club needs to sell to meet their goal?
(A) $8(t - 200) \geq 100$
(B) $8t \leq 300$
(C) $100t \geq 200 - 8$
(D) $8t + 100 \geq 200$
(E) $8t \geq 300$

11. Which inequality represents all possible solutions of $32x + 4(4x + 2) \geq 3x - 1$?
(A) $x \leq 5$
(B) $x \geq -5$
(C) $x \geq \dfrac{1}{5}$
(D) $x \geq -\dfrac{1}{5}$
(E) $x \leq -5$

12. Which inequality represents all possible solutions of $\dfrac{x}{6} \leq -3$?
(A) $x \leq 3$
(B) $x \leq -18$
(C) $x \leq -2$
(D) $x \geq 18$
(E) $x \leq -3$

13. Samantha has $20 for a cab home. The cab has a base price of $5, then is $2 per mile after that. Which of the following inequalities represents the the maximum number of miles, m, Samantha will be able to travel in the cab?
(A) $7m \leq 20$
(B) $2m + 5 < 20$
(C) $2m + 5 \leq 20$
(D) $2m - 5 \leq 20$
(E) $7m < 5$

14. Which inequality represents all possible solutions of $-5y < 25$?
(A) $y > 5$
(B) $y > -5$
(C) $y < -5$
(D) $y > 1$
(E) $y < -1$

15. Consider the inequality $ax + 3 \leq -18$. Which value of a will result in the solution $x \geq 7$?
(A) -5
(B) $-\dfrac{15}{7}$
(C) -3
(D) 3
(E) 5

16. If $\frac{2}{9} < x < \frac{3}{4}$, which fraction could be the value of x?
    (A) $\frac{9}{10}$
    (B) $\frac{9}{11}$
    (C) $\frac{4}{5}$
    (D) $\frac{7}{10}$
    (E) $\frac{1}{10}$

17. Which inequality represents all possible solutions of $-3y < 24$?
    (A) $y > 72$
    (B) $y < -72$
    (C) $y > -8$
    (D) $y < -8$
    (E) $y > 8$

Scientific Notation

1. Which expression has a value of 42,900?
   (A) 42.9×10^2
   (B) 4.29×10^3
   (C) 4.29×10^5
   (D) 4.29×10^4
   (E) 4.29×10^{-4}

2. What is $\frac{1}{8,000}$ written in scientific notation?
   (A) 1.25×10^{-5}
   (B) 1.25×10^{-4}
   (C) 12.5×10^{-4}
   (D) 1.25×10^{-3}
   (E) 1.25×10^4

3. What is the value of 0.0628×10^4?
   (A) 0.0628
   (B) 0.628
   (C) 6.28
   (D) 62.8
   (E) 628

4. Which is the sum of 9.5×10^6 and 5.9×10^5?
   (A) 1.09×10^6
   (B) 1.009×10^7
   (C) 1.09×10^7
   (D) 15.4×10^{11}
   (E) 1.009×10^{-7}

5. Which expression is the product of 3.8×10^4 and 5?
   (A) 8.8×10^4
   (B) 1.9×10^5
   (C) 1.9×10^4
   (D) 1.9×10^6
   (E) 1.9×10^3

6. Which expression is equivalent to $(4.1 \times 10^4)^2$?
   (A) 8.2×10^8
   (B) 1.681×10^9
   (C) 1.6×10^8
   (D) 8.2×10^2
   (E) 4.1×10^8

7. Which expression is equivalent to the difference of 7.3×10^6 and 3.7×10^5?
   (A) 6.93×10^5
   (B) 3.6×10
   (C) 3.6×10^5
   (D) 3.6×10^6
   (E) 6.93×10^6

8. Earth's circumference is approximately 4.07×10^7 meters. Earth's radius is approximately 6.378×10^6 meters. How much greater, in meters, is Earth's circumference than its radius?
   (A) 1.4522×10^4
   (B) 2.981×10^7
   (C) 3.7411×10^6
   (D) 3.4322×10^7
   (E) 2.308×10^7

9. A rectangular city park has a length of 9.2×10^3 feet and a width of 1.32×10^4 feet. What is the perimeter, in feet, of the park?
   (A) 4.48×10^4
   (B) 3.56×10^4
   (C) 1.052×10^4
   (D) 7.88×10^4
   (E) 1.121×10^4

The Tutorverse

10. Neptune is approximately 4.4×10^9 km from the sun. Venus is approximately 1.1×10^8 km from the sun. How many times farther, in km, from the sun is Neptune than Venus?
    (A) 3.3×10
    (B) 40
    (C) 4.29×10^9
    (D) 4
    (E) 4×10^2

11. The deepest part of the Pacific Ocean, the Mariana Trench, is 3.6201×10^4 feet deep. Mount Everest's highest elevation is 2.90317×10^4 feet. What would be the vertical distance from the peak of Mount Everest to the bottom of the Mariana Trench, in feet?
    (A) 6.52327×10^8
    (B) 6.52327×10^5
    (C) 6.52327×10^4
    (D) 7.1693×10^4
    (E) 7.1693×10^3

Geometry & Measurements

Pythagorean Theorem

1. Which is the missing length of the side in this right triangle?

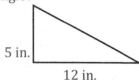

5 in.

12 in.

   (A) 9 in.
   (B) 11 in.
   (C) 13 in.
   (D) 17 in.
   (E) 19 in.

2. What is the length of the hypotenuse of the right triangle if its area is 9 cm²?

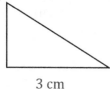

3 cm

   (A) $3\sqrt{2}$ cm
   (B) $3\sqrt{5}$ cm
   (C) 6 cm
   (D) 9 cm
   (E) 12 cm

3. A *Pythagorean Triple* is any set of three numbers *a*, *b*, and *c* such that $a^2 + b^2 = c^2$. Which of the following sets is NOT a Pythagorean Triple?
   (A) 3, 4, 5
   (B) $\sqrt{5}, \sqrt{7}, \sqrt{12}$
   (C) 6, 10, 24
   (D) $\sqrt{81}$, 12, 15
   (E) 6, 8, 10

4. What is the distance between the two points shown?

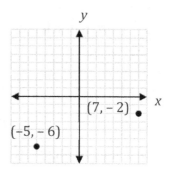

   (A) 9 units
   (B) 12 units
   (C) $4\sqrt{10}$ units
   (D) 16 units
   (E) $16\sqrt{10}$ units

5. What is the distance between two points located at (−5, −3) and (3, −5) on a coordinate plane?
   (A) $2\sqrt{17}$ units
   (B) $4\sqrt{7}$ units
   (C) 5 units
   (D) 10 units
   (E) 17 units

6. A triangle has an area of 16 ft². The length of the base is 4 ft. What is the perimeter of the triangle in feet?
   (A) 8
   (B) $4\sqrt{5}$
   (C) $12 + 4\sqrt{5}$
   (D) 16
   (E) $20 + 4\sqrt{17}$

The Tutorverse

7. What is the distance between the two points shown?

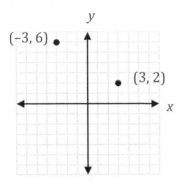

(A) 2√13 units
(B) 4√13 units
(C) 6 units
(D) 10 units
(E) 52 units

8. What is the distance between two points located at (–5, 8) and (3, –2) on a coordinate plane?
(A) 2√41
(B) 4√11
(C) 6
(D) 12
(E) 13

9. What is the perimeter of this right triangle if its area is 6 cm²?

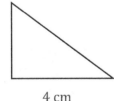

4 cm

(A) 2 + √5 cm
(B) 3 cm
(C) 5 cm
(D) 7 + 2√6 cm
(E) 12 cm

10. What is the perimeter of this right triangle if its area is 14 cm²?

4 cm

(A) 11 + √65 cm
(B) 7 cm
(C) √65 cm
(D) 2√7 cm
(E) 4 + 2√7 cm

11. What is the shortest distance between point X and point Y?

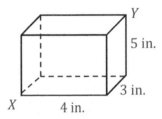

(A) 5
(B) 5√2
(C) √41
(D) √34
(E) 25

12. A 16-foot long ladder is placed 4 feet away from a building so that it reaches the top of the building's first story. If the building is 4 stories tall and each story is the same height, how tall is the building?

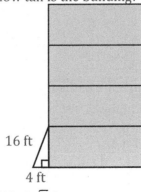

16 ft

4 ft

(A) 2√5 ft
(B) 4√15 ft
(C) 15 ft
(D) 16 ft
(E) 16√15 ft

The Tutorverse

Perimeter, Area, Volume

1. A circle is inscribed in a square, as shown. What is the area of the shaded region?

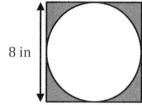

8 in

(A) 16 – 4π sq in
(B) 16 – 16π sq in
(C) 64 – 8π sq in
(D) 64 – 16π sq in
(E) 64 – 64π sq in

2. A right triangle is inscribed inside circle O. What is the area of the circle?

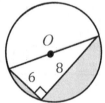

(A) 10π
(B) 25π
(C) 49π
(D) 50π
(E) 100π

3. The length of a rectangle is 8 inches. Its area is 56 square inches. What is the perimeter of the rectangle?
(A) 7 in
(B) 14 in
(C) 15 in
(D) 28 in
(E) 30 in

4. What is the area, in mm², of the figure shown?

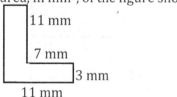

(A) 28
(B) 56
(C) 77
(D) 110
(E) 2,541

5. What is the perimeter, in mi, of the figure shown?

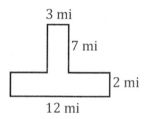

(A) 24
(B) 33
(C) 37.5
(D) 42
(E) 45

6. What is the circumference, in terms of π, of a circle with area 100π meters²?
(A) 10π meters
(B) 20π meters
(C) 25π meters
(D) 50π meters
(E) 2,500π meters

7. The isosceles triangle shown below has a perimeter of 32 centimeters. What is the area of the triangle, in square centimeters?

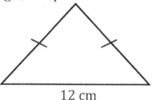

12 cm

(A) 24
(B) 30
(C) 48
(D) 60
(E) 96

8. A garden is 63 yards long and 21 yards wide. The farmer wants to place fencing around the entire garden, and he also wants to add two lengths of fencing inside the garden to split it into three congruent squares. How many yards of fencing will he need in all?
(A) 56
(B) 70
(C) 168
(D) 189
(E) 210

The Tutorverse

9. Circle X has a circumference of π feet and Circle Y has a circumference of 4π feet. What is the difference in the length, in feet, of the radius of Circle Y and the radius of Circle X?
   (A) 1
   (B) 1.5
   (C) √3
   (D) 3
   (E) 3π

10. What is the area of a square with perimeter 36 inches?
    (A) 18 sq in
    (B) 24 sq in
    (C) 36 sq in
    (D) 81 sq in
    (E) 324 sq in

11. What is the perimeter of a square with area 36 inches?
    (A) 18 in
    (B) 24 in
    (C) 36 in
    (D) 81 in
    (E) 324 in

12. An isosceles triangle has a base of 10 inches and a height of 12 inches, as shown below. What is the perimeter, in inches?

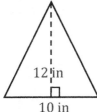

12 in

10 in

    (A) 2√61
    (B) 4√61
    (C) 34
    (D) 36
    (E) 60

13. A dinner plate is placed on top of a circular place mat. The placemat has a radius of 12 inches, and the dinner plate has a diameter of 16 centimeters. Find the area of the placemat that is not covered by the dinner plate.
    (A) 16π
    (B) 20π
    (C) 40π
    (D) 80π
    (E) 112π

14. Right triangle ABC has two legs measuring 6 inches and 8 inches. Right triangle XYZ is similar to triangle ABC and has a hypotenuse measuring 30 inches. Find the difference in the perimeters, in inches, of the two triangles.
    (A) 6
    (B) 16
    (C) 24
    (D) 48
    (E) 72

15. A cubic cardboard box has a volume of 64 cubic inches. Find the length of one side.
    (A) 4
    (B) 5
    (C) 6
    (D) 7
    (E) 8

16. How many more cubic cm of water can fit into a container with dimensions 4 cm × 5 cm × 6 cm than into a container with dimensions 3 cm × 4 cm × 5 cm?
    (A) 12 cm³
    (B) 30 cm³
    (C) 36 cm³
    (D) 60 cm³
    (E) 120 cm³

17. The volume of a box is 385 cubic inches. Its width is 5 inches, and its height is 11 inches. Find its length, in inches.
    (A) 5
    (B) 7
    (C) 9
    (D) 11
    (E) 13

18. A rectangular prism has a volume of 504 cubic centimeters. Which could NOT be its dimensions?
    (A) 9 cm by 8 cm by 7 cm
    (B) 12 cm by 6 cm by 7 cm
    (C) 14 cm by 6 cm by 6 cm
    (D) 16 cm by 9 cm by 4 cm
    (E) 18 cm by 7 cm by 4 cm

The Tutorverse

19. The three dimensions of a rectangular prism are all distinct odd integers. Which of the following could NOT be a possible volume for this prism?
    (A) 27 cubic inches
    (B) 35 cubic inches
    (C) 49 cubic inches
    (D) 105 cubic inches
    (E) 125 cubic inches

20. What is the volume of the right triangular prism below?

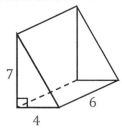

7
6
4

    (A) 17
    (B) 42
    (C) 84
    (D) 168
    (E) 336

21. The product of the height and width of a rectangular prism is 6. The product of its height and length is 10. The product of its width and length is 15. Find the volume of the whole prism.
    (A) 30
    (B) 60
    (C) 300
    (D) 450
    (E) 900

22. A small cube has a side length of 3 inches. How many small cubes are needed to completely fill a larger cube whose base has a perimeter of 60 inches?
    (A) 15
    (B) 20
    (C) 45
    (D) 60
    (E) 125

Problems Using Shapes and Angles

1. Each exterior angle of a square has which measure?
   (A) 90°
   (B) 120°
   (C) 180°
   (D) 270°
   (E) 360°

2. What is the measure of each angle in a regular hexagon?
   (A) 45°
   (B) 90°
   (C) 120°
   (D) 180°
   (E) 270°

3. Which of the following could be the lengths of the sides of a triangle?
   (A) 1, 2, 3
   (B) 3, 3, 6
   (C) 7, 8, 9
   (D) 3, 5, 8
   (E) 2, 5, 1

4. In the figure, B is the center of the circle and ∠ABC is a 45° angle. Vertices A and B of the triangle are on the circle. If the length of AB is 12, what is the area of the shaded region?

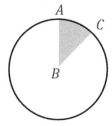

   (A) 18π
   (B) 12π
   (C) 8π
   (D) 4π
   (E) It cannot be determined from the given information.

The Tutorverse

5. In the figure, *AB* and *CD* are parallel, and *WX* and *YZ* are parallel. What the value of *x*?

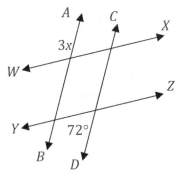

(A) 108
(B) 98
(C) 72
(D) 45
(E) 36

6. In the figure below, what is the value of *x*?

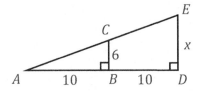

(A) 10
(B) 12
(C) 16
(D) 20
(E) It cannot be determined from the given information.

7. A certain isosceles triangle has exactly one angle measuring 42°. What could be the measure, in degrees, of another angle?
(A) 40
(B) 42
(C) 69
(D) 96
(E) 138

8. Let *h* represent the height of a triangle. Which expression would represent the area of this triangle if the base is 4 less than the height?
(A) $A = \frac{1}{2}bh$
(B) $A = \frac{1}{2}b(h-4)$
(C) $A = \frac{1}{2}(b-4)h$
(D) $A = \frac{1}{2}b(b-4)$
(E) $A = \frac{1}{2}h(h-4)$

9. What is the arc measure of ∠*AC*?

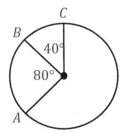

(A) 120
(B) 80
(C) 50
(D) 40
(E) 20

10. In the figure, if *b* is a whole number and *PR* = *RQ*, which of the following could be the length of segment *PQ*?

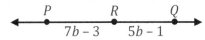

(A) 1
(B) 2
(C) 3
(D) 4
(E) 8

11. A parallelogram has one angle that measures 46°. What could be the measure of another angle?
(A) 20°
(B) 44°
(C) 67°
(D) 127°
(E) 134°

12. On the figure shown, point *X* is located at the midpoint of side *AB* and point *Y* will be located at the midpoint of side *AC*. Which could be a line segment that passes through centroid *Q*?

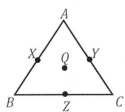

(A) *XY*
(B) *XC*
(C) *ZX*
(D) *YC*
(F) *ZY*

13. *AB* and *CD* are both diameters of the circle. What is the measure of ∠*CEF*?

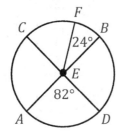

(A) 54°
(B) 62°
(C) 66°
(D) 58°
(E) 82°

14. What is the measure of each angle in a regular octagon?
(A) 45°
(B) 90°
(C) 120°
(D) 135°
(E) 180°

15. In the figure, lines *A* and *B* intersect, as shown. What is the value of *x*?

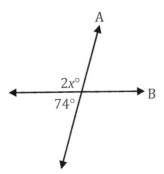

(A) 37
(B) 42
(C) 53
(D) 91
(E) 106

16. What is the value of *x*?

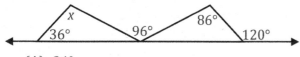

(A) 34°
(B) 60°
(C) 84°
(D) 94°
(E) 124°

17. *ABCD* is a parallelogram. What is the measure of ∠*ADC*?

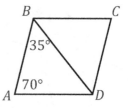

(A) 35°
(B) 70°
(C) 75°
(D) 110°
(E) 180°

18. Point *A* is at the center of the circle. Segment *AC* is equal to 8. What is the area of triangle *ABC*?

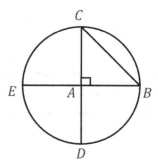

(A) 24
(B) 32
(C) 64
(D) 66
(E) 112

19. What is the value of *x*? (*Note: Figure not drawn to scale.*)

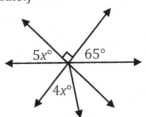

(A) 5
(B) 20
(C) 25
(D) 65
(E) 115

Coordinates

1. A line parallel to $y = 2x + 3$ passes through $(4, 7)$. What is the equation of the line?
   (A) $y = 2x - 1$
   (B) $y = \frac{x}{2} + 5$
   (C) $y = -2x + 15$
   (D) $y = -\frac{x}{2} + 9$
   (E) $y = 2x + 1$

2. The area of a triangle with vertices at $(0,0)$, $(4,0)$ and $(0,5)$ is
   (A) 5
   (B) 9
   (C) 10
   (D) 20
   (E) 40

3. Find the x–intercept of the line perpendicular to $y = -4x + 3$ passing through $(8, 3)$.
   (A) -4
   (B) -2
   (C) $-\frac{1}{4}$
   (D) $\frac{1}{4}$
   (E) 1

4. A square has a center at $(4, 1)$. Its sides are parallel to the x and y axes. Its area is 36. Which point is a vertex of the square?
   (A) $(4, 4)$
   (B) $(7, 4)$
   (C) $(4, 7)$
   (D) $(10, 1)$
   (E) $(1, 1)$

5. Which point solves the following inequality $x + 2y < -5$?
   (A) $(1, -3)$
   (B) $(2, -3)$
   (C) $(0, -3)$
   (D) $(1, -2)$
   (E) $(1, 2)$

6. Find the intersection of the lines $y = 3x + 4$ and $y = 5x - 2$.
   (A) $(3, 5)$
   (B) $(3, 13)$
   (C) $(13, 3)$
   (D) $(5, 3)$
   (E) $(4, -2)$

7. On a coordinate plane, what is the distance between the points $(-1, 4)$ and $(4, -8)$?
   (A) 5
   (B) 12
   (C) 13
   (D) 17
   (E) 20

8. Find the perimeter of a triangle with vertices at $(0, 0)$, $(14, 0)$, and $(5, 12)$ on a coordinate plane.
   (A) 26
   (B) 31
   (C) 35
   (D) 40
   (E) 42

9. What is the area of the trapezoid with vertices at $(0, 0)$, $(4, 0)$, $(0, 4)$ and $(4, 6)$ on a coordinate plane?
   (A) 10
   (B) 12
   (C) 20
   (D) 24
   (E) 30

10. Which of the following is an integer?
    (A) The distance from $(0, 0)$ to $(1, 1)$
    (B) The distance from $(1, 0)$ to $(3, 1)$
    (C) The distance from $(2, 4)$ to $(4, 2)$
    (D) The distance from $(3, 2)$ to $(0, -2)$
    (E) The distance from $(2, 2)$ to $(-2, -2)$

Transformations

1. On an *xy*-coordinate plane, point *Q* (4, 2) is translated 3 units up and 2 units left. What are its new coordinates?
   (A) (2, 5)
   (B) (7, 0)
   (C) (2, -1)
   (D) (1, 0)
   (E) (7, 5)

2. On an *xy*-coordinate plane, point *P* (3, 5) is first reflected across the *y*-axis, then across the *x*-axis. What are the coordinates of the new point?
   (A) (−3, −5)
   (B) (−3, 5)
   (C) (3, −5)
   (D) (5, −3)
   (E) (−5, −3)

3. Point *R* is translated (*t* + 1) units down and *t* units left. If the original coordinates of *R* were (7, 5) and the coordinates of the resulting point were (−1, *y*), find the value of *y*.
   (A) 0
   (B) −1
   (C) −2
   (D) −3
   (E) −4

4. Point *T* (*a*, *b*) is reflected across the *x*-axis and then translated 3 units to the left onto point *T'*. In terms of *a* and *b*, what are the coordinates of *T'*?
   (A) (−*a* − 3, *b*)
   (B) (*a* − 3, −*b*)
   (C) (−*a* − 3, −*b*)
   (D) (3 − *a*, *b*)
   (E) (−*a*, *b* − 3)

5. Point *U* is translated 4 units up, then reflected across the *y*-axis. If the coordinates of the point after the sequence of transformations is (6, 8), where is point *U*?
   (A) (6, 4)
   (B) (4, 6)
   (C) (−6, 4)
   (D) (−4, 6)
   (E) (−6, 12)

6. A triangle with vertices *A* (0, 0), *B* (4, 0), and *C* (0, 3) is reflected across the line *x* = 2, then translated 2 units up onto triangle *A'B'C'*. What are the coordinates of *C'*?
   (A) (0, 3)
   (B) (4, 3)
   (C) (4, 1)
   (D) (4, 5)
   (E) (0, 5)

7. Point *W* (*a*, *b*) is reflected across the line *y* = −1, then reflected across the *y*-axis. The resulting point has coordinates (−5, 9). Find the coordinates of point *W*.
   (A) (5, −7)
   (B) (−5, −11)
   (C) (5, 11)
   (D) (3, 11)
   (E) (5, −11)

8. Point *F* (4, 7) is rotated 180° about the origin, and then translated 2 units up. What are the coordinates of the resulting point?
   (A) (4, 9)
   (B) (−4, −9)
   (C) (−4, −5)
   (D) (−5, −4)
   (E) (−7, −2)

9. Point *M* (4, 2) is rotated 90° counterclockwise about the origin, then it is translated 2 units to the left. What are the coordinates of the resulting point?
   (A) (−2, 2)
   (B) (−4, 4)
   (C) (2, −6)
   (D) (−2, −6)
   (E) (−2, −2)

10. Triangle *ABC* has vertices *A* (0, 0), *B* (4, 0), and *C* (0, 6). If the triangle is dilated by a factor of 2, what is its new area?
    (A) 6
    (B) 12
    (C) 24
    (D) 48
    (E) 96

11. Triangle *ABC* with vertices *A* (1, 2), *B* (2, 3), and *C* (3, 6) is dilated by a factor of 3 and translated 2 units up to create triangle *A'B'C'*. What are the coordinates of *B'*?
    (A) (5, 8)
    (B) (6, 8)
    (C) (6, 11)
    (D) (8, 11)
    (E) (12, 18)

12. The parallelogram *ABCD*, shown on the grid, is dilated by a factor of $\frac{1}{4}$ to create parallelogram *A'B'C'D'*.

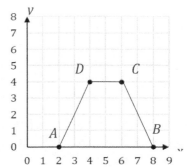

    What is the area of *A'B'C'D'*?
    (A) 4
    (B) 16
    (C) 64
    (D) 256
    (E) 1,024

Slope

1. Which is the slope of the line represented by the equation $y = \frac{5}{7}x + 6$?
   (A) −5
   (B) $-\frac{5}{7}$
   (C) $\frac{5}{7}$
   (D) $\frac{7}{5}$
   (E) 7

2. What is the slope of the line represented by the equation $7x - 5y = 30$?
   (A) $-\frac{7}{5}$
   (B) $-\frac{5}{7}$
   (C) $\frac{5}{7}$
   (D) $\frac{7}{5}$
   (E) 6

3. Which equation represents a line parallel to the graph of $12x + 4y = 10$?
   (A) $y = 3x + \frac{5}{2}$
   (B) $y = -\frac{6x+4}{3}$
   (C) $y = -\frac{9x+3}{4}$
   (D) $y = -\frac{9x+2}{3}$
   (E) $y = 12x + 10$

4. Which is the slope of the line represented by the equation $3x + 8y = 12$?
   (A) −8
   (B) $-\frac{3}{8}$
   (C) $\frac{3}{8}$
   (D) $\frac{8}{3}$
   (E) 3

5. Which is the slope of a line that has an *x*-intercept of (5, 0) and a *y*-intercept of (0, −2)?
   (A) 2
   (B) $\frac{5}{2}$
   (C) $\frac{2}{5}$
   (D) $-\frac{2}{5}$
   (E) $-\frac{2}{3}$

6. The points (1, 7) and (*x*, 4) lie on the same line. If the slope of the line is $\frac{1}{2}$, what is the value of *x*?
   (A) 7
   (B) 5
   (C) $\frac{1}{5}$
   (D) −5
   (F) −7

The Tutorverse

7. Which equation represents a line parallel to the graph of $-x + 2y = 5$ on the coordinate grid?

    (A) $y = \frac{1}{2}x + 9$

    (B) $y = 2x + 5$

    (C) $y = -\frac{1}{2}x + 6$

    (D) $y = \frac{x+3}{3}$

    (E) $y = -\frac{1}{3}x + 2$

8. In the xy-coordinate plane, what is the slope of a line that is perpendicular to the line with the equation $8x - 5y = 20$?

    (A) $y = \frac{8}{5}x + 6$

    (B) $y = 5x - 1$

    (C) $y = -8x - 5$

    (D) $y = -\frac{5}{8}x - 4$

    (E) $y = \frac{1}{5}x + 2$

9. What is the slope of the line represented by the equation $\frac{1}{2}x + 3y = 6$?

    (A) $-\frac{1}{6}$

    (B) $-\frac{1}{2}$

    (C) $\frac{1}{6}$

    (D) 3

    (E) 2

10. Which is the slope of the line passing through the points $(0, 8)$ and $(10, 5)$?

    (A) 4

    (B) 3

    (C) $\frac{3}{10}$

    (D) $-\frac{3}{10}$

    (E) $-\frac{10}{3}$

11. A line with a slope of $\frac{3}{5}$ passes through points $(k, 6)$ and $(-2, k)$. What is the value of k?

    (A) 12

    (B) 4

    (C) 3

    (D) $\frac{1}{3}$

    (E) -3

12. What is the equation of a line perpendicular to $3y + 2x = 6$ and that shares the same y-intercept?

    (A) $2y + 3x = 6$

    (B) $y = \frac{3}{2}x + 2$

    (C) $y = \frac{3}{2}x - 6$

    (D) $y - 8 = \frac{3}{2}(x - 4)$

    (E) $y = -\frac{2}{3}x + 2$

Spatial Reasoning

1. What shape is made by the cross-section of the figure below?

    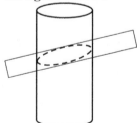

    (A) ellipse
    (B) circle
    (C) sphere
    (D) cylinder
    (E) arc

2. An equilateral triangle is drawn below. Its vertices are P, Q, and R. The midpoint of PQ is T, the midpoint of QR is U, and the midpoint of PR is S. How many different triangles can be drawn with 3 vertices chosen from P, Q, R, S, T, and U?

    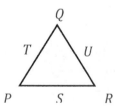

    (A) 6
    (B) 17
    (C) 20
    (D) 216
    (E) 729

The Tutorverse

3. How many triangles are in the figure below?

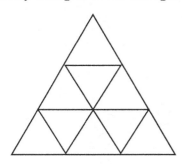

(A) 9
(B) 10
(C) 11
(D) 12
(E) 13

4. Dan lives 8 miles south and 15 miles east of his brother Dave. If there were a straight path paved from Dan's house to Dave's, how long would it be?
(A) 7 miles
(B) 12.5 miles
(C) 15 miles
(D) 17 miles
(E) 23 miles

5. The dimensions of each segment are shown below. How many squares are there in total?

(A) 5
(B) 6
(C) 7
(D) 8
(E) 9

6. Which figure is a possible net for the cube shown?

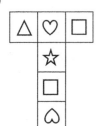

(A)   (B) 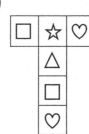 (C) 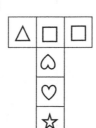 (D) 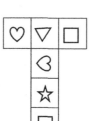 (E)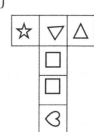

7. Which figure is a possible cube for the net shown?

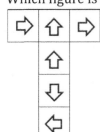

(A)   (B)   (C)   (D)   (E)

The Tutorverse

8. Which figure is a possible net for the cube?

(A)    (B) 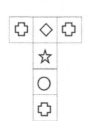   (C)    (D) 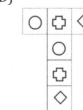   (E)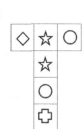

Data Analysis & Probability

Mean, Median, Mode

Use the information below to answer the next 3 problems:

The ages of the first ten people to enter an amusement park one day were 8, 38, 36, 5, 3, 65, 62, 37, 31, and 5.

1. What was their mean age?
    (A) 28
    (B) 29
    (C) 36
    (D) 57
    (E) 65

2. What was their median age?
    (A) 31
    (B) 32.5
    (C) 33.5
    (D) 34
    (E) 36

3. What was the range of their ages?
    (A) 10
    (B) 31
    (C) 35
    (D) 62
    (E) 65

The following 4 questions are based on the below table, which displays the number of visitors at a library each day for one week.

Day	Number of Visitors
Monday	98
Tuesday	59
Wednesday	57
Thursday	85
Friday	58
Saturday	57
Sunday	69

4. What is the mean number of visitors during the 7-day period?
    (A) 50
    (B) 57
    (C) 69
    (D) 80
    (E) 98

5. What is the median number of visitors during the 7-day period?
    (A) 57
    (B) 59
    (C) 60
    (D) 69
    (E) 81

6. What is the mode of the data?
   (A) 57
   (B) 58
   (C) 59
   (D) 69
   (E) 70

7. What is the range of the data?
   (A) 28
   (B) 36
   (C) 40
   (D) 41
   (E) 57

8. The average distance Jolene jogged per day in April, May and June was 4.5 miles. The average distance she jogged per day in July and August was 5.5 miles. What was the average distance, in miles, she jogged per day over all five months?
   (A) 4
   (B) 4.9
   (C) 6.1
   (D) 5
   (E) 4.5

9. If the average of 4 consecutive even integers is 53, what is the smallest number?
   (A) 50
   (B) 52
   (C) 56
   (D) 58
   (E) 200

10. A hotel offers five different room types. The nightly prices of the first four are $70, $90, $150, and $240. If the nightly price of the fifth room type is the range of prices the first four room types, what is the mean of all five prices?
    (A) $140
    (B) $144
    (C) $160
    (D) $170
    (E) $200

11. If all the factors of 24 were written as a list, then what is the range of the list?
    (A) 5
    (B) 8
    (C) 10
    (D) 23
    (F) 24

12. What is the median of all of the prime numbers under 20?
    (A) 7
    (B) 9
    (C) 11
    (D) 16
    (E) 17

13. Consider the data set {4, 7, 27, 3, 15, 6, 43}. Which number, if added to the set, will not change the mean?
    (A) 7
    (B) 11
    (C) 15
    (D) 18
    (E) 105

14. Consider the data set {4, 2, 9, 1, 9, 8, 8}. Which number, if added to the set, will not change the median?
    (A) 3
    (B) 6
    (C) 7
    (D) 8
    (E) 9

15. Susie was trying to calculate the mean of her five test scores. She forgot what she scored on the first 4 tests but knew the sum of those four scores was 375. If Susie scored a 95 on her fifth test, then what was the mean of all 5 scores?
    (A) 75
    (B) 85
    (C) 94
    (D) 94.375
    (E) 95

16. Paul took three tests. His grades were 92, 85, and 87. He will take one more test before the end of the semester. If he wants a test average of 90, what must he score on his fourth test?
    (A) 98
    (B) 97
    (C) 96
    (D) 95
    (E) 90

17. After three tests, Brandon had a test average of 87. After his fourth test, his average dropped to 83. What did he score on his fourth test?
    (A) 70
    (B) 71
    (C) 74
    (D) 83
    (E) 05

The Tutorverse

Probability

1. Events A, B, and C are independent, mutually exclusive events. Let P(A) = 25%, P(B) = 55%, and P(C) = 20%. What is P(A or B)?
   (A) 14%
   (B) 20%
   (C) 30%
   (D) 80%
   (E) 100%

2. Jenny plays a game in which there are 3 outcomes: win, loss, and tie. For each game, let P(win) = 0.3, P(loss) = 0.6, and P(tie) = 0.1. If Jenny plays the game 2 times, what is the probability that she will tie the first game, and NOT win the second game?
   (A) 0.9
   (B) 0.27
   (C) 0.054
   (D) 0.07
   (E) 0.06

3. What is the probability that a randomly selected positive integer greater than 4 and less than 20 will be prime?
   (A) $\frac{1}{8}$
   (B) $\frac{5}{16}$
   (C) $\frac{3}{8}$
   (D) $\frac{2}{5}$
   (E) $\frac{3}{5}$

4. At every school game, a student is chosen randomly to win a prize. At one game, there were 16 male students, 10 female students, 21 male adults, and 13 female adults. What is the probability the person chosen was a female student?
   (A) $\frac{1}{6}$
   (B) $\frac{4}{15}$
   (C) $\frac{7}{20}$
   (D) $\frac{13}{23}$
   (E) $\frac{10}{13}$

5. Freshmen at San Jose High School took a survey about classes they take. The results are displayed in the table below.

	Takes Algebra	Does Not Take Algebra
Takes Biology	48	35
Does Not Take Biology	61	56

   What is the probability that a randomly selected student likes takes neither algebra nor biology?
   (A) 17.5%
   (B) 20%
   (C) 24%
   (D) 28%
   (E) 48%

6. A deck contains 10 red cards, 5 yellow cards, 8 green cards, and 7 blue cards. What is the probability that a randomly selected card is red?
   (A) $\frac{1}{12}$
   (B) $\frac{1}{6}$
   (C) $\frac{1}{4}$
   (D) $\frac{1}{3}$
   (E) $\frac{2}{3}$

7. Sammy, Tim, and Betty are at a bowling alley. Their names will be chosen at random to determine the order in which they will bowl. What is the probability that Sammy will be chosen first, and Betty will be chosen second?
   (A) $\frac{1}{2}$
   (B) $\frac{1}{4}$
   (C) $\frac{1}{6}$
   (D) $\frac{1}{8}$
   (E) $\frac{1}{16}$

8. There are 8 cards in a set featuring 2 of each of these shapes: stars, circles, triangles, and squares. If 2 cards are chosen at random, what is the probability they will show the same shape?
   (A) $\frac{1}{56}$
   (B) $\frac{1}{28}$
   (C) $\frac{1}{8}$
   (D) $\frac{1}{7}$
   (E) $\frac{1}{5}$

9. Oscar plays baseball at school. His games are cancelled if it is below 50°. If the chance of being below 50° on Monday is 0.3, and the chance being below 50° on Friday is 0.4, what is the chance that Oscar's baseball games will be cancelled on both Monday and Friday, assuming the weather on one day has no effect on the other?
   (A) 1.2
   (B) 0.7
   (C) 0.12
   (D) 0.1
   (E) 0.012

10. In a certain city, there is a probability of 30% that it will snow on any given day. What is the probability that it will snow on 3 consecutive days?
   (A) 90%
   (B) 9%
   (C) 6%
   (D) 3%
   (E) 2.7%

11. Derek places 4 blue beads, 5 green beads, and 3 orange beads in a bowl. He randomly selects one, does not replace it, and randomly selects another. What is the probability that both beads are blue?
   (A) $\frac{4}{5}$
   (B) $\frac{1}{3}$
   (C) $\frac{3}{11}$
   (D) $\frac{1}{9}$
   (E) $\frac{1}{11}$

12. A survey was conducted at a mall to ask about the items that shoppers were purchasing at a certain store. The results are in the table.

	Pants	Not Pants
Shoes	26	40
Not Shoes	37	47

   What is the probability that a randomly selected shopper was buying shoes, but not pants?
   (A) $\frac{3}{20}$
   (B) $\frac{17}{100}$
   (C) $\frac{1}{4}$
   (D) $\frac{4}{15}$
   (E) $\frac{1}{3}$

13. The probability of picking a blue plate out of a cabinet is $\frac{5}{12}$. If there are 36 plates in the cabinet, how many are NOT blue?
   (A) 31
   (B) 21
   (C) 15
   (D) 12
   (E) 10

14. There are red and green apples in a bucket. The probability of picking a red apple is $\frac{2}{3}$. If 5 more green apples were added, the probability of picking a red apple would be $\frac{4}{7}$. How many total apples are in the bucket?
   (A) 20
   (B) 30
   (C) 35
   (D) 40
   (E) 50

15. Angela, Brad, Charlie, Debra, and Emily are giving a class presentation, for which the teacher is selecting names at random to present. What is the probability that Brad will be chosen first, and Emily will NOT be chosen second?
   (A) $\frac{1}{25}$
   (B) $\frac{1}{10}$
   (C) $\frac{1}{9}$
   (D) $\frac{3}{20}$
   (E) $\frac{1}{7}$

The Tutorverse

Counting

1. A letter sequence is 4 letters long and consists of letters K, L, M, and N. If letters may repeat, how many letter sequences are possible?
   (A) 256
   (B) 128
   (C) 81
   (D) 64
   (E) 24

2. A spinner has six equal sections labelled Cat, Dog, Bird, Sheep, Cow, and Pig. Another spinner has four equal sections colored red, green, blue, and yellow. A third spinner has five equal sections labelled 1, 2, 3, 4, and 5. If each wheel is spun once, how many different spin combinations are possible?
   (A) 20
   (B) 24
   (C) 30
   (D) 120
   (E) 720

3. A dinner party wants to pick 2 different appetizers out of a set of 8 to share for the table. In how many ways can they do this?
   (A) 64
   (B) 56
   (C) 36
   (D) 28
   (E) 16

4. A number is picked from set A, which contains the numbers 2, 4, 8, and 16. A number is picked from set B, which contains the numbers 3, 9, and 27. If the two numbers are multiplied, how many different products are possible?
   (A) 6
   (B) 12
   (C) 24
   (D) 144
   (E) 432

5. A certain identification code is composed of three symbols: a digit, a letter, and another digit, in that order. If repetition is allowed, how many possible identification codes exist?
   (A) 6,760
   (B) 2,600
   (C) 100
   (D) 62
   (E) 46

6. There are 5 boys and 5 girls in a committee. 2 boys and 2 girls must be chosen to create a panel of 4 judges. In how many ways can this be done?
   (A) 10
   (B) 100
   (C) 105
   (D) 210
   (E) 400

7. In how many ways can the letters in the word DEER be scrambled if the two E's may not be next to each other?
   (A) 6
   (B) 12
   (C) 16
   (D) 18
   (E) 24

8. A teacher wants to choose two students out of a class of 10 to run an errand. How many pairs can the teacher pick?
   (A) 5
   (B) 20
   (C) 45
   (D) 90
   (E) 100

9. A Norwegian citizen is planning a trip to the United States. He wants to visit 2 of the original 13 colony states. How many different pairs of states can he choose to see, if the order in which he sees the two states doesn't matter?
   (A) 26
   (B) 39
   (C) 78
   (D) 156
   (E) 169

10. How many 3-digit numbers are only composed of even digits?
    (A) 900
    (B) 648
    (C) 400
    (D) 125
    (E) 100

11. Out of a team of 11 baseball players, 9 take the field for any given game. How many different lineups are possible?
    (A) 110
    (B) 99
    (C) 55
    (D) 20
    (E) 9

12. How many ways can you scramble the word "Oaxaca" if two A's must never be adjacent?
    (A) 24
    (B) 72
    (C) 120
    (D) 144
    (E) 720

Set Theory

1. In Mrs. Wigginton's class, 10 students have glasses, 12 students have freckles, 6 students have glasses and freckles, and 8 have neither glasses nor freckles. How many students are in Mrs. Wigginton's class?
    (A) 20
    (B) 22
    (C) 24
    (D) 28
    (E) 32

2. In the set consisting of the integers from one through ten inclusive, how many distinct integers are in the union of the set of primes and the set of evens?
    (A) 6
    (B) 7
    (C) 8
    (D) 9
    (E) 10

3. Set G has 9 elements and Set H has 12 elements. The intersection of the sets has 4 elements. How many elements are in the union of Sets G and H?
    (A) 5
    (B) 8
    (C) 17
    (D) 21
    (E) 25

4. Set K has 11 numbers. The union of Sets K and L has 18 distinct numbers, and the intersection of the two sets has 5 numbers. How many numbers belong to Set L?
    (A) 6
    (B) 7
    (C) 12
    (D) 13
    (E) 16

5. Consider the following Venn diagram showing the following integer values. How many integers are in the union of Sets A and B?

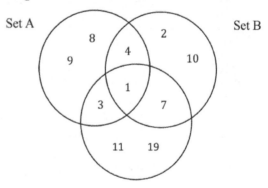

    (A) 4
    (B) 5
    (C) 7
    (D) 8
    (E) 10

6. The union of Sets A and B has 15 elements. Set A has 10 elements, and their intersection has 5 elements. How many elements does Set B have?
    (A) 0
    (B) 5
    (C) 10
    (D) 15
    (E) 20

7. Out of a group of 60 students, 40 of them have a cat and 23 of them have a dog. There are 6 students who have neither a cat nor a dog. How many students have both pets?
    (A) 3
    (B) 6
    (C) 7
    (D) 9
    (E) 21

The Tutorverse

8. Consider the following Venn diagram. What is the sum of the integers that make up the intersection of Sets N and O?

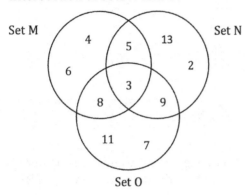

Set M   Set N

Set O

(A) 9
(B) 12
(C) 25
(D) 33
(E) 58

9. A teacher orders 25 pizzas for her class. Of these, 8 have onions and 18 have pepperoni. If 4 pizzas have no toppings at all, and these are the only toppings, how many pizzas have both onions and pepperoni?
(A) 4
(B) 5
(C) 6
(D) 7
(E) 8

10. What is the intersection of Set H and the union of Sets F and G?

Set F = {0, 1, 2, 3}

Set G = {0, 4, 9, 25}

Set H = {0, 1, 3, 6, 9, 12, 25}

(A) {0, 1}
(B) {0, 1, 3}
(C) {0, 1, 3, 4}
(D) {0, 1, 3, 9, 25}
(E) {0, 1, 2, 3, 4, 9, 25}

11. Consider the following Venn diagram. What is the sum of the integer values that make up the union of Sets C and D?

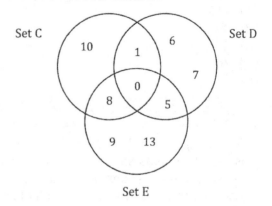

Set C   Set D

Set E

(A) 1
(B) 23
(C) 37
(D) 38
(E) 59

12. Set A consists of all the perfect squares less than or equal to 100. Set B consists of all the integers ending in 4, 6, or 9. How many integers are in the intersection of these two sets?
(A) 3
(B) 4
(C) 5
(D) 6
(E) 7

13. Set A consists of all prime numbers between 1 and 20, inclusive. Set B consists of all perfect squares between 1 and 20, inclusive. What is the difference between the number of integers in the union of the two sets and the number of integers in the intersection of the two sets?
(A) 0
(B) 4
(C) 8
(D) 12
(E) 16

Reading Charts & Graphs

The next two questions relate to the graph below.

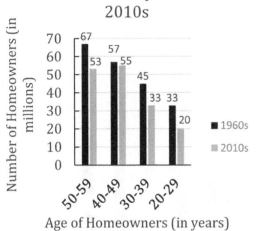

Home Ownership 1960s vs. 2010s

1. Which age group has the largest percent change of homeowners between 1960 and 2010?
   (A) 20-29
   (B) 30-39
   (C) 40-49
   (D) 50-59
   (E) Both 20-29 and 30-39

2. About what percentage of the 2010 homeowners are 30-39 years old?
   (A) 13%
   (B) 20%
   (C) 28%
   (D) 33%
   (E) 72%

The next two questions relate to the graph below.

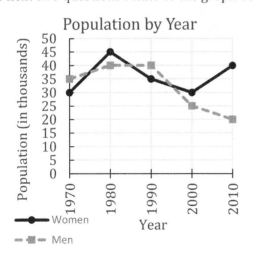

3. In which time period are the populations of women and men are both decreasing?
   (A) 1970-1980
   (B) 1980-1990
   (C) 1990-2000
   (D) 2000-2010
   (E) There is no time period in which both populations are decreasing

4. What is the difference in the number of men and women in 2010?
   (A) 0
   (B) 5,000
   (C) 10,000
   (D) 15,000
   (E) 20,000

5. How many more students have one sibling than have no siblings?

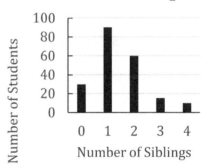

Students with Siblings

   (A) 3
   (B) 30
   (C) 60
   (D) 90
   (E) 120

The Tutorverse

6. What percent of the money in the account at the beginning of 2016 was withdrawn by the beginning of 2017 (rounded to the nearest tenth of a percent)?

Money in Savings Account

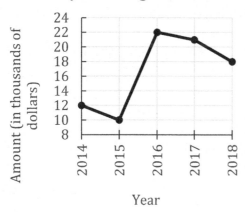

(A) 1.0%
(B) 4.5%
(C) 7%
(D) 8.3%
(E) 9%

The next two questions relate to the graph below.

7. Which of the following statements can NOT be determined by the histogram?

Student Test Scores

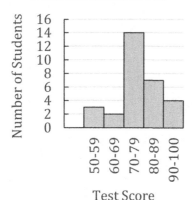

(A) The fraction of students who scored below 80.
(B) The number of students who scored above a 79.
(C) The percent of students who scored between 80 and 100.
(D) The number of students who scored below a 65.
(E) The percent of students who scored at least a 70.

8. How many students scored less than 70 on the test?
(A) 2
(B) 3
(C) 4
(D) 5
(E) 19

The next two questions relate to the graph below.

Can Collection

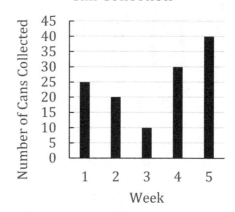

9. How many more cans were collected in week 4 than in week 1?
(A) 5
(B) 10
(C) 15
(D) 20
(E) 30

10. What is the percent decrease in the number of cans collected in week 2 compared to the number of cans collected in week 1?
(A) 4%
(B) 5%
(C) 11%
(D) 20%
(E) 25%

Verbal

Overview

The Verbal section is comprised of synonyms and analogies. Synonym questions assess a student's ability to recognize words and reason through different relationships and subtle differences among words. The analogies measure how well students can relate words and ideas to each other using logic. Together, these questions are designed to test students' vocabulary and reasoning skills.

Students will have 30 minutes to answer 30 synonyms and 30 analogy questions.

On the Actual Test

Synonym questions consist of a single word in capital letters, followed by five answer choices labeled A through E. Students must select the answer choice that has the same or most nearly the same meaning as the word in capital letters.

Analogy questions ask students to look at a pair of words and select another pair of words with a matching relationship. Analogy questions are presented on the Upper Level SSAT in two different ways:

- ☞ Two-part stem: "A" is to "B" as…

    In these types of questions, students are given two words in the stem of the question, and are asked to select the pair of words with the same relationship as demonstrated between words "A" and "B."

- ☞ Three-part stem: "A" is to "B" as "C" is to…

    In these types of questions, students are given three words in the stem of the question; words "A" and "B" form one relationship, and are asked to complete the same relationship between word "C" and your answer choice.

There are many different types of relationships featured in the analogies. The most common ones are described below:

- ☞ Antonym relationships: Words that have the opposite, or nearly the opposite, meaning.
- ☞ Association relationships: One word in a pair is connected to the other word of the pair by association.
- ☞ Cause-and-Effect relationships: One word in a pair is a cause that may produce the other word.
- ☞ Defining relationships: Words that are related by a verb or verbal relationship.
- ☞ Degree/Intensity relationship: One word in a pair is related to the other word of the pair by a higher or lower degree.
- ☞ Function relationships: Words that define the function of an object.
- ☞ Grammatical relationships: Words that are related by a grammatical rule (e.g. plurality, tense, person, etc.).
- ☞ Individual to Object relationships: One word in a pair indicates a person or type of person, while the other word in the pair indicates the object which that person uses.
- ☞ Noun/Verb relationships: One word in a pair indicates a noun, while the other word of the pair indicates an action associated with that noun.
- ☞ Part/Whole relationships: The first word in a pair is a part of the second word of the pair.
- ☞ Purpose relationships: Words that have a common purpose when used together in a task.
- ☞ Type/Kind relationships: One word in a pair that is a type or kind of the other word of the pair.
- ☞ Whole/Part relationships: The first word in a pair is the whole, of which the second word is a part

☞ Synonym relationships: Words that have very similar meaning (NOTE: not the same as the questions featured in the synonyms portion of the Verbal section).

Unlike in this workbook, the questions on the actual test will **not** indicate which type of relationship each analogy represents.

In This Practice Book

Synonym questions are given their own section and are generally presented in order of difficulty (the harder questions appear toward the end of the section).

Analogy questions are also given their own section and are also generally presented in order from less to more challenging. However, analogy questions are further subdivided as follows:

☞ Guided Practice – 14 units, one each for the individual types of analogies listed above. Each unit will only include a specific type of analogy. This allows students to focus on a particular type of analogy, if needed.

☞ Mixed Practice – 10 units of mixed practice. Each unit will include a mix of analogy types, which mirrors the format of the actual test. This allows students to see how well they know the different types of analogies.

There are additional instructions and recommendations at the beginning of each of the Synonyms and Analogies sections, which students should review before starting.

There are many ways to tackle this section of the test. Use the results from the diagnostic practice test to develop a plan. For instance, students may want to try the analogies Mixed Practice 1 to get a sense for which areas to focus on. Then, dive into the relevant Guided Practice sections. If students already know what need further work, they may jump right in to a Guided Practice section.

Tutorverse Tips!

Knowing whether or not to guess can be tricky. The Upper Level SSAT gives students 1 point for each question that is answered correctly. However, if students answer a question incorrectly, ¼ of a point will be deducted from the total score (see example below). No points will be awarded or deducted for questions that are left unanswered. Therefore, answer easy questions first, and come back to tougher questions later.

The formula for determining the raw score is:
(Number of Questions Answered Correctly × 1) – (Number of Questions Answered Incorrectly × ¼)

How Guessing Impacts A Score

Since there are 150 scored questions (167 total questions – 1 writing prompt – 16 experimental questions), the highest possible raw score is 150 points. This would be awarded to students who answer all 150 questions correctly.

If a student answers 110 questions correctly **but answers 40 questions incorrectly**, he or she will have earned (110 × 1) – (40 × ¼), or 110 – 10 = 100 points.

If a student answers 110 questions correctly **but leaves 40 questions unanswered**, he or she will have earned (110 × 1) – (40 × 0), or 110 – 0 = 110 points.

Therefore, it is important to refrain from making wild guesses. Instead, try to use process of elimination to make an educated guess.

The Tutorverse

Synonyms

Overview

Synonym questions consist of a single word in capital letters, followed by five answer choices labeled A through E. Students must select the answer choice that most nearly has the same meaning as the word in capital letters.

How to Use This Section

How much time students should spend on this section should be based on the diagnostic practice test results as well as the student's study plan. For most students, even those who score very well on the diagnostic practice test, we recommend practicing at least 10-15 questions per week in preparing for the exam. Those who score well on the diagnostic practice test and have an expansive vocabulary may wish to focus more on intermediate and advanced questions, while other students may wish to focus on introductory and intermediate questions.

The purpose of this section is to introduce students to new words. Some may find many of the words in this section to be challenging. Students should not be surprised to have to look up many of the words encountered in this section! We encourage students to make a list of difficult or challenging words, whether they appear in questions or answer choices. Write down the definition of each word as well as a sentence using the word. Students might also want to consider writing down positive or negative associations, any root words that can help them remember the word, or any words that are commonly encountered with that word.

Tutorverse Tips!

Sometimes, words can have more than one meaning. Don't be confused! Look at the answer choices to make an educated guess as to which meaning is being used in the question. Then, use reasoning skills to select the word that most nearly means the same as the word in capital letters.

Use it in a Sentence

As you read the question words in capital letters, think of a word that you might use instead of the question word.

If you don't know what a word means, try using it in a sentence. This will often help you see which word can be used to replace the question word. If this doesn't help, see if you can figure out whether or not the word has any positive or negative associations that match those of the answer choices.

Study Roots, Prefixes, & Suffixes

Many English words are derived from a single Greek or Latin root word. Sometimes, these root words relate to many different English words. In addition, knowing common prefixes and suffixes can help with very long or unfamiliar words, which can inform on the word's connotation or meaning.

Read, Read, Read!

Finally, there is no better preparation for the Synonym section than spending time reading. The practice of reading, whether for school or for pleasure, will help you build up your vocabulary. It will give you practice in utilizing context clues and figuring out what unknown words might mean. Reading at or above your current grade level will help you make better sense of more complicated words and sentences.

The Tutorverse

Introductory

Directions – Select the one word or phrase whose meaning is closest to the word in capital letters.

1. DIAGRAM:
   (A) complicated test
   (B) writing implement
   (C) body part
   (D) simple drawing
   (E) popular movie

2. ILLEGITIMATE:
   (A) illogical
   (B) unauthorized
   (C) sickly
   (D) official
   (E) receptive

3. IMMATURE:
   (A) undeveloped
   (B) believable
   (C) established
   (D) sensitive
   (E) happy

4. POSTPONE:
   (A) point out
   (B) recall that
   (C) put off
   (D) run from
   (E) hurry up

5. PREDICTION:
   (A) guess
   (B) recommendation
   (C) memory
   (D) speech
   (E) advice

6. TRANSFER:
   (A) squabble
   (B) own
   (C) presume
   (D) give
   (E) require

7. UNIFY:
   (A) attack
   (B) put together
   (C) protect
   (D) prevent
   (E) pull apart

8. STRENGTHEN:
   (A) fortify
   (B) minimize
   (C) diminish
   (D) outweigh
   (E) compile

9. DISRESPECTFUL:
   (A) considerate
   (B) unhappy
   (C) unhelpful
   (D) generous
   (E) impolite

10. DISTINCTIVE:
    (A) expansive
    (B) fundamental
    (C) intuitive
    (D) ordinary
    (E) special

11. DISMISSIVE:
    (A) certain
    (B) indifferent
    (C) unbiased
    (D) interested
    (E) unsure

12. EMIT:
    (A) put away
    (B) go to
    (C) guess that
    (D) leave out
    (E) give off

13. INNOVATIVE:
    (A) appealing
    (B) noteworthy
    (C) powerful
    (D) groundbreaking
    (E) indistinct

14. EXPORT:
    (A) buy from
    (B) send to
    (C) make from
    (D) receive from
    (E) return to

15. VACANT:
    (A) unoccupied
    (B) closed
    (C) restful
    (D) expensive
    (E) inhabited

16. REVITALIZE:
    (A) provide
    (B) acknowledge
    (C) invigorate
    (D) mitigate
    (E) observe

17. OBJECTIVE:
    (A) quarrelsome
    (B) expressive
    (C) neutral
    (D) biased
    (E) savage

18. PLAUSIBLE:
    (A) disturbing
    (B) impossible
    (C) reasonable
    (D) boring
    (E) passing

19. PRECLUDE:
  (A) connect to
  (B) confirm
  (C) write on
  (D) consist of
  (E) rule out

20. SUBJUGATE:
  (A) study
  (B) conquer
  (C) narrate
  (D) teach
  (E) define

21. ASPIRE:
  (A) leave from
  (B) sweat
  (C) hope for
  (D) intervene in
  (E) obey

22. SOLIDIFY:
  (A) determine
  (B) fragment
  (C) melt
  (D) reinforce
  (E) undermine

23. BOYCOTT:
  (A) refuse
  (B) buy
  (C) embarrass
  (D) relate
  (E) sell

24. COMMEMORATE:
  (A) show respect
  (B) ponder
  (C) showcase
  (D) rebuild
  (E) estimate

25. ENTHUSIASTIC:
  (A) accurate
  (B) complacent
  (C) spiritual
  (D) eager
  (E) insistent

26. FORMIDABLE:
  (A) timely
  (B) creative
  (C) immaculate
  (D) oblivious
  (E) intimidating

27. IMMUNE:
  (A) harmless
  (B) uncommon
  (C) healthy
  (D) invulnerable
  (E) frail

28. SACRIFICE:
  (A) accompany
  (B) save
  (C) accommodate
  (D) exterminate
  (E) forfeit

29. STRATEGY:
  (A) dangerous conflict
  (B) plan of action
  (C) unwilling
       cooperation
  (D) permanent rules
  (E) game of chance

30. UNANIMOUS:
  (A) opposing
  (B) divided
  (C) contradictory
  (D) correct
  (E) united

31. AFFECT:
  (A) outcome
  (B) impact
  (C) facilitate
  (D) govern
  (E) deject

32. ALTER:
  (A) amend
  (B) fix
  (C) constrict
  (D) improve
  (E) worship

33. APPROPRIATE:
  (A) valuable
  (B) incorrect
  (C) gentle
  (D) rough
  (E) proper

34. ARRANGE:
  (A) spill
  (B) travel
  (C) organize
  (D) reach
  (E) beautify

35. ASSESS:
  (A) spend
  (B) evaluate
  (C) map
  (D) evict
  (E) accumulate

36. DEMONSTRATE:
  (A) expend
  (B) argue
  (C) respond
  (D) refute
  (E) reveal

37. DEVISE:
  (A) catch
  (B) invent
  (C) edit
  (D) share
  (E) demand

38. EFFECT:
  (A) end product
  (B) detail
  (C) reason for
  (D) cause
  (E) affect

39. CRITIQUE:
  (A) recognition
  (B) authenticity
  (C) pattern
  (D) quarrel
  (E) assessment

40. EXCLUDE:
    (A) admit
    (B) describe
    (C) escape
    (D) deny
    (E) exhaust

41. IMPLY:
    (A) simplify
    (B) criminalize
    (C) suggest
    (D) disappoint
    (E) accuse

42. INFLUENCE:
    (A) comfort
    (B) shape
    (C) power
    (D) compliment
    (E) talent

43. INQUIRE:
    (A) reply
    (B) tell
    (C) mandate
    (D) question
    (E) approve

44. INTENTION:
    (A) evidence
    (B) good
    (C) retention
    (D) goal
    (E) unknown

45. INTERACT:
    (A) claim
    (B) communicate
    (C) improvise
    (D) compete
    (E) defend

46. INVOLVE:
    (A) include
    (B) appreciate
    (C) welcome
    (D) intrigue
    (E) complicate

47. PERSUADE:
    (A) legalize
    (B) plagiarize
    (C) suave
    (D) convince
    (E) circulate

Intermediate

Directions – Select the one word or phrase whose meaning is closest to the word in capital letters.

1. BINARY:
   (A) perceptive
   (B) frequent
   (C) single
   (D) irate
   (E) paired

2. ENACT:
   (A) put in place
   (B) veto
   (C) get rid of
   (D) cross out
   (E) dissolve

3. HYPERBOLE:
   (A) mistake
   (B) accuracy
   (C) opinion
   (D) exaggeration
   (E) suggestion

4. IRRATIONAL:
   (A) invaluable
   (B) sparse
   (C) valid
   (D) audacious
   (E) preposterous

5. INTERIM:
   (A) infrequent
   (B) temporary
   (C) permanent
   (D) final
   (E) beginning

6. MICRON:
   (A) excess
   (B) speck
   (C) distance
   (D) tradition
   (E) colossus

The Tutorverse

7. MONOTONY:
   (A) single ownership
   (B) excitement
   (C) lack of variety
   (D) melody
   (E) vast expanse

8. NONESSENTIAL:
   (A) crucial
   (B) premature
   (C) indecisive
   (D) superfluous
   (E) selective

9. PERIPHERAL:
   (A) priceless
   (B) superb
   (C) primary
   (D) outlying
   (E) inferior

10. PROTOTYPE:
    (A) imitation
    (B) brand
    (C) improvement
    (D) mock-up
    (E) category

11. SUBTLETY:
    (A) gratification
    (B) nuance
    (C) hostility
    (D) confusion
    (E) bravery

12. SYNCHRONIZE:
    (A) dance
    (B) swim
    (C) place in order
    (D) stand in place
    (E) cooperate with

13. PICTURESQUE:
    (A) motionless
    (B) delightful
    (C) imperceptible
    (D) capture
    (E) comical

14. EXEMPLIFY:
    (A) ambush
    (B) leave
    (C) stimulate
    (D) represent
    (E) explain

15. VERSATILE:
    (A) decrepit
    (B) flexible
    (C) honorable
    (D) practiced
    (E) brilliant

16. CONTEMPTUOUS:
    (A) fragile
    (B) enviable
    (C) derisive
    (D) admiring
    (E) inflexible

17. RELINQUISH:
    (A) obtain
    (B) adore
    (C) recruit
    (D) relish
    (E) abandon

18. LUCID:
    (A) coherent
    (B) headstrong
    (C) elusive
    (D) inconceivable
    (E) fraternal

19. MANDATORY:
    (A) voluntary
    (B) delirious
    (C) irreversible
    (D) indiscreet
    (E) unavoidable

20. MINISCULE:
    (A) infinitesimal
    (B) transcendent
    (C) exuberant
    (D) dauntless
    (E) countless

21. PANDEMONIUM:
    (A) healthy resilience
    (B) dire consequence
    (C) imposing presence
    (D) perfect order
    (E) complete chaos

22. PATERNAL:
    (A) protective
    (B) punishing
    (C) demeaning
    (D) gratuitous
    (E) impatient

23. SENTIMENTAL:
    (A) crazy
    (B) memorable
    (C) ridiculous
    (D) emotional
    (E) inexpressible

24. SUBTERRANEAN:
    (A) worldly
    (B) isolated
    (C) restorative
    (D) underground
    (E) private

25. ENVISION:
    (A) overhear
    (B) imagine
    (C) humiliate
    (D) touch
    (E) learn

26. INCONTROVERTIBLE:
    (A) undeniable
    (B) malleable
    (C) controversial
    (D) immaterial
    (E) ignoble

27. PRECIPITOUS:
    (A) substantial
    (B) steep
    (C) wet
    (D) irritating
    (E) intensive

The Tutorverse

28. RECIPROCAL:
  (A) singular
  (B) robust
  (C) mutual
  (D) inaccessible
  (E) adverse

29. ECLECTIC:
  (A) chosen
  (B) varied
  (C) corporeal
  (D) imaginary
  (E) required

30. JOVIAL:
  (A) rare
  (B) precious
  (C) opulent
  (D) garish
  (E) merry

31. TRANQUILITY:
  (A) discomfort
  (B) sadness
  (C) efficiency
  (D) peace
  (E) chaos

32. TUMULT:
  (A) widespread peace
  (B) accident
  (C) skilled acrobatics
  (D) harmony
  (E) commotion

33. ANALYZE:
  (A) oversee
  (B) dispel
  (C) devote
  (D) medicate
  (E) scrutinize

34. CONCEIVE:
  (A) convenient to
  (B) double cross
  (C) agree to
  (D) think up
  (E) renovate

35. DEDUCE:
  (A) produce
  (B) figure out
  (C) detract from
  (D) deteriorate
  (E) waive

36. SIGNIFICANCE:
  (A) radiance
  (B) substance
  (C) presumption
  (D) triviality
  (E) impudence

37. SPECULATE:
  (A) give respect
  (B) learn about
  (C) know certainly
  (D) understand deeply
  (E) guess randomly

38. COUNTERFEIT:
  (A) sincere
  (B) immeasurable
  (C) preventative
  (D) invincible
  (E) phony

39. PLACID:
  (A) lakefront
  (B) beautiful
  (C) calm
  (D) unruly
  (E) dissatisfied

40. TANGIBLE:
  (A) cherished
  (B) imperceptible
  (C) real
  (D) incoherent
  (E) feeble

41. ENIGMA:
  (A) evil
  (B) propaganda
  (C) mystery
  (D) thrill
  (E) enemy

42. TENACIOUS:
  (A) resolute
  (B) secure
  (C) tender
  (D) wavering
  (E) starving

43. OBLITERATE:
  (A) convey
  (B) craft
  (C) destroy
  (D) read
  (E) rate

44. TENTATIVE:
  (A) cosmetic
  (B) provisional
  (C) coincidental
  (D) sturdy
  (E) appointment

45. CURTAIL:
  (A) flourish
  (B) cover up
  (C) falter
  (D) begin quickly
  (E) pare down

46. RESPITE:
  (A) relief from
  (B) movement toward
  (C) physique
  (D) hatred of
  (E) havoc

47. HINDER:
  (A) sinister
  (B) kindle
  (C) impede
  (D) rigorous
  (E) authorize

Advanced

<u>Directions</u> – Select the one word or phrase whose meaning is closest to the word in capital letters.

1. DISSUADE:
   (A) motivate
   (B) evade
   (C) dilute
   (D) deter
   (E) misplace

2. EXORCISE:
   (A) apply
   (B) pray for
   (C) scare
   (D) athletic
   (E) drive out

3. EXTRANEOUS:
   (A) irrelevant
   (B) numerous
   (C) significant
   (D) lukewarm
   (E) conservative

4. INNATE:
   (A) acquired
   (B) normal
   (C) scrupulous
   (D) emergent
   (E) hereditary

5. MALEDICTION:
   (A) spiteful word
   (B) established patriarchy
   (C) praiseworthy idea
   (D) rambling thought
   (E) masculine phrase

6. UNAMBIGUOUS:
   (A) intangible
   (B) vague
   (C) clear
   (D) gigantic
   (E) critical

7. CONSCIENTIOUS:
   (A) objectionable
   (B) superior
   (C) ignorant
   (D) fortuitous
   (E) aware

8. CHRONIC:
   (A) painful
   (B) lasting
   (C) evanescent
   (D) dubious
   (E) precarious

9. INCREDULOUS:
   (A) conceivable
   (B) preeminent
   (C) inquisitive
   (D) doubtful
   (E) demonstrable

10. DICTUM:
    (A) fervent idea
    (B) safe shelter
    (C) mistaken belief
    (D) burning desire
    (E) formal statement

11. ENGENDER:
    (A) separate by
    (B) split apart
    (C) seal in
    (D) bring about
    (E) classify as

12. OMNIPOTENT:
    (A) cosmic
    (B) effective
    (C) extravagant
    (D) bountiful
    (E) almighty

13. PATRONIZE:
    (A) impersonate
    (B) hoard
    (C) donate
    (D) condescend
    (E) request

14. EMPATHY:
    (A) insanity
    (B) compassion
    (C) enmity
    (D) emphasis
    (E) preeminence

15. CACOPHONY:
    (A) slanderous words
    (B) discordant din
    (C) quiet solitude
    (D) profanity
    (E) harmonious symphony

16. TRANSCRIBE:
    (A) abridge
    (B) copy
    (C) condense
    (D) confound
    (E) apply

17. INSCRIPTION:
    (A) established law
    (B) solid stone
    (C) fanciful lyrics
    (D) carved message
    (E) simple explanation

18. SENSATIONALIZE:
    (A) feel
    (B) embellish
    (C) flaunt
    (D) hurt
    (E) anticipate

The Tutorverse

19. PROTRACTED:
   (A) measured
   (B) immutable
   (C) mathematical
   (D) angular
   (E) extended

20. QUANDARY:
   (A) unpleasant sensation
   (B) unnavigable swamp
   (C) confused idea
   (D) impossible dilemma
   (E) strong moral

21. VACILLATE:
   (A) eliminate from
   (B) vacuum up
   (C) evoke that
   (D) reflect upon
   (E) waver between

22. ACUMEN:
   (A) sharp pain
   (B) insistence
   (C) good judgment
   (D) precise aim
   (E) paucity

23. AUSPICIOUS:
   (A) questionable
   (B) devious
   (C) troublesome
   (D) favorable
   (E) explosive

24. UNDULATE:
   (A) congratulate
   (B) aquatic
   (C) extol
   (D) swell
   (E) consistent

25. ARTICULATE:
   (A) extemporaneous
   (B) meandering
   (C) eloquent
   (D) boastful
   (E) indirect

26. CLARIFY:
   (A) obscure
   (B) interrogate
   (C) elucidate
   (D) pontificate
   (E) denigrate

27. COMPLEMENT:
   (A) harmonize with
   (B) flatter
   (C) conspire against
   (D) repress
   (E) commend for

28. CONCISE:
   (A) persuasive
   (B) estimable
   (C) deplorable
   (D) pithy
   (E) indivisible

29. LOGICAL:
   (A) cogent
   (B) nonsensical
   (C) paramount
   (D) raucous
   (E) ephemeral

30. REQUISITE:
   (A) necessary
   (B) exquisite
   (C) incoherent
   (D) perfect
   (E) contingent

31. NOXIOUS:
   (A) hale
   (B) sibilant
   (C) odor
   (D) stout
   (E) disgusting

32. HARANGUE:
   (A) make an example of
   (B) pay tribute to
   (C) berate
   (D) fine-tune
   (E) hang from

33. REPLETE:
   (A) exhausted
   (B) sated
   (C) partial
   (D) incompetent
   (E) disgruntled

34. REPREHENSIBLE:
   (A) theoretical
   (B) innocent
   (C) complete
   (D) representative
   (E) unacceptable

35. CYNICAL:
   (A) pessimistic
   (B) fervent
   (C) positive
   (D) extravagant
   (E) unsophisticated

36. POIGNANT:
   (A) vapid
   (B) satirical
   (C) impervious
   (D) touching
   (E) cinematic

37. TERSE:
   (A) courageous
   (B) spontaneous
   (C) ardent
   (D) stressed
   (E) brusque

38. LANGUID:
   (A) sanguine
   (B) rapid
   (C) insufficient
   (D) leisurely
   (E) wet

39. RESPLENDENT:
   (A) waning
   (B) dismal
   (C) dutiful
   (D) pious
   (E) glorious

40. PONDEROUS:
    (A) contemplate
    (B) pervasive
    (C) scholarly
    (D) tedious
    (E) personable

41. TIMOROUS:
    (A) colorful
    (B) inevitable
    (C) nervous
    (D) bold
    (E) scintillating

42. OBSOLETE:
    (A) resilient
    (B) electronic
    (C) lavish
    (D) fashionable
    (E) archaic

43. RETICENT:
    (A) candid
    (B) incompatible
    (C) elderly
    (D) taciturn
    (E) primitive

44. AFFABLE:
    (A) economical
    (B) pleasant
    (C) sedate
    (D) pompous
    (E) laughable

45. OBSEQUIOUS:
    (A) subservient
    (B) insulting
    (C) extraordinary
    (D) inopportune
    (E) pretentious

46. SUPERCILIOUS:
    (A) instantaneous
    (B) arrogant
    (C) secondary
    (D) desultory
    (E) intricate

47. CHICANERY:
    (A) deception
    (B) fashionable
    (C) property
    (D) sweetness
    (E) crazy plan

Analogies

Overview

Analogy questions ask students to look at a pair of words and select another pair of words with a matching relationship. Analogy questions are presented on the Upper Level SSAT in two different ways:

🐾 Two-part stem: "A" is to "B" as...
   In these types of questions, students are given two words in the stem of the question, and are asked to select the pair of words with the same relationship as demonstrated between words "A" and "B."

🐾 Three-part stem: "A" is to "B" as "C" is to...
   In these types of questions, students are given three words in the stem of the question; words "A" and "B" form one relationship, and are asked to complete the same relationship between word "C" and your answer choice.

How to Use This Section

How much time students spend on this section should be based on their diagnostic practice test results as well as their study plan. For most students, even those who score very well on the diagnostic practice test, we recommend practicing at least 5-10 questions per week in preparing for the exam.

One study plan might be to try a Mixed Practice section to get a sense for which areas to focus on. Based on those results, work on the relevant Guided Practice sections. If students already know what they need to work on, they can jump right in to a Guided Practice section.

The purpose of this section is to introduce students to new words. Some may find many of the words in this section to be challenging. Students should not be surprised to have to look up many of the words encountered in this section! We encourage students to make a list of difficult or challenging words, whether they appear in questions or answer choices. Write down the definition of each word as well as a sentence using the word. Students might also want to consider writing down positive or negative associations, any root words that can help them remember the word, or any words that are commonly encountered with that word.

Tutorverse Tips!

The key to success on the analogies section is practice. Students should know the common types of analogies by heart and be able to quickly categorize the question stem provided into one of these types.

Write down the relationship in the margin and see which of the choices creates an analogy that matches that of the question stem.

Guided Practice

Directions: For each question, select the answer choice that best completes the meaning of the sentence.

Antonyms

1. Optional is to required as
   (A) vital is to unimportant
   (B) mandatory is to obligatory
   (C) suspicious is to untrustworthy
   (D) safe is to secure
   (E) happy is to content

2. North is to south as
   (A) run is to race
   (B) hot is to warm
   (C) empty is to blank
   (D) black is to white
   (E) jump is to rope

3. Brief is to lasting as
   (A) evening is to midnight
   (B) short is to message
   (C) lengthy is to day
   (D) complete is to partial
   (E) explanation is to satisfactory

4. Benign is to malignant as
   (A) hateful is to despicable
   (B) pious is to profane
   (C) tumor is to illness
   (D) attitude is to person
   (E) beneficial is to helpful

5. Exuberant is to languid as
   (A) deliberate is to methodical
   (B) lethargic is to groggy
   (C) unbelievable is to excitable
   (D) boisterous is to animated
   (E) fundamental is to superfluous

6. Merciful is to pitiless as merciless is to
   (A) forgiving
   (B) judge
   (C) obedient
   (D) harsh
   (E) pathetic

7. Eternal is to transitory as quarrelsome is to
   (A) amenable
   (B) confrontational
   (C) pugnacious
   (D) immortal
   (E) argumentative

8. Malady is to cure as consensus is to
   (A) agreement
   (B) illness
   (C) disparity
   (D) decision
   (E) solution

9. Verdant is to barren as candid is to
   (A) forthright
   (B) fertile
   (C) restrained
   (D) arable
   (E) friendly

10. Pretentious is to modest as ominous is to
    (A) menacing
    (B) cloudy
    (C) dark
    (D) promising
    (E) humble

Association

1. Open is to sesame as
   (A) sardine is to swordfish
   (B) unicycle is to exquisite
   (C) implore is to defer
   (D) pretty is to please
   (E) reptile is to whale

2. Null is to void as
   (A) forgive is to forget
   (B) mend is to break
   (C) remember is to photograph
   (D) blame is to accuse
   (E) close is to conclude

The Tutorverse

3. Fun is to games as supply is to
   (A) amount
   (B) provide
   (C) carnival
   (D) demand
   (E) enjoyment

4. Under is to weather as bite is to
   (A) fish
   (B) bullet
   (C) chew
   (D) bitten
   (E) mouth

5. Salesman is to traveling as pig is to
   (A) clean
   (B) chicken
   (C) suckling
   (D) cowering
   (E) wandering

6. Lamb is to mutton as chicken is to
   (A) coop
   (B) dinner
   (C) egg
   (D) nugget
   (E) poultry

7. Reference is to obscure as
   (A) feline is to dog
   (B) fear is to lion
   (C) alien is to human
   (D) beast is to mythical
   (E) cat is to canine

8. Walking is to shoe as
   (A) spot is to tight
   (B) garbage is to can
   (C) paper is to printer
   (D) handle is to door
   (E) bowl is to cereal

9. Pork is to pig as beef is to
   (A) cow
   (B) bun
   (C) steak
   (D) animal
   (E) hamburger

10. Dagger is to cloak as
    (A) tape is to rip
    (B) cement is to glue
    (C) sheath is to casing
    (D) weapon is to knife
    (E) mortar is to brick

Cause-and-Effect

1. Moon is to tides as
   (A) bicycle is to wheel
   (B) orbit is to path
   (C) ocean is to vast
   (D) pigment is to colors
   (E) smell is to sight

2. Growth is to fertilizer as
   (A) gloves is to protection
   (B) manure is to compost
   (C) farm is to farmer
   (D) field is to stones
   (E) oxygen is to plants

3. Nectar is to flower as
   (A) lift is to wing
   (B) bees is to pollen
   (C) sugar is to sweetness
   (D) camera is to security
   (E) seed is to petal

4. Bread is to baker as article is to
   (A) constitution
   (B) bakery
   (C) news
   (D) draft
   (E) reporter

5. Speed is to cessation as
   (A) vivaciousness is to vitality
   (B) swiftness is to alacrity
   (C) humility is to arrogance
   (D) moisture is to humidity
   (E) velocity is to haste

6. Rain is to drought as
   (A) lamp is to glow
   (B) deluge is to flood
   (C) light is to darkness
   (D) precipitation is to snow
   (E) hurricane is to water

The Tutorverse

7. Instability is to balance as isolation is to
    (A) community
    (B) privacy
    (C) personality
    (D) loneliness
    (E) prison

8. Proficiency is to training as conflict is to
    (A) disagreement
    (B) tolerance
    (C) approval
    (D) evidence
    (E) resolution

9. Assurance is to confidence as doubt is to
    (A) conviction
    (B) principle
    (C) uncertainty
    (D) appreciation
    (E) theory

10. Negligence is to precision as hesitation is to
    (A) confidence
    (B) courage
    (C) outcomes
    (D) defiance
    (E) certainty

Defining

1. Playwright is to script as
    (A) actor is to role
    (B) poem is to teacher
    (C) author is to novel
    (D) library is to literature
    (E) reader is to literacy

2. Tower is to signal as computer is to
    (A) inbox
    (B) email
    (C) satellite
    (D) orbit
    (E) location

3. Moon is to earth as earth is to
    (A) sky
    (B) sun
    (C) meteor
    (D) comet
    (E) planet

4. Mask is to sight as
    (A) dirty is to clean
    (B) fog is to vista
    (C) filter is to air
    (D) mist is to damp
    (E) smell is to nose

5. Mechanic is to vehicle as
    (A) conductor is to painting
    (B) plumber is to van
    (C) goldsmith is to hinge
    (D) blacksmith is to horseshoe
    (E) grape is to wine

6. Hair is to barber as
    (A) barrier is to impassible
    (B) dam is to levee
    (C) writing is to eraser
    (D) homework is to paper
    (E) hypothermia is to lifejacket

7. Vegetation is to garden as
    (A) soil is to seed
    (B) flower is to petal
    (C) birch is to tree
    (D) moss is to rock
    (E) fungus is to mushroom

8. Sorcerer is to incantation as monk is to
    (A) monastery
    (B) prayer
    (C) magic
    (D) wizard
    (E) religion

9. Shovel is to arborist as wheel is to
    (A) car
    (B) spin
    (C) gear
    (D) spoke
    (E) driver

10. River is to confluence as street is to
    (A) map
    (B) alley
    (C) intersection
    (D) union
    (E) highway

The Tutorverse

Degree/Intensity

1. Trickle is to deluge as
   - (A) ocean is to drown
   - (B) burn is to mark
   - (C) water is to damp
   - (D) singe is to char
   - (E) dam is to river

2. Unlikely is to impossible as
   - (A) suspected is to suspicious
   - (B) muddled is to obvious
   - (C) incorrigible is to obedient
   - (D) vague is to incomprehensible
   - (E) forgetful is to inconsiderate

3. Pink is to red as gray is to
   - (A) clear
   - (B) tone
   - (C) color
   - (D) blue
   - (E) black

4. Smart is to omniscient as
   - (A) strong is to omnipotent
   - (B) intelligent is to knowing
   - (C) powerful is to weak
   - (D) clever is to careful
   - (E) dumb is to lame

5. Small is to microscopic as
   - (A) elephant is to elephantine
   - (B) space is to occluded
   - (C) miniscule is to minutia
   - (D) finite is to infinite
   - (E) big is to capacious

6. Dislike is to detest as
   - (A) empathize is to love
   - (B) argument is to agreement
   - (C) debase is to criminalize
   - (D) like is to adore
   - (E) conflict is to fight

7. Slow is to glacial as calm is to
   - (A) fast
   - (B) rapid
   - (C) halcyon
   - (D) blaring
   - (E) clumsy

8. Fib is to lie as difficult is to
   - (A) alleged
   - (B) arduous
   - (C) overt
   - (D) maladroit
   - (E) ostentatious

9. Pesky is to insufferable as lengthy is to
   - (A) incompetent
   - (B) interminable
   - (C) inexhaustible
   - (D) infernal
   - (E) incentive

10. Plush is to comfortable as indestructible is to
   - (A) paramount
   - (B) viscous
   - (C) comfortable
   - (D) durable
   - (E) temporary

Function/Object

1. Pen is to write as
   - (A) utensil is to eat
   - (B) marker is to erase
   - (C) paper is to shred
   - (D) water is to dirty
   - (E) plate is to dish

2. Caricature is to ridicule as
   - (A) picture is to photograph
   - (B) count is to abacus
   - (C) scorn is to enemy
   - (D) calculator is to compute
   - (E) animation is to fault

The Tutorverse

3. Key is to unlock as edict is to
    (A) proclaim
    (B) undermine
    (C) whine
    (D) employ
    (E) enrage

4. Sycophant is to flatter as
    (A) colleague is to maximize
    (B) representative is to spy
    (C) emissary is to represent
    (D) contrarian is to diversify
    (E) accountant is to overestimate

5. Helmet is to protect as
    (A) clean is to soap
    (B) flag is to designate
    (C) mirror is to glass
    (D) magnet is to magnetic
    (E) pinch is to tweezer

6. Sanctuary is to harbor as
    (A) mercenary is to armor
    (B) dispensary is to medicinal
    (C) rehabilitation is to infirmary
    (D) monastery is to vow
    (E) aviary is to flight

7. Control is to regulator as
    (A) blessing is to benediction
    (B) praise is to revel
    (C) regress is to advance
    (D) radio is to transmit
    (E) therapist is to calm

8. Compass is to locate as epitaph is to
    (A) banish
    (B) scribble
    (C) repulse
    (D) commemorate
    (E) epitome

9. Wing is to fly as nutrient is to
    (A) display
    (B) vitamin
    (C) drink
    (D) sustain
    (E) ailment

10. Salve is to relieve as incision is to
    (A) pinpoint
    (B) exact
    (C) sear
    (D) combine
    (E) separate

Grammar

1. Man is to men as
    (A) human is to being
    (B) duck is to gander
    (C) goose is to geese
    (D) cow is to bull
    (E) women is to woman

2. Walk is to walks as
    (A) are is to is
    (B) talks is to talk
    (C) is is to are
    (D) be is to being
    (E) skip is to skipping

3. Seek is to sought as sell is to
    (A) ask
    (B) buy
    (C) find
    (D) sold
    (E) bought

4. Ran is to run as
    (A) ate is to eat
    (B) running is to sprinting
    (C) eating is to eaten
    (D) run is to stop
    (E) go is to gone

5. Flown is to flew as
    (A) forbidden is to forbade
    (B) forget is to forgotten
    (C) forgave is to forgiven
    (D) freeze is to frozen
    (E) fell is to fall

6. Did is to do as
    (A) knew is to know
    (B) drew is to drawn
    (C) counted is to counting
    (D) feel is to felt
    (E) cost is to costs

7. Cactus is to cacti as fungus is to
   (A) funguses
   (B) fungus
   (C) fungusy
   (D) fungi
   (E) fungi

8. Spoken is to speak as sprung is to
   (A) sprang
   (B) springs
   (C) spring
   (D) springing
   (E) springy

9. Stolen is to steal as stunk is to
   (A) stinks
   (B) stink
   (C) stank
   (D) stinky
   (E) stinking

10. Chose is to choose as blew is to
    (A) blown
    (B) blow
    (C) blewn
    (D) blowing
    (E) blows

Individual/Object

1. Butcher is to knife as
   (A) carnivore is to meat
   (B) cook is to ingredients
   (C) actor is to actress
   (D) hunter is to prey
   (E) dishwasher is to stove

2. Seamstress is to thimble as astronomer is to
   (A) telescope
   (B) celestial
   (C) sky
   (D) constellation
   (E) astrology

3. Scientist is to microscope as maid is to
   (A) service
   (B) housekeeper
   (C) child
   (D) hotel
   (E) duster

4. Navigator is to compass as
   (A) fortuneteller is to spectacles
   (B) lattice is to weaver
   (C) legislator is to attorney
   (D) miser is to asset
   (E) miller is to grindstone

5. Pharmacist is to drug as
   (A) thermometer is to technician
   (B) mason is to hammer
   (C) fabric is to designer
   (D) programmer is to metallurgy
   (E) stethoscope is to surgeon

6. Soldier is to rifle as
   (A) purveyor is to vendor
   (B) bible is to pontiff
   (C) reaper is to sickle
   (D) surrogate is to exception
   (E) submarine is to navy

7. Sculptor is to chisel as
   (A) biographer is to biography
   (B) husbandry is to animal
   (C) stenographer is to keyboard
   (D) map is to cartographer
   (E) funeral is to eulogy

8. Extraterrestrial is to spacecraft as chemist is to
   (A) mad
   (B) intelligent
   (C) occupation
   (D) explosion
   (E) vial

9. Investigator is to clues as linguist is to
   (A) sounds
   (B) languages
   (C) suspects
   (D) sights
   (E) thoughts

10. Tanner is to leather as viper is to
    (A) deadly
    (B) rattlesnake
    (C) intoxicate
    (D) venom
    (E) slither

The Tutorverse

Noun/Verb

1. Money is to deposit as
   (A) listen is to telegram
   (B) send is to computer
   (C) withdraw is to decrease
   (D) machine is to automatic
   (E) email is to type

2. Bouquet is to arrange as
   (A) sell is to return
   (B) boutique is to vendor
   (C) graffiti is to vandalize
   (D) rose is to tulip
   (E) merchandise is to purchase

3. Shopper is to purchase as trickster is to
   (A) agree
   (B) clarify
   (C) enjoy
   (D) foretell
   (E) connive

4. Intimidate is to bully as befriend is to
   (A) companion
   (B) bereave
   (C) enemy
   (D) truth
   (E) teacher

5. Adversary is to compete as
   (A) accuser is to allege
   (B) protagonist is to condemn
   (C) assistant is to dominate
   (D) edifice is to tall
   (E) collector is to disperse

6. Advocate is to attorney as
   (A) compensate is to employer
   (B) rebel is to instigate
   (C) introvert is to solitude
   (D) confuse is to vertigo
   (E) deduct is to employee

7. Imperfection is to tarnish as
   (A) bulldozer is to raze
   (B) debater is to rebuttal
   (C) abyss is to drain
   (D) antecedent is to supersede
   (E) dictator is to acquiesce

8. Tyrant is to dominate as rain is to
   (A) water
   (B) weather
   (C) fall
   (D) season
   (E) snow

9. Protect is to roof as direct is to
   (A) location
   (B) surround
   (C) normal
   (D) deviate
   (E) funnel

10. Validate is to hypothesis as weave is to
    (A) garment
    (B) experiment
    (C) laboratory
    (D) factory
    (E) wood

Part/Whole

1. Act is to play as
   (A) chalk is to board
   (B) line is to recite
   (C) stanza is to poem
   (D) diary is to secret
   (E) stage is to actor

2. Lyric is to song as
   (A) letter is to grade
   (B) marker is to correct
   (C) paragraph is to essay
   (D) liquid is to rain
   (E) memorize is to sing

The Tutorverse

3.   Ship is to fleet as wolf is to
(A) pack
(B) predator
(C) coyote
(D) howl
(E) sea

4.   Strand is to hair as drawer is to
(A) dresser
(B) shed
(C) room
(D) storage
(E) closet

5.   Mother is to family as
(A) matriarch is to familial
(B) planet is to terrain
(C) atmosphere is to air
(D) galaxy is to universe
(E) gun is to bullet

6.   Accessory is to outfit as
(A) sole is to shoe
(B) folder is to cabinet
(C) lamp is to light
(D) glacier is to cube
(E) music is to musician

7.   Droplet is to puddle as grain is to
(A) water
(B) dune
(C) granular
(D) microscopic
(E) fertilize

8.   Name is to roster as pupil is to
(A) student
(B) proposal
(C) study
(D) test
(E) eye

9.   Room is to home as seat is to
(A) sleep
(B) rest
(C) sit
(D) theater
(E) stand

10.   Symbol is to cipher as worker is to
(A) task
(B) staff
(C) manage
(D) weekend
(E) promotion

Purpose/Object

1.   Glove is to baseball as
(A) net is to butterfly
(B) football is to fan
(C) microscope is to laboratory
(D) asteroid is to danger
(E) umpire is to unbiased

2.   Matches is to candle as brush is to
(A) wax
(B) detangle
(C) tidy
(D) beautiful
(E) fur

3.   Violin is to bow as drum is to
(A) key
(B) note
(C) stick
(D) music
(E) sound

4.   Shovel is to snow as spoon is to
(A) eat
(B) kitchen
(C) soup
(D) fork
(E) table

5.   Eraser is to paper as broom is to
(A) mop
(B) rag
(C) ground
(D) sink
(E) sponge

6.   Basketball is to hoop as
(A) photograph is to image
(B) paper is to write
(C) lure is to ensnare
(D) arrow is to target
(E) barometer is to temperature

The Tutorverse

7. Rag is to mess as
   (A) balloon is to anchor
   (B) mop is to floor
   (C) appetizer is to beverage
   (D) confetti is to clean
   (E) tablecloth is to cocktail

8. Stick is to puck as fuse is to
   (A) hockey
   (B) string
   (C) fusion
   (D) explosive
   (E) chemistry

9. Glue is to pieces as staple is to
   (A) paper
   (B) glue
   (C) office
   (D) copier
   (E) combine

10. Syringe is to injection as testimony is to
    (A) evidence
    (B) allege
    (C) medication
    (D) promise
    (E) motivate

Type/Kind

1. Swan is to bird as
   (A) spaghetti is to pasta
   (B) woodpecker is to hawk
   (C) penguin is to aquatic
   (D) linguine is to clam
   (E) tomato is to basil

2. Bag is to backpack as
   (A) avenue is to map
   (B) instrument is to saxophone
   (C) purse is to woman
   (D) drum is to percussion
   (E) harp is to harpist

3. Poodle is to dog as puma is to
   (A) stripe
   (B) spotted
   (C) feral
   (D) cat
   (E) lion

4. Baguette is to bread as soda is to
   (A) carbonation
   (B) water
   (C) beverage
   (D) sugar
   (E) hydrate

5. Pigeon is to bird as
   (A) manor is to structure
   (B) estate is to inheritance
   (C) comb is to style
   (D) vegetable is to carrot
   (E) keepsake is to memento

6. Scientist is to physicist as
   (A) shoe is to sneaker
   (B) photo is to photographer
   (C) alibi is to excuse
   (D) oaf is to giant
   (E) ape is to primate

7. Arm is to appendage as
   (A) thumb is to toe
   (B) cranium is to torso
   (C) wolf is to lupine
   (D) sapphire is to gemstone
   (E) legend is to mythos

8. Slang is to language as governor is to
   (A) politician
   (B) trustworthy
   (C) president
   (D) powerful
   (E) senator

9. Jazz is to music as poetry is to
   (A) poet
   (B) essay
   (C) figurative
   (D) writing
   (E) interpretation

10. Dandelion is to weed as ballet is to
    (A) performer
    (B) ballerina
    (C) tutu
    (D) dance
    (E) interpretive

The Tutorverse

Whole/Part

1. Chain is to link as
   (A) motorcycle is to helmet
   (B) windshield is to truck
   (C) skeleton is to bone
   (D) roof is to convertible
   (E) toy is to pinwheel

2. List is to item as
   (A) pants is to sweater
   (B) sofa is to furniture
   (C) dress is to closet
   (D) collection is to piece
   (E) handle is to drawer

3. Jacket is to collar as tooth is to
   (A) dentist
   (B) fluoride
   (C) decay
   (D) brush
   (E) enamel

4. Company is to employee as
   (A) job is to work
   (B) protest is to protestor
   (C) parade is to celebrate
   (D) improvement is to demotion
   (E) performance is to accomplishment

5. Week is to day as
   (A) work is to play
   (B) stag is to antler
   (C) ash is to fireplace
   (D) holiday is to vacation
   (E) Saturday is to weekend

6. Garden is to plant as
   (A) bird is to hatch
   (B) nest is to honeycomb
   (C) queen is to subject
   (D) beehive is to colony
   (E) swarm is to insect

7. Month is to week as school is to
   (A) bus
   (B) grade
   (C) district
   (D) classroom
   (E) curriculum

8. Cheese is to rind as avocado is to
   (A) pit
   (B) plant
   (C) ferment
   (D) vegetable
   (E) seedling

9. Film is to story as competition is to
   (A) speed
   (B) height
   (C) distance
   (D) compete
   (E) competitor

10. Essay is to paragraphs as building is to
    (A) levels
    (B) engineer
    (C) lobby
    (D) elevators
    (E) cameras

Synonym

1. Precede is to lead as
   (A) flaunt is to gaunt
   (B) exceed is to limit
   (C) dissolve is to solidify
   (D) deflect is to absorb
   (E) forgo is to decline

2. Incapacity is to powerlessness as
   (A) sensation is to numbness
   (B) invasion is to invitation
   (C) likelihood is to guarantee
   (D) preference is to aversion
   (E) insight is to awareness

The Tutorverse

3. Eloquent is to expressive as
   (A) rare is to unique
   (B) presumptuous is to presume
   (C) fanatical is to fanfare
   (D) cosmic is to cosmetic
   (E) diverse is to uniform

4. Analysis is to evaluation as gesture is to
   (A) smile
   (B) action
   (C) nod
   (D) wave
   (E) frown

5. Subjective is to personal as approximate is to
   (A) exact
   (B) opinion
   (C) objective
   (D) imprecise
   (E) fact

6. Ignominious is to disgraceful as
   (A) derivative is to original
   (B) sporadic is to systematic
   (C) consecutive is to alternating
   (D) culpable is to culprit
   (E) laudable is to praiseworthy

7. Rife is to rampant as
   (A) extensive is to limited
   (B) plentiful is to sparse
   (C) transient is to permanent
   (D) wild is to domestic
   (E) potent is to influential

8. Cursory is to perfunctory as infallible is to
   (A) flawed
   (B) everlasting
   (C) detailed
   (D) ceaseless
   (E) perfect

9. Wane is to diminish as
   (A) edify is to edifice
   (B) espouse is to marry
   (C) accomplish is to accomplice
   (D) circulate is to conceal
   (E) relate is to understand

10. Malevolent is to wicked as insidious is to
    (A) interior
    (B) agreeable
    (C) sinister
    (D) blatant
    (E) evident

Mixed Practice

Directions: For each question, select the answer choice that best completes the meaning of the sentence.

Mixed 1

1. Skis is to poles as bicycle is to
   (A) path
   (B) snow
   (C) chain
   (D) helmet
   (E) handlebars

2. Conductor is to baton as mathematician is to
   (A) calculate
   (B) solve
   (C) hypothesize
   (D) estimate
   (E) equation

3. Shot is to shoot as sat is to
   (A) sit
   (B) sits
   (C) seats
   (D) seat
   (E) sitting

4. Set is to placemat as
   (A) dish is to wash
   (B) feast is to banquet
   (C) agenda is to plan
   (D) surprise is to celebration
   (E) schedule is to meeting

The Tutorverse

5. Goose is to flock as
   (A) chicken is to egg
   (B) saddle is to rider
   (C) stirrup is to mare
   (D) cow is to milk
   (E) horse is to herd

6. Fish is to salmon as utensil is to
   (A) plate
   (B) spatula
   (C) chop
   (D) china
   (E) napkin

7. Theoretical is to physics as
   (A) green is to color
   (B) mad is to scientist
   (C) hypothesis is to belief
   (D) helmet is to visor
   (E) experiment is to research

8. Sprinter is to race as
   (A) athlete is to marathon
   (B) swimmer is to pool
   (C) runner is to jogger
   (D) dancer is to partner
   (E) spectator is to sport

9. Message is to word as anthology is to
   (A) novel
   (B) protagonist
   (C) subject
   (D) publisher
   (E) reader

10. Zephyr is to gale as ripple is to
    (A) pond
    (B) tsunami
    (C) tributary
    (D) thunderstorm
    (E) lake

11. Soothe is to lotion as
    (A) thimble is to sew
    (B) hole is to shovel
    (C) sauce is to flavor
    (D) tape is to connect
    (E) compress is to clamp

12. Sound is to silence as
    (A) hygiene is to filth
    (B) volume is to loudness
    (C) bathing is to cleanliness
    (D) quiet is to peace
    (E) deafness is to noise

13. Exemplary is to admirable as immutable is to
    (A) booming
    (B) fluctuating
    (C) permanent
    (D) marvelous
    (E) flawless

14. Sweltering is to frigid as
    (A) viable is to possible
    (B) extravagant is to lavish
    (C) elusive is to obvious
    (D) freezing is to frozen
    (E) wealthy is to affluent

Mixed 2

1. Broom is to sweep as dynamite is to
   (A) create
   (B) explode
   (C) stick
   (D) danger
   (E) fuse

2. Headache is to migraine as cut is to
   (A) gash
   (B) suffer
   (C) itch
   (D) rash
   (E) injury

3. Gardener is to shears as
   (A) cyclist is to wheel
   (B) patron is to visit
   (C) alcohol is to goblet
   (D) waiter is to tray
   (E) canvas is to painter

4. Drink is to beverage as
   (A) seasoning is to mix
   (B) spaghetti is to slurp
   (C) tenderize is to bread
   (D) knead is to bake
   (E) chew is to food

The Tutorverse

5. Stars is to constellation as pane is to
   (A) shatter
   (B) window
   (C) transparent
   (D) glass
   (E) sun

6. Song is to rhythm as
   (A) sound is to pleasant
   (B) voice is to speech
   (C) tea is to leaf
   (D) coffee is to bean
   (E) gallon is to cup

7. Leaves is to rake as hair is to
   (A) wig
   (B) leaf
   (C) mess
   (D) comb
   (E) clean

8. Pompous is to arrogant as
   (A) sacrilegious is to sacred
   (B) veracious is to deceitful
   (C) witless is to mindful
   (D) studious is to student
   (E) squalid is to fetid

9. Deride is to admire as appease is to
   (A) provoke
   (B) negotiation
   (C) cowardly
   (D) give
   (E) satisfy

Mixed 3

1. Grief is to joy as tolerance is to
   (A) acceptance
   (B) bigotry
   (C) love
   (D) indifference
   (E) patience

2. Bottomless is to abyss as
   (A) aluminum is to foil
   (B) endless is to limited
   (C) cavern is to explore
   (D) plastic is to recycle
   (E) fragrant is to foul

10. Havoc is to wreak as amok is to
    (A) run
    (B) place
    (C) sow
    (D) terror
    (E) rampage

11. Play is to finale as story is to
    (A) epilogue
    (B) prologue
    (C) forward
    (D) introduction
    (E) dedication

12. Brass is to metal as water is to
    (A) liquid
    (B) ice
    (C) life
    (D) air
    (E) pollution

13. Sworn is to swore as taken is to
    (A) take
    (B) takes
    (C) took
    (D) taking
    (E) swearing

14. Gluttony is to obesity as labor is to
    (A) exhaustion
    (B) requirement
    (C) excess
    (D) camp
    (E) chore

3. Ideas is to thinker as novel is to
   (A) movie
   (B) writer
   (C) usual
   (D) speech
   (E) different

4. Bee is to honey as bird is to
   (A) nest
   (B) worm
   (C) fly
   (D) tree
   (E) cat

The Tutorverse

5. Fanaticism is to enthusiasm as decree is to
   (A) royalty
   (B) question
   (C) command
   (D) customer
   (E) achiever

6. Synopsis is to summarize as blanket is to
   (A) rug
   (B) abridge
   (C) recreate
   (D) weave
   (E) warm

7. Steal is to stolen as
   (A) lie is to liar
   (B) break is to broke
   (C) began is to begun
   (D) cut is to cutting
   (E) break is to broken

8. Strawberry is to fruit as
   (A) dessert is to cake
   (B) banana is to peel
   (C) avocado is to pit
   (D) grape is to seed
   (E) croissant is to pastry

9. Singer is to microphone as
   (A) textbook is to pupil
   (B) spy is to espionage
   (C) musician is to instrument
   (D) farmer is to vegetables
   (E) parent is to child

10. Screwdriver is to screw as mallet is to
    (A) dinner
    (B) bovine
    (C) stake
    (D) wager
    (E) vampire

11. Toxin is to poison as pinnacle is to
    (A) pedestal
    (B) venom
    (C) slope
    (D) side
    (E) summit

12. Year is to month as hour is to
    (A) minute
    (B) time
    (C) day
    (D) length
    (E) type

13. Yolk is to egg as spoke is to
    (A) wheel
    (B) speak
    (C) rotate
    (D) discuss
    (E) support

14. Collect is to memento as peruse is to
    (A) organize
    (B) reuse
    (C) recycle
    (D) report
    (E) underline

Mixed 4

1. Resilient is to feeble as sedate is to
   (A) energetic
   (B) anesthesia
   (C) nurse
   (D) hospitalize
   (E) tired

2. Sun is to light as chicken is to
   (A) roast
   (B) egg
   (C) rooster
   (D) hen
   (E) dinner

3. Florist is to flower as
   (A) peace is to war
   (B) librarian is to book
   (C) sea is to water
   (D) insurance is to business
   (E) groceries is to supermarket

4. Compliment is to fawn as explain is to
   (A) praise
   (B) query
   (C) approve
   (D) pontificate
   (E) hesitate

The Tutorverse

5. Referee is to whistle as
   (A) criminal is to police
   (B) athlete is to uniform
   (C) carpenter is to hammer
   (D) driver is to tire
   (E) cinematographer is to picture

6. Believe is to believing as
   (A) folded is to folding
   (B) believer is to believed
   (C) read is to read
   (D) read is to reading
   (E) imagining is to imagine

7. Fence is to separate as plunger is to
   (A) soak
   (B) free
   (C) equipment
   (D) plumber
   (E) bathroom

8. Wallet is to money as folder is to
   (A) storage
   (B) student
   (C) teacher
   (D) organizer
   (E) document

9. State is to county as floor is to
   (A) board
   (B) carpet
   (C) polish
   (D) stair
   (E) wax

10. Prim is to proper as
    (A) front is to center
    (B) reprehensible is to shameful
    (C) pamper is to pander
    (D) etiquette is to propriety
    (E) manners is to behavior

11. Tone is to brusque as preposition is to
    (A) is
    (B) are
    (C) from
    (D) front
    (E) opposed

12. Appellation is to identify as
    (A) classification is to dispose
    (B) cessation is to continue
    (C) intermission is to interval
    (D) communication is to transmission
    (E) respite is to recover

13. Venerate is to revere as assert is to
    (A) insert
    (B) guess
    (C) worship
    (D) adore
    (E) declare

14. Headline is to article as cell is to
    (A) prison
    (B) bar
    (C) prisoner
    (D) warden
    (E) doctor

Mixed 5

1. Rapid is to gradual as reckless is to
   (A) careless
   (B) daredevil
   (C) prudent
   (D) decisive
   (E) lawyer

2. Suffocation is to air as
   (A) hunger is to food
   (B) life is to breath
   (C) vision is to sight
   (D) atmosphere is to planet
   (E) brightness is to light

3. Plug is to drain as bandage is to
   (A) hospital
   (B) doctor
   (C) nurse
   (D) bleeding
   (E) pain

4. Book is to tome as
   (A) swamp is to swampy
   (B) clue is to solution
   (C) maze is to labyrinth
   (D) limb is to prosthetic
   (E) maverick is to individuality

5. Lens is to focus as bulb is to
    (A) incandescent
    (B) illuminate
    (C) peer
    (D) zoom
    (E) fluorescent

6. Knife is to knives as
    (A) loaf is to loaves
    (B) loaf is to loafs
    (C) halves is to half
    (D) wife is to wifes
    (E) halfs is to halves

7. Game is to play as
    (A) wear is to uniform
    (B) friend is to teammate
    (C) lose is to win
    (D) point is to score
    (E) rank is to division

8. Dilemma is to predicament as
    (A) grimace is to expression
    (B) campaign is to manager
    (C) commotion is to harmony
    (D) phenomenon is to marvel
    (E) conformist is to protestor

9. Camera is to picture as education is to
    (A) teacher
    (B) instruct
    (C) diploma
    (D) student
    (E) school

10. Student is to class as
    (A) pigeon is to dove
    (B) fish is to water
    (C) lake is to ocean
    (D) bird is to flock
    (E) kitty is to cat

11. Shoe is to boot as
    (A) jewelry is to earring
    (B) ring is to diamond
    (C) necklace is to silver
    (D) sneaker is to cleat
    (E) gem is to gold

12. Camper is to tent as
    (A) monolith is to architecture
    (B) mountaineer is to harness
    (C) wolf is to sheep
    (D) house is to nomad
    (E) boots is to hiker

13. Grid is to columns as movie is to
    (A) film
    (B) color
    (C) scenes
    (D) money
    (E) budget

14. Beck is to call as bread is to
    (A) spoon
    (B) butter
    (C) smile
    (D) shake
    (E) pepper

Mixed 6

1. Emerge is to vanish as coddle is to
    (A) neglect
    (B) spoil
    (C) disappear
    (D) materialize
    (E) pamper

2. Rank is to file as cut is to
    (A) snip
    (B) glue
    (C) scissor
    (D) paste
    (E) cabinet

3. Flame is to wax as heat is to
    (A) beach
    (B) desert
    (C) arctic
    (D) freezer
    (E) chocolate

4. Fete is to celebrate as philanthropy is to
    (A) skepticism
    (B) charity
    (C) share
    (D) hoard
    (E) laud

5. Thespian is to script as guide is to
(A) landmark
(B) attraction
(C) tour
(D) tourist
(E) map

6. Counselor is to advise as spectator is to
(A) binoculars
(B) participate
(C) shun
(D) define
(E) observe

7. Bystander is to crowd as
(A) volunteer is to volunteering
(B) repeat is to chorus
(C) harpist is to orchestra
(D) contestant is to participate
(E) guitarist is to drummer

8. Sock is to foot as coat is to
(A) warm
(B) jacket
(C) paint
(D) car
(E) torso

9. Red is to color as bee is to
(A) termite
(B) butterfly
(C) insect
(D) hive
(E) sting

10. Menu is to entrée as pie is to
(A) flaky
(B) baked
(C) dessert
(D) crust
(E) oven

11. Deviate is to veer as transpire is to
(A) sweat
(B) point
(C) transfer
(D) happen
(E) transport

12. Exercise is to frailty as
(A) blanket is to mattress
(B) workout is to physique
(C) sleep is to fatigue
(D) dream is to nightmare
(E) weakness is to feebleness

13. Take is to took as see is to
(A) seen
(B) saw
(C) sought
(D) seeing
(E) sawn

14. Think is to ruminate as
(A) confirm is to demystify
(B) ponder is to decide
(C) fire is to conflagration
(D) wonder is to debunk
(E) question is to believe

Mixed 7

1. Mischievous is to respectful as obligatory is to
(A) essential
(B) mandatory
(C) law
(D) naughty
(E) optional

2. Hearty is to hale as salad is to
(A) meal
(B) soup
(C) appetizer
(D) cucumber
(E) vegetable

3. Warmth is to heater as health is to
(A) healthy
(B) wealth
(C) hunger
(D) sickness
(E) exercise

4. Excuse is to mistake as lie is to
(A) fib
(B) liar
(C) plea
(D) truth
(E) explain

5. Snip is to cut as tear is to
   (A) fray
   (B) blow
   (C) scrape
   (D) shred
   (E) combine

6. Get is to got as give is to
   (A) gave
   (B) given
   (C) receive
   (D) thank
   (E) offer

7. Speech is to lecturer as formula is to
   (A) solution
   (B) variable
   (C) equation
   (D) expression
   (E) mathematician

8. Oppose is to competitor as win is to
   (A) victory
   (B) rank
   (C) succeed
   (D) boxer
   (E) champion

9. Patch is to quilt as ant is to
   (A) eater
   (B) hill
   (C) queen
   (D) annoying
   (E) colony

10. Snorkel is to air as effort is to
    (A) flipper
    (B) doubt
    (C) oxygen
    (D) result
    (E) person

11. Orchid is to flower as octagon is to
    (A) sign
    (B) prism
    (C) geometry
    (D) shape
    (E) eight

12. Paragraph is to sentence as country is to
    (A) state
    (B) planet
    (C) president
    (D) continent
    (E) congressman

13. Confide is to reveal as perceive is to
    (A) receive
    (B) deceive
    (C) offer
    (D) detect
    (E) confess

14. Rebellion is to overthrow as psychic is to
    (A) envisage
    (B) relinquish
    (C) disillusion
    (D) sympathize
    (E) probe

Mixed 8

1. Volleyball is to hand as baseball is to
   (A) bat
   (B) base
   (C) player
   (D) mound
   (E) dugout

2. Knight is to lance as coach is to
   (A) gym
   (B) school
   (C) player
   (D) whistle
   (E) field

3. Terrible is to terribly as sneaky is to
   (A) sneaks
   (B) sneakily
   (C) sneakier
   (D) snuck
   (E) sneak

4. Instructor is to curriculum as baker is to
   (A) pie
   (B) dessert
   (C) flour
   (D) contest
   (E) chef

The Tutorverse

5. Actor is to perform as merchant is to
   (A) sell
   (B) tax
   (C) merchandise
   (D) customer
   (E) actress

6. Pane is to window as tile is to
   (A) linoleum
   (B) mosaic
   (C) key
   (D) carpet
   (E) pattern

7. Cloth is to surface as napkin is to
   (A) food
   (B) towel
   (C) water
   (D) mouth
   (E) tissue

8. Snake is to reptile as radish is to
   (A) red
   (B) potato
   (C) salad
   (D) vegetable
   (E) spicy

9. Transcript is to documentation as diversion is to
   (A) focus
   (B) distraction
   (C) goal
   (D) evidence
   (E) destination

10. Magazine is to article as sentence is to
    (A) essay
    (B) word
    (C) article
    (D) question
    (E) command

11. Learning is to education as is strength to
    (A) intelligence
    (B) compression
    (C) reduction
    (D) exercising
    (E) stagnation

12. Vigilante is to avenge as apprentice is to
    (A) apply
    (B) educate
    (C) artisan
    (D) discourage
    (E) train

13. Bizarre is to strange as steadfast is to
    (A) irresolute
    (B) strenuous
    (C) aberrant
    (D) protective
    (E) dependable

14. Inept is to skilled as
    (A) fickle is to stable
    (B) dunce is to corner
    (C) artisan is to tool
    (D) hammer is to sickle
    (E) ocean is to weather

Mixed 9

1. Blizzard is to snowfall as downpour is to
   (A) overflow
   (B) monsoon
   (C) tempest
   (D) puddle
   (E) rain

2. Frivolously is to frivolous as graciously is to
   (A) gratitude
   (B) gracious
   (C) gracefully
   (D) gratuitous
   (E) graceful

3. Curator is to art as composer is to
   (A) harmonize
   (B) notes
   (C) atmosphere
   (D) sing
   (E) orchestral

4. Physician is to diagnose as narrator is to
   (A) reliable
   (B) trustworthy
   (C) heal
   (D) exaggerate
   (E) describe

The Tutorverse

5. Razor is to beard as knife is to
   - (A) sharp
   - (B) bread
   - (C) juice
   - (D) lunch
   - (E) weapon

6. Year is to decade as note is to
   - (A) marker
   - (B) instrument
   - (C) band
   - (D) music
   - (E) musician

7. Knife is to potato as scissors is to
   - (A) dagger
   - (B) paper
   - (C) sword
   - (D) glue
   - (E) tape

8. Consult is to discuss as recur is to
   - (A) pirate
   - (B) repeat
   - (C) discussion
   - (D) prevent
   - (E) consultation

9. Letter is to alphabet as blade is to
   - (A) dissect
   - (B) tooth
   - (C) language
   - (D) sharper
   - (E) propeller

10. Octopus is to invertebrate as
    - (A) ocean is to oxygen
    - (B) bird is to winged
    - (C) tree is to sequoia
    - (D) nature is to ecosystem
    - (E) acorn is to nut

11. Prank is to bamboozle as narration is to
    - (A) implore
    - (B) coerce
    - (C) denote
    - (D) elucidate
    - (E) interrogate

12. Bacteria is to decomposition as allergen is to
    - (A) pollen
    - (B) airborne
    - (C) natural
    - (D) disease
    - (E) irritation

13. Jester is to derision as idol is to
    - (A) ridicule
    - (B) animosity
    - (C) bitterness
    - (D) veneration
    - (E) mockery

14. Specific is to vague as
    - (A) transitory is to provisional
    - (B) nebulous is to indefinite
    - (C) indelible is to erasable
    - (D) ineffaceable is to enduring
    - (E) precise is to unambiguous

Mixed 10

1. Immemorial is to time as wrought is to
   - (A) decorated
   - (B) iron
   - (C) road
   - (D) rope
   - (E) intended

2. Shade is to trees as flame is to
   - (A) ice
   - (B) matches
   - (C) sapling
   - (D) paper
   - (E) wind

3. Ride is to rode as ring is to
   - (A) rang
   - (B) rose
   - (C) finger
   - (D) rung
   - (E) ridden

4. Illustrator is to marker as photographer is to
   - (A) zoom
   - (B) studio
   - (C) camera
   - (D) scenery
   - (E) layout

5. Travel is to adventurer as fight is to
   (A) joust
   (B) duel
   (C) warrior
   (D) match
   (E) pacifist

6. Unit is to textbook as slice is to
   (A) piece
   (B) serve
   (C) knife
   (D) separate
   (E) cake

7. Bait is to fisher as gold is to
   (A) bar
   (B) jeweler
   (C) bullion
   (D) bank
   (E) tooth

8. Aroma is to scent as distinction is to
   (A) difference
   (B) pleasant
   (C) instinct
   (D) odor
   (E) choice

9. Hat is to fedora as machinery is to
   (A) factory
   (B) tractor
   (C) utilize
   (D) gears
   (E) repairman

10. Facsimile is to manuscript as clone is to
    (A) replica
    (B) person
    (C) duplicate
    (D) imitation
    (E) twin

11. Empty is to desolate as
    (A) full is to complacent
    (B) wasteland is to barren
    (C) unforgiving is to plentiful
    (D) inferior is to proficient
    (E) poor is to destitute

12. Network is to connect as metaphor is to
    (A) abbreviate
    (B) simile
    (C) word
    (D) express
    (E) poem

13. Pilot is to airplane
    (A) father is to daughter
    (B) clown is to party
    (C) criminal is to danger
    (D) policeman is to order
    (E) child is to kite

14. Bucket is to water as
    (A) greenhouse is to contain
    (B) cat is to bird
    (C) animal is to plant
    (D) garden is to yard
    (E) album is to photograph

Reading

Overview

In the Reading section, students will read passages and answer questions that pertain to those passages. The passages will vary; some passages will be short poems, while others will be longer essays. All of the questions are designed to measure how well a student understands what he or she reads.

Students will have 40 minutes to answer 40 reading comprehension questions.

On the Actual Test

There are two main types of passages on the Upper Level SSAT: fiction and non-fiction.

Fiction passages can include short stories, poems, novels, or even personal essays. Non-fiction passages can include informative or persuasive essays and can cover topics ranging from the humanities to the sciences.

The Reading section features questions that highlight the four major topics below. The questions on the test will **not** indicate which topic is being tested. Five answer choices are presented with letters A through E. The questions are **NOT** ordered according to level of difficulty.

- *Main Idea/Theme* – What is the general message, premise, or idea of the passage? What is the author trying to tell the reader?
- *Details* – What happens in the passage, and why? What do certain words or phrases mean?
- *Inferences* – What are some conclusions that can be drawn from the passage? What can a reader infer based on the passage?
- *Mood, Tone, Style, and Figurative Language* – What feeling is the author trying to convey? How does the author use figurative language, such as metaphors and similes, to establish a mood, or set a tone?

In This Practice Book

There are 25 passages in this section from a variety of sources, which reflect what students will see on the actual Upper Level SSAT. These passages have been divided into Fiction and Non-Fiction sections. The corresponding questions will test students' ability to pinpoint some or all of the major topics that were outlined above.

We recommend that students practice several passages per week in preparing for the exam.

See an unfamiliar word? Look it up! Many words and concepts in this section might be challenging. It's a good habit to keep a list of vocabulary learned in passages, questions, or answer choices. Write down the definition of the word and use it in a sentence. Other notes that might help are positive or negative associations of the word, root words, or any phrases that are commonly encountered with the new word.

Tutorverse Tips!

Practice Active Reading

We recommend that you read the passage first before attempting to answer the questions. As you read, underline or circle key information like main ideas. Draw arrows between related ideas, or examples that support main ideas. Consider outlining the passage to get a sense for the structure of the passage as well as how the different parts of the passage are related to each other.

The Tutorverse

Because the questions on each passage will be similar to those that you have practiced, you can keep an eye out for important themes and ideas as you read. This will help save time when you answer the questions.

Identifying Main Ideas & Themes

Think about what the main idea might be as you read the passage. Ask yourself these questions as you read:

- What is the point of this passage? What is the author trying to tell me?
- What is the author's point of view on the topic?
- Is there a lesson or moral that I am supposed to learn from the passage?

Referring Back to the Text

- When the question refers back to the text with a quotation, make sure to read a little bit before and after the quoted text. Many times, the quote itself can have an ambiguous meaning if read by itself. Therefore, use context clues to help answer the questions.
- The same advice applies to questions that ask about a word or phrase's meaning. Use context clues, as the word or phrase will almost certainly have more than one possible definition.

Prove It!

Think you have the right answer? Prove it! You should be able to cite evidence from the text to support your answer for <u>every single question</u> – even inference questions! If you can't prove it to yourself, you probably haven't picked the right choice. Ask yourself, "How do I know this is true? What evidence is there from the passage that I can point to?"

Guessing

Knowing whether or not to guess can be tricky. The Upper Level SSAT gives you 1 point for each question that is answered correctly. However, if you answer a question incorrectly, ¼ of a point will be deducted from your total score (see example below).

The formula for determining the raw score is:
(Number of Questions Answered Correctly × 1) – (Number of Questions Answered Incorrectly × ¼)

No points will be awarded or deducted for questions that are left unanswered. Therefore, answer easy questions first, and come back to tougher questions later.

<u>How Guessing Impacts A Score</u>

Since there are 150 scored questions (167 total questions – 1 writing prompt – 16 experimental questions), the highest possible raw score is 150 points. This would be awarded to students who answer all 150 questions correctly.

If a student answers 110 questions correctly **but answers 40 questions incorrectly**, he or she will have earned (110 × 1) – (40 × ¼), or 110 – 10 = 100 points.

If a student answers 110 questions correctly **but leaves 40 questions unanswered**, he or she will have earned (110 × 1) – (40 × 0), or 110 – 0 = 110 points.

Therefore, it is important to refrain from making wild guesses. Instead, try to use process of elimination to make an educated guess.

Fiction

This section contains fiction passages. These passages have been adapted from short stories, novels, and poems, to help students become comfortable with the types of passages they will encounter on the actual test. Carefully read each passage and then answer the questions about it. For each question, select the choice that best answers the question based on the passage.

Passage #1

It seemed to her many years since he had begun to prepare her mind for "the place," as she always called it. Her mother had died when she was born, so she had never known or missed her. Her young, handsome, rich, doting father seemed to be the only relation she had in the world. They had always played together and been fond of each
5   other. She only knew he was rich because she had heard people say so when they thought she was not listening, and she had also heard them say that when she grew up she would be rich, too. She did not know all that being rich meant. She had always lived in a beautiful bungalow, and had been used to seeing many servants who made salaams to her and called her "Missee Sahib," and gave her her own way in everything. She had had toys and
10   pets and an *ayah* who worshipped her, and she had gradually learned that people who were rich had these things. That, however, was all she knew about it.

During her short life only one thing had troubled her, and that thing was "the place" she was to be taken to someday. The climate of India was very bad for children, and as soon as possible they were sent away from it – generally to England and to school.
15   She had seen other children go away, and had heard their fathers and mothers talk about the letters they received from them. She had known that she would be obliged to go also, and though sometimes her father's stories of the voyage and the new country had attracted her, she had been troubled by the thought that he could not stay with her.

"Couldn't you go to that place with me, papa?" she had asked when she was five
20   years old. "Couldn't you go to school, too? I would help you with your lessons."

1. As described in the passage, Missee Sahib appears to be
   (A) naïve
   (B) eloquent
   (C) destitute
   (D) plaintive
   (E) precocious

2. The "place" (line 13) that the narrator refers to is most likely
   (A) a school in India
   (B) an *ayah* in India
   (C) an *ayah* In England
   (D) a school in England
   (E) a beautiful bungalow

3. The main reason why Missee Sahib does not wish to go to "the place" is because
   (A) she would miss the *ayah*
   (B) she would be separated from her father
   (C) she did not want to live without servants
   (D) she did not want to leave her toys and pets behind
   (E) she heard fearful things from other children and their parents

4. From Missee Sahib's point of view, her upbringing most probably seemed
   (A) spartan
   (B) ordinary
   (C) privileged
   (D) unfortunate
   (E) cosmopolitan

The Tutorverse

Passage #2

> I returned from the City about three o'clock on that May afternoon pretty well disgusted with life. I had been three months in the Old Country, and was fed up with it. If anyone had told me a year ago that I would have been feeling like that I should have laughed at him; but there was the fact. The weather made me liverish, the talk of the
> 5   ordinary Englishman made me sick. I couldn't get enough exercise, and the amusements of London seemed as flat as soda-water that has been standing in the sun. "Richard Hannay," I kept telling myself, "you have got into the wrong ditch, my friend, and you had better climb out."
>
>   It made me bite my lips to think of the plans I had been building up those last
> 10   years in Bulawayo, Zimbabwe. I had my fortune – not one of the big ones, but good enough for me; and I had figured out all kinds of ways of enjoying myself. My father had brought me out from Scotland at the age of six, and I had never been home since; so England was a sort of Arabian Nights to me, and I counted on stopping there for the rest of my days.
>
> 15   But from the first I was disappointed with it. In about a week, I was tired of seeing sights, and in less than a month I had had enough of restaurants and theatres and race-meetings. I had no real pal to go about with, which probably explains things. Plenty of people invited me to their houses, but they didn't seem much interested in me. They would fling me a question or two about South Africa, and then get on their own affairs. A
> 20   lot of Imperialist ladies asked me to tea to meet schoolmasters from New Zealand and editors from Vancouver, and that was the most dismal business of all. Here was I, thirty-seven years old, sound in wind and limb, with enough money to have a good time, yawning my head off all day. I had just about settled to clear out and get back to the African countryside, for I was the best bored man in the United Kingdom.

1. According to the passage, the narrator is originally from
   (A) Scotland
   (B) Bulawayo
   (C) Vancouver
   (D) New Zealand
   (E) South Africa

2. The narrator is "disgusted with life" (line 2)
   (A) because he feels very old
   (B) because he is disappointed by his plans
   (C) because he is in poor physical condition
   (D) because he was injured falling into a ditch
   (E) because he does not have enough money to enjoy London

3. The phrase "the amusements of... the sun" (lines 5-6) is an example of
   (A) simile
   (B) allegory
   (C) metaphor
   (D) hyperbole
   (E) personification

4. All of the following are reasons why the narrator calls himself the "best bored man in the United Kingdom" (line 24) EXCEPT that he
   (A) dislikes the weather
   (B) feels listless and idle
   (C) has no traveling companion
   (D) finds the conversation boring
   (E) never really wanted to visit London

5. The narrator's use of the which of the following words is an example of a hyperbole?
   (A) "ordinary Englishman" (line 5)
   (B) "I was tired" (line 15)
   (C) "fling me a question" (line 19)
   (D) "sound in wind and limb" (line 22)
   (E) "yawning my head off all day" (line 23)

The Tutorverse

Passage #3

We were looking for quail, each with a shotgun, but we had only one dog.
...Suddenly, we heard, at a little distance to our right, and partly in front, a noise as of
some animal thrashing about in the bushes, which we could see were violently agitated.
"We've startled a deer," I said. "I wish we had brought a rifle."
5   Morgan, who had stopped and was intently watching the agitated brush, said
nothing, but had cocked both barrels of his gun, and was holding it in readiness to aim. I
thought him a trifle excited, which surprised me, for he had a reputation for exceptional
coolness, even in moments of sudden and imminent peril.
    Catching sight of his face as he turned it slightly toward me, I was struck by the
10   pallor of it. Then I understood that we had serious business on hand, and my first
conjecture was that we had "jumped" a grizzly.
    The bushes were now quiet, and the sounds had ceased, but Morgan was as
attentive to the place as before.
    "What is it? What the devil is it?" I asked.
15   "That Infernal Thing!" he replied, without turning his head. His voice was husky
and unnatural. He trembled visibly.
    I was about to speak further, when I observed the wild oats near the place of the
disturbance moving in the most inexplicable way. I can hardly describe it. It seemed as if
stirred by a streak of wind, which not only bent it, but pressed it down – crushed it so that
20   it did not rise, and this movement was slowly extending itself directly toward us...
    The slow, undeviating approach of the line of disturbance was distinctly
disquieting. My companion appeared actually frightened, and I could hardly credit my
senses when I saw him suddenly throw his gun to his shoulders and fire both barrels at
the agitated grass! Before the smoke of the discharge had cleared away I heard a loud
25   savage cry – a scream like that of a wild animal – and, flinging his gun upon the ground,
Morgan sprang away and ran swiftly from the spot. At the same instant I was thrown
violently to the ground by the impact of something unseen in the smoke – some soft,
heavy substance that seemed thrown against me with great force.

1. Why does the narrator mention Morgan's reputation (lines 7-8)?
(A) It explains why the pair startled a deer.
(B) It foreshadows how Morgan later reacts.
(C) It explains why the narrator is hunting with Morgan.
(D) It shows why there is only one dog with the group.
(E) It provides a frame of comparison for later actions.

2. The passage focuses on the
(A) excitement of a hunt
(B) best way to prepare for a hunt
(C) friendship between two hunters
(D) sights and sounds of the outdoors
(E) experience of encountering danger

3. The sensory information most important to this passage is
(A) the sound of a gunshot
(B) the strength of the Thing
(C) the movement in the grass
(D) the smell of smoke in the air
(E) the sound of thrashing in bushes

4. Over the course of the passage, the mood of the narrator changes from
(A) puzzled to worried to hostile
(B) enraged to envious to surprised
(C) dismissive to tense to terrified
(D) nonchalant to scared to relaxed
(E) exhilarated to dreamy to desperate

The Tutorverse

Passage #4

> "Here, hand me the crowbar," said Tom. "Now, by using this little round knob which projects from the cliff here as a fulcrum, we may be able to lever it off. Yes; there it goes. I never thought it could have come so easily. Now, Jack, the sooner we get back to our hut and then down to Cape Town, the better."
>
> 5   We wrapped up our treasure, and made our way across the hills toward home.
>
> "We'll take it down to Cape Town," said Tom, "and if we can't dispose of it with advantage there, it will be worth our while to bring it to London with us. Let us go along to Madison's first, though; he knows something of these things, and can perhaps give us some idea of what we may consider a fair price for our treasure."
>
> 10   We turned off from the track accordingly, before reaching our hut, and kept along the narrow path leading to Madison's farm. He was at lunch when we entered; and in a minute we were seated at each side of him, enjoying South African hospitality.
>
> "Well," he said, after the servants were gone, "what's in the wind now? I see you have something to say to me. What is it?"
>
> 15   Tom produced his packet, and solemnly untied the handkerchiefs which enveloped it. "There!" he said, putting his crystal on the table. "What would you say was a fair price for that?"
>
> Madison took it up and examined it critically. "Well," he said, laying it down again, "in its crude state, about twelve shillings per ton."
>
> 20   "Twelve shillings!" cried Tom, starting to his feet. "Don't you see what it is?"
>
> "Rock-salt!"
>
> "Rock-salt be damned! A diamond!"
>
> "Taste it!" said Madison.
>
> Tom put it to his lips, dashed it down with a dreadful exclamation, and rushed out
>
> 25 of the room.

1. As used in line 6, "dispose" most nearly means
   (A) toss
   (B) sell
   (C) destroy
   (D) recycle
   (E) provide

2. Before meeting with Madison, the narrator and Tom believed the "treasure" (lines 5, 9) to be a
   (A) shilling
   (B) fulcrum
   (C) crowbar
   (D) diamond
   (E) salt crystal

3. As described in the passage, Tom appears to have rushed out of the room (lines 24-25) because
   (A) Madison insulted him greatly
   (B) he was disappointed in learning the truth
   (C) the narrator urged him to rush off to London
   (D) Jack threatened to steal the treasure from him
   (E) he was excited about the great sum of money to be earned

Passage #5

Tomorrow would be Christmas Day, and she had only $1.87 with which to buy Jim a present. She had been saving every penny she could for months, with this result. Twenty dollars a week doesn't go far. Expenses had been greater than she had calculated. They always are. Only $1.87 to buy a present for Jim. Her Jim.

5   Suddenly she whirled from the window and stood before her mirror. Her eyes were shining brilliantly, but her face had lost its color within twenty seconds. Rapidly she pulled down her hair and let it fall to its full length.

Now, there were two possessions of the James Dillingham Youngs in which they both took a mighty pride. One was Jim's gold watch that had been his father's and his

10   grandfather's. The other was Della's hair. Had the queen of Sheba lived in the flat across the airshaft, Della would have let her hair hang out the window someday to dry just to depreciate Her Majesty's jewels and gifts.

So now Della's beautiful hair fell about her, rippling and shining like a cascade of brown waters. It reached below her knee and made itself almost a garment for her. And

15   then she did it up again nervously and quickly. Once, she faltered for a minute and stood still where a tear or two splashed on the worn red carpet.

On went her old brown jacket; on went her old brown hat. With a whirl of skirts and with the brilliant sparkle still in her eyes, she fluttered out the door and down the stairs to the street.

20   Where she stopped the sign read: "Mme. Sofronie, Hair Goods of All Kinds." One flight up Della ran, and collected herself, panting. Madame, large, too white, chilly, hardly looked the "Sofronie."

"Will you buy my hair?" asked Della.

"I buy hair," said Madame. "Take yer hat off and let's have a sight at the look of it."

25   Down rippled the brown cascade.

"Twenty dollars," said Madame, lifting the mass with a practiced hand.

"Give it to me quick," said Della.

Oh, and the next two hours tripped by on rosy wings. She was ransacking the stores for Jim's present.

1. Della's face likely loses its color (line 6) because
   (A) she cuts all her hair off to sell
   (B) Mme. Sofronie offers to buy all her hair
   (C) she has an idea that she doesn't like but feels compelled to act upon
   (D) she realizes that she will never be able to afford or find Jim a good present
   (E) she feels as though she has just seen the queen of Sheba

2. In line 29, "ransacking the stores" most likely refers to
   (A) frantic shopping
   (B) stealing from stores
   (C) destroying storefronts
   (D) terrifying shopkeepers
   (E) making a mess in stores

3. The author includes mention of "Her Majesty's jewels and gifts" (line 12) in order to
   (A) express the beauty of Della's hair
   (B) compare them to Jim's gold watch
   (C) contrast them to the queen of Sheba
   (D) describe Della's fervent desire to meet royalty
   (E) show Della's desperation to find Jim a good present

4. The author uses the simile "like a cascade of brown waters" (lines 13-14) in order to describe
   (A) Della's brown jacket
   (B) Della's beautiful hair
   (C) Jim's watch
   (D) Della's tears splashing on the carpet
   (E) Her Majesty's jewels and gifts

The Tutorverse

Passage #6

Truly he had a grave time that first winter. The rod of power was new to him, and he felt it his "duty" to use it more frequently than might have been thought necessary by those upon whose sense the privilege had palled. Tears and sulky faces, and impotent fists doubled fiercely when his back was turned, were the rewards of his
5   conscientiousness; and the boys – and girls too – were glad when working time came round again, and the master went home to help his father on the farm.

Let it not be supposed that Master Horner was of a cruel and ogrish nature – a babe-eater – a Herod—one who delighted in torturing the helpless. Such souls there may be, among those endowed with the awful control of the whip, but they are rare in the
10   fresh and natural regions we describe. It is, we believe, where young gentlemen are to be crammed for college, that the process of hardening heart and skin together goes on most vigorously. Yet among the uneducated there is so high a respect for bodily strength, that it is necessary for the schoolmaster to show, first of all, that he possesses this inadmissible requisite for his place. The rest is more readily taken for granted. Brains he may have – a
15   strong arm he must have: so he proves the more important claim first. We must therefore make all due allowance for Master Horner, who could not be expected to overtop his position so far as to discern at once the philosophy of teaching.

He was sadly brow-beaten during his first term of service by a great broad-shouldered lout of some eighteen years or so, who thought he needed a little more
20   "schooling," but at the same time felt quite competent to direct the manner and measure of his attempts.

"You ought to begin with print, Joshua," said Master Horner to this youth.

"What should I want print for?" said the disciple, with great contempt. "Print won't never do me no good. I want a copy in cursive."
25   The master looked at the infant giant, and did as he wished, but we say not with what secret resolutions.

1. As used in the sentence, "grave" (line 1) most nearly means
   (A) tomb
   (B) trivial
   (C) jaunty
   (D) deadly
   (E) challenging

2. According to the passage, it is most reasonable to infer that Horner felt compelled to wield "the rod of power" (line 1) because
   (A) he is ogrish and cruel
   (B) he enjoyed torturing the helpless, like Herod
   (C) that is how, in his youth, he was taught by his teacher
   (D) that is the only way to motivate students to cram for college
   (E) he must demonstrate strength and dominance in order to control his class

3. The "inadmissible requisite" (lines 13-14) refers to
   (A) unending patience
   (B) physical dominance
   (C) friendly appearance
   (D) relatable personality
   (E) impressive intelligence

4. After Joshua replies to Horner in lines 22-23, Horner most likely feels
   (A) validation
   (B) resentment
   (C) appreciation
   (D) disappointed
   (E) embarrassment

5. The phrase "infant giant" (line 25) refers to
   (A) Joshua
   (B) Horner
   (C) Herod
   (D) Horner's nickname for his students
   (E) The students' nickname for Horner

The Tutorverse

Passage #7

There is an air of easy sociality among the guests at the Brant House, a disposition on the part of all to contribute to the general amusement, that makes a summer sojourn on the beach far more agreeable than in certain larger, more frequented watering-places, where one is always in danger of discovering that the gentlemanly person with whom he

5   has been fraternizing is a scoundrel...Still, some consider the Brant rather slow, and many good folk were a trifle surprised when Mr. Edwin Salsbury and Mr. Charles Burnham arrived from Wikhasset Station, with overstuffed trunks and a most unexceptionable butler in gray livery, in charge of two beautiful setter-dogs.

These gentlemen seemed to have imagined that they were about visiting some

10   backwoods wilderness, some savage tract of country, "remote, unfriended, melancholy, slow," for they brought almost everything with them that men of elegant leisure could require, as if the hotel were but four walls and a roof, which they must furnish with their own chattels. I am sure it took Thomas, the butler, a whole day to unpack the awnings, the bootjacks, the game-bags, the cigar-boxes, the guns, the camp-stools, the liquor-cases, the

15   bathing-suits, and other paraphernalia that these pleasure-seekers brought. It must be owned, however, that their room, a large one in the Bachelors' Quarter, facing the sea, wore a very comfortable, sportsmanlike look when all was arranged.

Thus surrounded, the young men betook themselves to the deliberate pursuit of idle pleasures. They arose at nine and went down the shore, invariably returning at ten

20   with one unfortunate snipe, which was preserved on ice, with much ceremony, till wanted. At this rate it took them a week to shoot a breakfast; but to see them forge ahead, splendid in velveteen and corduroy, with top-boots and a complete harness of green cord and patent-leather straps, you would have imagined that all game-birds were about to become extinct in that region. Their dogs, even, recognized this great-cry-little-wool

25   condition of things, and bounded off joyously at the start, but came home crestfallen, with an air of canine humiliation.

1. The "watering-places" (line 3) probably refer to
    (A) hunting trips
    (B) amusement parks
    (C) vacation destinations
    (D) backwoods wilderness
    (E) savage tracts of country

2. From the details, you can tell that the narrator finds Salsbury and Burnham a poor fit for Brant House because
    (A) they were fraternizing with suspicious men
    (B) all of the other guests are wealthy men of leisure
    (C) their butler, Thomas, was rude and unfriendly
    (D) the location did not permit animals or allow hunting
    (E) they brought an extravagant air to an otherwise casual location

3. In line 13, "chattels" most nearly means
    (A) animals
    (B) awnings
    (C) activities
    (D) belongings
    (E) conversations

4. The narrator implies which of the following about Salsbury and Burnham's hunting excursions?
    (A) The men were not as good at hunting as they thought they were.
    (B) They were so successful that no game-birds remained in the region.
    (C) The hunters would not have been successful without their dogs.
    (D) Salsbury and Burnham were humiliated by their lack of success.
    (E) The prey they hunted fed all the guests staying at the Brant House for a week.

Passage #8

How unwise had the wanderers been, who had deserted their shelter, entangled themselves in the web of society, and entered on what men of the world call "life," – that labyrinth of evil, that scheme of mutual torture. To live, according to this sense of the word, we must not only observe and learn, we must also feel; we must not be mere
5   spectators of action, we must act; we must not describe, but be subjects of description. Deep sorrow must have been the inmate of our bosoms; fraud must have lain in wait for us; the artful must have deceived us; sickening doubt and false hope must have checkered our days; hilarity and joy, that lap the soul in ecstasy, must at times have possessed us. Who that knows what "life" is, would pine for this feverish species of existence? I have
10   lived. I have spent days and nights of festivity; I have joined in ambitious hopes, and exulted in victory: now, – shut the door on the world, and build high the wall that is to separate me from the troubled scene enacted within its precincts. Let us live for each other and for happiness; let us seek peace in our dear home, near the inland murmur of streams, and the gracious waving of trees, the beauteous vesture of earth, and sublime
15   pageantry of the skies. Let us leave "life," that we may live.

1. In line 9, the word "pine" refers to a
   (A) type of tree
   (B) strong desire
   (C) beautiful place
   (D) profound regret
   (E) powerful reminder

2. The author's use of which of the following words is an example of personification?
   (A) "web of society" (line 2)
   (B) "spectators of action" (line 5)
   (C) "doubt and false hope" (line 7)
   (D) "nights of festivity" (line 10)
   (E) "murmur of streams" (lines 13-14)

3. Which of the following does the author cite as personal experience to support her central claim?
   (A) "spectators of action" (line 5)
   (B) "hilarity and joy" (line 8)
   (C) "days and nights of festivity" (line 10)
   (D) "beauteous vesture of earth" (line 14)
   (E) "sublime pageantry" (lines 14-15)

4. The author's attitude toward society is best described as
   (A) hostile
   (B) modest
   (C) fervent
   (D) hopeful
   (E) ambivalent

5. The author's goal in writing the passage is to
   (A) relate a humorous story
   (B) tell about a personal anecdote
   (C) give specific and detailed instructions
   (D) describe two different ways of living life
   (E) describe a problem and recommend a solution

The Tutorverse

Passage #9

An old man going a lone highway
Came at the evening, cold and gray,
To a chasm vast and wide and steep,
With waters rolling cold and deep.
5   The old man crossed in the twilight dim,
The sullen stream had no fears for him;
But he turned when safe on the other side,
And built a bridge to span the tide.

"Old man," said a fellow pilgrim near,
10   "You are wasting your strength with building here.
Your journey will end with the ending day,
You never again will pass this way.
You've crossed the chasm, deep and wide,
Why build you this bridge at eventide?"

15   The builder lifted his old gray head.
"Good friend, in the path I have come," he said,
"There followeth after me today
A youth whose feet must pass this way.
The chasm that was as nought to me
20   To that fair-haired youth may a pitfall be;
He, too, must cross in the twilight dim –
Good friend, I am building this bridge for him."

1. The author uses the analogy of the bridge to illustrate that
    (A) people can only rely on themselves
    (B) you cannot cross a river without a bridge
    (C) life is long and spent with pointless activities
    (D) each generation can make life better for the next
    (E) one should never burn make enemies and burn bridges

2. The author would most likely agree with which of the following statements?
    (A) The young should be suspicious of the old and their actions.
    (B) People should travel around rivers, not across them.
    (C) You learn to overcome obstacles as you get older.
    (D) It's better to spend your time living as opposed to working.
    (E) People should focus on themselves and not worry about others.

3. In the passage, the chasm (lines 3, 13, 19) represents
    (A) the simple pleasures of life
    (B) the beauty and joy of youth
    (C) an opportunity to make money
    (D) a toll one must pay to grow older
    (E) challenges one encounters in life

4. In the context of the passage, you can tell that "twilight" (line 5) refers to
    (A) a difficult challenge
    (B) the end of a person's life
    (C) the sun reflecting off the river
    (D) the light shining through the trees
    (E) morning

5. As described in the passage, the old man appears to be
    (A) naïve
    (B) rushed
    (C) selfless
    (D) carefree
    (E) preoccupied

The Tutorverse

Passage #10

> Fall, leaves, fall; die, flowers, away;
> Lengthen night and shorten day;
> Every leaf speaks bliss to me,
> Fluttering from the autumn tree.
> 5   I shall smile when wreaths of snow
> Blossom where the rose should grow;
> I shall sing when night's decay
> Ushers in a drearier day.

1. The author's tone can best be described as
   (A) comical
   (B) frustrated
   (C) indifferent
   (D) impassioned
   (E) contemptuous

2. In line 3, the phrase "Every leaf speaks bliss" is an example of
   (A) ethos
   (B) simile
   (C) metaphor
   (D) metonymy
   (E) personification

3. The passage is primarily about
   (A) the biology of plants
   (B) roses and other blossoms
   (C) the comforts of warmer weather
   (D) reflecting on the changing season
   (E) the effects of daylight saving time

Passage #11

> I wandered lonely as a cloud
> That floats on high o'er vales and hills
> When all at once I saw a crowd,
> A host, of golden daffodils;
> 5   Beside the lake, beneath the trees,
> Fluttering and dancing in the breeze.
>
> Continuous as the stars that shine
> And twinkle on the milky way,
> They stretched in never-ending line
> 10   Along the margin of a bay:
> Ten thousand saw I at a glance,
> Tossing their heads in sprightly dance.
>
> The waves beside them dance; but they
> Out-did the sparkling waves in glee:
> 15   A poet could not but be gay,
> In such a jocund company:
> I gazed – and gazed – but little thought
> What wealth the show to me had brought:
>
> For oft, when on my couch I lie
> 20   In vacant or in pensive mood,
> They flash upon that inward eye
> Which is the bliss of solitude;
> And then my heart with pleasure fills,
> And dances with the daffodils.

1. In line 1, the phrase "I wandered lonely as a cloud" is an example of
   (A) alliteration
   (B) onomatopoeia
   (C) personification
   (D) simile
   (E) synecdoche

2. The "[t]en thousand" (line 11) probably refers
   (A) to beautiful flowers
   (B) to the stars that shine
   (C) to people in the crowd
   (D) to the trees by the lake
   (E) to the waves on the lake

3. In line 16, the word "jocund" most nearly mean
   (A) cheerful
   (B) crowded
   (C) fetid
   (D) humorous
   (E) ironic

4. When the speaker writes "the bliss of solitude" (line 22), he is most likely referring to
   (A) individual liberty
   (B) a tranquil home life
   (C) being a person in a crowd
   (D) time to reflect on nature's beauty
   (E) escaping the drudgery of the week

5. Which of the following is an example of personification?
   (A) "A host, of golden daffodils" (line 4)
   (B) "And twinkle on the milky way" (line 8)
   (C) "They stretched in never-ending line" (line 9)
   (D) "The waves beside them dance" (line 13)"
   (E) "In vacant or in pensive mood" (line 20)

The Tutorverse

Passage #12

> I met a traveler from an antique land
> Who said: "Two vast and trunkless legs of stone
> Stand in the desert...Near them, on the sand,
> Half sunk, a shattered visage lies, whose frown,
> 5   And wrinkled lip, and sneer of cold command,
> Tell that its sculptor well those passions read
> Which yet survive, stamped on these lifeless things,
> The hand that mocked them, and the heart that fed:
> And on the pedestal these words appear:
> 10   'My name is Ozymandias, king of kings:
> Look on my works, ye Mighty, and despair!'
> Nothing beside remains. Round the decay
> Of that colossal wreck, boundless and bare
> The lone and level sands stretch far away."

1. In line 4, the word "visage" means
    (A) face
    (B) sight
    (C) statue
    (D) person
    (E) landscape

2. In which of the following lines does the author describe the sculptor's skill in carving the statue?
    (A) Line 2
    (B) Line 6
    (C) Line 12
    (D) Line 13
    (E) Line 14

3. Which of the following conclusions can best be drawn from the passage?
    (A) The traveler was an antiques dealer.
    (B) The traveler got lost on his way home.
    (C) The sculptor was a good friend of Ozymandias.
    (D) The traveler encountered the ruins of a great civilization.
    (E) The traveler was an archaeologist who studies old statues.

4. As described in the passage, Ozymandias appears to have been
    (A) artistic
    (B) elderly
    (C) powerful
    (D) despairing
    (E) compassionate

5. The main reason the author describes the words on the pedestal (lines 10–11) is to
    (A) compare the statue with its surroundings
    (B) provide historical context for the poem
    (C) help the reader understand the narrator's background
    (D) cast doubt on the reliability of the traveler as a storyteller
    (E) show how the statue would be described in a museum

6. Which of the following summarizes the main idea of the passage?
    (A) Ozymandias was the greatest king in all of history.
    (B) Ancient sculptors are more skilled than today's sculptors.
    (C) Deserts are not an appropriate environment for statues.
    (D) Only the largest and most impressive works of art remain forever.
    (E) Even the greatest accomplishments will eventually be lost or forgotten.

The Tutorverse

Non-Fiction

This section contains non-fiction passages that can explain an idea or attempt to persuade the reader. Carefully read each passage and then answer the questions about it. For each question, select the choice that best answers the question based on the passage.

Passage #1

> Dream delivers us to dream, and there is no end to illusion. Life is a train of moods like a string of beads, and, as we pass through them, they prove to be many-colored lenses which paint the world their own hue, and each shows only what lies in its focus. From the mountain you see the mountain. We animate what we can, and we see only what we
> 5 animate. Nature and books belong to the eyes that see them. It depends on the mood of the man, whether he shall see the sunset or the fine poem. There are always sunsets, and there is always genius; but only a few hours so serene that we can relish nature or criticism. The more or less depends on structure or temperament. Temperament is the iron wire on which the beads are strung.

1. The author's use of which of the following words is an example of a metaphor?
    (A) "dream delivers us to dream" (line 1)
    (B) "life is a train of moods" (line 1)
    (C) "many-colored lenses" (line 2)
    (D) "paint the world their own hue" (line 3)
    (E) "we see only what we animate" (lines 4-5)

2. The "beads" (line 9) probably refer to
    (A) an iron wire
    (B) a person's mood
    (C) a type of decoration
    (D) a person's temperament
    (E) the interpretation of a book

3. It is most reasonable to infer from the passage that a person who experiences a negative life event
    (A) should welcome constructive criticism
    (B) thinks about it with a long-term point of view
    (C) focuses on how it makes him or her feel in the moment
    (D) deserves to suffer for not adequately preparing in advance
    (E) should reflect upon it in the peacefulness of nature

4. This passage was probably taken from
    (A) a historical novel
    (B) a scientific report
    (C) a personal journal or diary
    (D) an advertisement for beads
    (E) a commercial for national parks

5. Which of the following questions is the author most likely to answer next?
    (A) Should people stop trying to control their lives?
    (B) Where can a person go to reflect on life's events?
    (C) How does a person's personality affect his outlook on life?
    (D) What time of day is the best time to think about one's life?
    (E) Who needs to spend time contemplating life's mysteries?

The Tutorverse

Passage #2

> Though an essay must state a proposition, there are other requirements to be fulfilled. The bones of subject and predicate must be dressed in a certain way. The basis of the essay is meditation, and it must in a measure admit the reader to the meditative process. (This procedure is frankly hinted in all those titles that used to begin with "Of" or
>
> 5   "On": "Of Truth," "Of Riches," "On the Graces and Anxieties of Pig-Driving," "On the Knocking at the Gate in 'Macbeth'," "On the Enjoyment of Unpleasant Places".) An essay, to some extent, thinks aloud; though not in the loose and pointless way to which the "stream of consciousness" addicts have accustomed us. The author must have made up his mind – otherwise, where is his proposition? But the essay, I think, should show how and why he
>
> 10   made up his mind as he did; should engagingly rehearse the steps by which he came to his conclusions.
>
>   The essay, then, having persuasion for its object, states a proposition; its method is meditation; it is subjective rather than objective, critical rather than creative. It can never be a mere marshaling of facts; for it struggles, in one way or another, for truth; and
>
> 15   truth is something one arrives at by the help of facts, not the facts themselves. Meditating on facts may bring one to truth; facts alone will not. Nor can there be an essay without a point of view and a personality.

1. "Proposition" (line 1) most nearly means
   - (A) bid
   - (B) fact
   - (C) premise
   - (D) project
   - (E) request

2. The author's tone in lines 4-6 can best be described as
   - (A) humorous
   - (B) sincere
   - (C) solemn
   - (D) virtuous
   - (E) vindictive

3. The author is primarily concerned with
   - (A) providing a critique of certain essays
   - (B) quantifying the qualities of a good title
   - (C) sharing a point of view on a literary genre
   - (D) analyzing the topics of different pieces of writing
   - (E) explaining how best to write the perfect essay

4. According to author, an essay must include all of the following EXCEPT
   - (A) an opinion
   - (B) a catchy title
   - (C) a clear purpose and aim
   - (D) reasoning and explanation
   - (E) the author's personality and voice

5. According to the passage, the purpose of an essay is to
   - (A) entertain the reader using stories
   - (B) share thoughts as if thinking aloud
   - (C) be as creative and inventive as possible
   - (D) coach the reader toward a particular conclusion
   - (E) showcase one's ability to use literary devices effectively

6. Without changing the author's meaning, "marshaling" (line 15) could be replaced by which of the following?
   - (A) arranging and critiquing
   - (B) gathering and stating
   - (C) corralling and analyzing
   - (D) collecting and evaluating
   - (E) organizing and assessing

Passage #3

Medicine has made great strides in this generation, especially during the last four years. We owe much to the skill and devotion of the medical profession. In spite of great scientific progress, however, each year we lose many more persons from preventable and premature deaths than we lost in battle or from war injuries during the entire war.

5   We are proud of past reductions in our death rates. But these reductions have come principally from public health and other community services. We have been less effective in making available to all of our people the benefits of medical progress in the care and treatment of individuals.

       In the past, the benefits of modern medical science have not been enjoyed by our
10   citizens with any degree of equality. Nor are they today. Nor will they be in the future – unless government is bold enough to do something about it.

       People with low or moderate incomes do not get the same medical attention as those with high incomes. The poor have more sickness, but they get less medical care. People who live in rural areas do not get the same amount or quality of medical attention
15   as those who live in our cities.

       Our new Economic Bill of Rights should mean health security for all, regardless of residence, station, or race – everywhere in the United States.

       We should resolve now that the health of this Nation is a national concern; that financial barriers in the way of attaining health shall be removed; that the health of all its
20   citizens deserves the help of all the Nation.

1. The author's primary purpose is to
    (A) share specific details and facts
    (B) present a particular point of view
    (C) build empathy by sharing a story
    (D) criticize an opposing point of view
    (E) highlight a problem without a solution

2. Based on the passage, it can be inferred that the author's main concern with medicine is
    (A) that not everyone who needs it can get it
    (B) that too many people still die of curable diseases
    (C) that the wealthy need more medical attention than the poor
    (D) that those who live in cities are unable to access quality healthcare
    (E) that public health and community services are not robust enough

3. As used in line 17, "station" refers to
    (A) a person's creed or ethnicity
    (B) a type of expensive medicine
    (C) one's economic or social standing
    (D) an obstacle to medical advancement
    (E) a place to ride on public transportation

4. According to evidence from the passage, the author would most likely agree with which of the following statements?
    (A) More people should move to cities for access to better healthcare.
    (B) Access to healthcare should not be a matter of money.
    (C) Quality healthcare treatment can only be achieved by spending more money.
    (D) Hospitals should not get in trouble if they refuse to treat someone who can't pay.
    (E) The government should not be involved in a person's medical treatment.

5. Which of the following is the author most likely to discuss next?
    (A) The people responsible for healthcare inequality.
    (B) An account of premature and preventable deaths.
    (C) Specific examples where poor people were unable to be treated.
    (D) Reasons why the government should ensure healthcare for everyone.
    (E) Particular areas in medicine which have made the greatest advancements.

Passage #4

In 2014, *The Washington Post* conducted a poll and found that 26% of registered American voters claimed to be "too busy" to vote on Election Day. It gets worse: the percentage of eligible voters that cast their ballots during presidential elections rarely exceeds 60%.

5   It is a sad state of affairs when fellow citizens find themselves without enough time to determine the leaders of our democracy. The fact that the United States trails most developed countries in voter turnout is embarrassing and damaging to both our democracy at home and our reputation abroad. Yet, there is hope to be found in looking abroad; holding elections during the weekend or on national holidays has helped other

10   democracies ensure a high voter turnout.

In the 1800s, when America was an agrarian society, American elections were scheduled on Tuesdays to accommodate farming schedules. In today's more industrialized America, less than 2 percent of the population is employed in agriculture, and the vast majority of the citizenry must work on Tuesdays. Faced with interminable

15   voting lines, long commutes to polling stations, or even the possibility of getting fired, some voters just can't afford to take time off to vote on Tuesdays. This may help explain why American voter turnout is so dismally low. Other countries appear to have preempted these potential deterrents by holding elections on weekends or holidays. Austria, Belgium, France, and Germany are just some of the developed countries that have

20   made it easier for their citizens to vote, and all of them boast significantly higher voter turnout than that of the United States.

The truth is that Congress must mandate an election schedule that is more accommodating to the American public. In doing so, they will communicate to voters the importance of Election Day and reinforce the notion that every vote is important. What's

25   more, moving elections to weekends or holidays could transform the mundane act of casting a ballot into a genuine cultural event. Election Day would not only be a day to exercise political power, but would be a chance for people to come together and celebrate democracy itself. Imagine an Election Day that isn't overshadowed by the possibility of missed job deadlines, but is instead celebrated in the streets with food and music.

30   The ability to express one's opinion through voting is the most sacred right of any citizen of a democracy. It's time for our elections to reflect that.

1. Which of the following is the best title for the selection?
    (A) The Advantages of Life Abroad
    (B) The End of Agricultural Societies
    (C) The Importance of the Right to Vote
    (D) A Necessary Change to America's Voting Calendar
    (E) Democracy Gone Awry: The Problem with American Congress

2. It can be inferred from the passage that an "agrarian society" (line 11)
    (A) does not guarantee citizens the right to vote
    (B) requires farmers to work on Tuesdays
    (C) gives more power to factory workers than farmers
    (D) promotes a voting system similar to European countries
    (E) is marked by an absence of widely developed industries

(continued on next page)

The Tutorverse

3. The author of the passage is primarily concerned with
   (A) increasing voter turnout
   (B) copying the lifestyles of European citizens
   (C) creating positive messaging for young voters
   (D) highlighting the social potential of Election Day
   (E) showcasing obvious contradictions in voting habits

4. As used in line 18, the word "deterrents" most nearly means
   (A) anomalies
   (B) assessments
   (C) difficulties
   (D) establishments
   (E) incentives

5. According to the passage, what is a possible result of scheduling Election Day on a holiday or weekend?
   (A) Voting day would become a festive event.
   (B) People would be too busy to bother voting.
   (C) Voter turnout would remain largely the same.
   (D) Congress would finally gain the trust of citizens.
   (E) America would reestablish its position as a global superpower.

6. The author's style is most similar to writing that can be found in
   (A) a novel
   (B) an editorial
   (C) a movie script
   (D) a personal memoir
   (E) an instructional pamphlet

The Tutorverse

Passage #5

> Tonight I call the roll – the roll of honor of those who stood with us in 1932 and still stand with us today.
>
> Written on it are the names of millions who never had a chance – men at starvation wages, women in sweatshops, children at looms.
>
> 5   Written on it are the names of those who despaired, young men and young women for whom opportunity had become a will-o'-the-wisp.
>
> Written on it are the names of farmers whose acres yielded only bitterness, business men whose books were portents of disaster, home owners who were faced with eviction, frugal citizens whose savings were insecure.
>
> 10   Written there in large letters are the names of countless other Americans of all parties and all faiths, Americans who had eyes to see and hearts to understand, whose consciences were burdened because too many of their fellows were burdened, who looked on these things four years ago and said, "This can be changed. We will change it."
>
> For twelve years this Nation was afflicted with hear-nothing, see-nothing, do-
> 15 nothing Government. The Nation looked to Government but the Government looked away. Nine mocking years with the golden calf and three long years of the scourge! Nine crazy years at the ticker and three long years in the breadlines! Nine mad years of mirage and three long years of despair! Powerful influences strive today to restore that kind of government with its doctrine that Government is best which is most indifferent.
>
> 20   For nearly four years you have had an Administration which instead of twirling its thumbs has rolled up its sleeves. We will keep our sleeves rolled up.
>
> We had to struggle with the old enemies of peace – business and financial monopoly, speculation, reckless banking, class antagonism, sectionalism, war profiteering.
>
> 25   They had begun to consider the Government of the United States as a mere appendage to their own affairs. We know now that Government by organized money is just as dangerous as Government by organized mob.
>
> Never before in all our history have these forces been so united against one candidate as they stand today. They are unanimous in their hate for me – and I welcome
> 30 their hatred.

1. The author's repeated use of the phrase "written on it" (lines 3, 5, 7) is an example of
   (A) simile
   (B) metaphor
   (C) anaphora
   (D) hyperbole
   (E) personification

2. In the author's opinion, the "things four years ago" (line 13) were
   (A) abysmal
   (B) beneficial
   (C) necessary
   (D) unavoidable
   (E) unremarkable

3. Which of the following does the author use to describe a period of plenty?
   (A) "women in sweatshops" (line 4)
   (B) "years of the scourge" (line 16)
   (C) "years at the ticker" (line 17)
   (D) "years of despair" (line 18)
   (E) "organized money" (line 26)

4. The author lists all of the following as unequivocally dangerous EXCEPT
   (A) selfishness
   (B) unchecked greed
   (C) organized crime
   (D) the government
   (E) excessive wealth

The Tutorverse

Passage #6

There is no record of any European vessel having passed the Narrows until nearly a hundred years after the brief visit of Verrazano and his *Delfina*. When another century opened, then came the first rude stage of the grand movement of civilization. The *Haalve Maan*, a yacht of forty tons bearing the colors of the Netherlands commanded by a bold
5   English skipper, came sailing along the coast in the summer of 1609. Her object was that of every other exploring vessel sailing westward at that day: seeking a passage to Cathay. Moving northward from the Chesapeake in the last days of August, her commander, Hendrick Hudson, noted that what he surveyed was "a very good land to fall in with, and a pleasant land to see."
10   Finding what he believed to be the mouths of "three great rivers," Hudson entered a fine harbor, and anchored just within Sandy Hook. There he saw "many salmon and mullets, and rays very great." The next day, Friday, September 4th, his crew moved farther into the outer harbor, and "caught ten great mullets, and a ray as great as four men could haul into the ship."
15   A small party from the *Haalve Maan* landed, went into the woods, and saw "great stores of very goodly oaks, and some currants." These last were probably whortle-berries; currants ripen earlier. "The land was very pleasant with grass, and flowers, and goodly trees, and very sweet smells came from them." One can fancy those rough old sea-dogs, English and Dutch, gazing up at the "many tall and goodly oaks," which so greatly
20   excited their admiration, and then perchance stooping to pick a "posy," some gay-colored autumn flower, a golden-rod, or a daisy.

1. According to the passage, why did the *Haalve Maan* sail through the Narrows?
   (A) to fight in a war
   (B) to race the *Delfina*
   (C) to find a distant land
   (D) to find a better place to fish
   (E) to find a better place to hunt

2. The passage was probably written in order to
   (A) tell the story of a particular person
   (B) describe an historic event in detail
   (C) convince the reader to visit a certain place
   (D) compare and contrast two different events
   (E) explain the reason why something important happened

3. In the third paragraph, the author describes
   (A) the bounty of the land
   (B) why the *Haalve Maan* sailed the Narrows
   (C) who the *Haalve Maan* met on its voyage
   (D) what was obtained from the sea
   (E) disagreements between Hudson and Verrazano

4. The writer's style is best described as
   (A) poetic
   (B) succinct
   (C) journalistic
   (D) economical
   (E) conversational

The Tutorverse

Passage #7

> The isolation of every human soul and the necessity of self-dependence must give each individual the right to choose his own surroundings.
>
> The strongest reason for giving woman all the opportunities for higher education, for the full development of her faculties, forces of mind and body; for giving her the most
> 5   enlarged freedom of thought and action; a complete emancipation from all forms of bondage, of custom, dependence, superstition; from all the crippling influences of fear, is the solitude and personal responsibility of her own individual life. The strongest reason why we ask for woman a voice in the government under which she lives; in the religion she is asked to believe; equality in social life, where she is the chief factor; a place in the
> 10   trades and professions, where she may earn her bread, is because of her birthright to self-sovereignty; because, as an individual, she must rely on herself. No matter how much women prefer to lean, to be protected and supported, nor how much men desire to have them do so, they must make the voyage of life alone, and for safety in an emergency they must know something of the laws of navigation. To guide our own craft, we must be
> 15   captain, pilot, engineer; with chart and compass to stand at the wheel; to match the wind and waves and know when to take in the sail, and to read the signs in the firmament over all. It matters not whether the solitary voyager is man or woman.

1. In the author's opinion, an education
    (A) is vital to being able to sail or pilot a ship
    (B) is not necessary for women who wish to be supported by men
    (C) should be controlled by women to ensure equal access
    (D) is something that everyone must have in order to be self-reliant
    (E) is the sole domain of women, who should keep men away from it

2. The "laws of navigation" (line 14) probably refers to
    (A) the rules of sailing boat
    (B) something only learned in higher education
    (C) the skill needed to safely sail around the world
    (D) a person's ability to survive and make good decisions
    (E) knowledge necessary for employment in certain professions

3. The author's use of which of the following words is an example of a metaphor?
    (A) "forms of bondage" (line 5-6)
    (B) "crippling influences of fear" (line 6)
    (C) "birthright to self-sovereignty" (line 10-11)
    (D) "safety in an emergency" (line 13)
    (E) "guide our own craft" (line 14)

4. Which of the following is the best title for the selection?
    (A) Why Women Need Men
    (B) Tips on Navigating a Dangerous World
    (C) More Different Than Alike: Men vs. Women
    (D) On Preserving Traditional Customs and Beliefs
    (E) Self-Sovereignty: The Need for Gender Equality

5. The author would most likely agree with which of the following?
    (A) a law enabling women to pursue an education
    (B) a belief that women should stay at home instead of work
    (C) the notion that men and women are born with different abilities
    (D) the idea that women should rely on men to be protected and supported
    (E) an argument in favor of limiting a woman's right to equal opportunity

Passage #8

We have in part, lost our ancient respect for you: a sorry fact to chronicle. There were once various statements floating about our cradle, complimentary to your supposed virtues. You were Phoebe, twin to Phoebus: a queen, having a separate establishment, coming into a deserted court by night, and kindling it into more than daytime revelry. You
5   were an enchantress, the tutelary divinity of water-sprites and greensward fairies. Your presence was indispensable for felicitous dreams. To be moonstruck, then, meant to be charmed inexpressibly, to be lifted off our feet.

Now, we allow that you have suffered by misrepresentation, or else are we right in detecting your arts; for, by all your starry handmaidens, you are not what we took you
10   to be! We are informed that you are a timid dependent only of the sun, afraid to show yourself while he is on his journey; that you slyly steal the garb of his splendor as he lays it aside, and blaze forthwith in your borrowed finery. That you are no friend to innocent goblins, but abettor to housebreakers; conspirator in many direful deeds, attending base nocturnal councils, and tacitly arraigning yourself against the law…

15   Your inconstancy, to come on delicate ground, shines above your other characteristics. Since we have seen your color come and go, we surmise that there is no dearth of intrigue up there; and in a red or a grey veil, you masquerade periodically, at unseasonable hours. Of painting your complexion, we are disposed to acquit you; yet it is a severe blow to us to learn, from the most trustworthy sources, that you wax.

1. Based on the passage, it can be inferred that Phoebe is the name of
(A) a star
(B) a fairy
(C) a sprite
(D) the sun
(E) the moon

2. As used in line 2, "our cradle" refers to
(A) creative stories
(B) a rocking motion
(C) scientific evidence
(D) furniture for a baby
(E) early human society

3. In line 12, "borrowed finery" refers to
(A) legal troubles
(B) stolen clothing
(C) red or grey veils
(D) light, or brightness
(E) sprite and fairy clothes

4. The author's primary purpose of the passage is to
(A) compare and contrast two different objects
(B) share a lesson or moral that can be learned
(C) celebrate something mysterious and misunderstood
(D) criticize housebreakers, conspirators, and those that help them
(E) explain the movements and appearances of heavenly bodies

5. The author's tone can best be described as which of the following?
(A) reverential
(B) concerned
(C) confused
(D) offended
(E) irate

Passage #9

5   This month, our nation recognizes National Poetry Month, a celebration of poetry and its place in American society. Like spring, poetry offers man a rebirth of his inner spirit. Poetry expresses our humanity, and, through meter, makes music of the spoken world as it rhythmically sways and floats through our imaginations. It is the laughter of children, the gentle rustle of an autumn breeze, and the pitter-patter of a sun shower. Poetry, simply put, is beauty defined...

10   Whether constructed with long cadenced lines or intricate stanzas, conventional or openhanded sonnetry, light quatrains or heavy ballads, or the age-old epic yarns of Homer and Virgil, the power of poetry surrounds us. It tells of love, of death, of things temporal or spiritual, and of the hereafter. It speaks of the most common of occurrences and the most revealing of emotions, and it flows like a symphony, its meter enhancing the expressiveness of its words...

15   I have often found that a good poet helps me to examine my inner self through the poet's use of words, meter, and rhyme. Such poets enable their readers to look within and to confront their own vexations and perplexities, and then sort out the wheat from the chaff and deal with the inevitable dilemmas of life...

20   The lines of a poem contain the timeless power of concentrated thought. Whether a poem is as ancient as the "Aeneid" by Virgil or as straightforward as the verses of Emily Dickinson or Ella Wheeler Cox, poetry can evoke the full range of human emotions from joy to sadness. Poems are, as William Butler Yeats once said, "monuments of unaging intellect." Poems may also be monuments to historical eras – speaking for every man and woman of the time...

25   Nothing has the capacity of poetry to condense the pain and the beauty of living and to reach the spiritual side of our natures. A talented poet can elicit tears with only a few lines of verse, while the novelist must reach for plot twists and character development to garner a similar response. In no form of expression is the choice of each word so important...

Poetry is man's attempt to reach up and out of his human skin, and connect, just for a moment, with something perfect and eternal.

1. In terms of meaning, "meter" (line 3) is most like the word
   (A) mile
   (B) yard
   (C) rhythm
   (D) emotion
   (E) imagination

2. In which of the following does the author use a simile to describe poetry?
   (A) "It is the laughter of children" (lines 4-5)
   (B) "poetry surrounds us" (line 9)
   (C) "it flows like a symphony" (line 11)
   (D) "pain and beauty of living" (line 23)
   (E) "perfect and eternal" (line 29)

3. The author uses all of the words to refer to poetry EXCEPT
   (A) yarns
   (B) verses
   (C) natures
   (D) ballads
   (E) monuments

4. In lines 15-16, "wheat" and "chaff" refer to
   (A) types of food
   (B) good and bad choices
   (C) physical nourishment
   (D) topics of famous poems
   (E) common literary devices

(continued on next page)

The Tutorverse

5. The author states that all of the following are reasons to read poetry EXCEPT
   (A) becoming a wiser person
   (B) achieving fame and immortality
   (C) making sense of life's happenings
   (D) learning about bygone time periods
   (E) improving the skill of self-reflection

6. In the author's opinion, poetry is the greatest of art forms because
   (A) it is an ancient form of writing
   (B) it uses music to help engage the reader
   (C) it accomplishes a great deal with very little
   (D) it is widely read by children and adults alike
   (E) it tells interesting and often complex stories

Passage #10

> I rise today to ask Americans to give our children a choice of educational opportunities. I am a strong supporter of college education, but our children should have a wider range of post-high school educational choices in addition to college education. We should include the trade and technical school education as one of our national education
> 5   priorities.
> With the growth of technology and our commitment to international commerce, trade and technical training education is vital to our society. This type of specific education is indispensable to the expansion of career opportunities in the United States. While college and post-graduate programs are appropriate avenues for many students,
> 10   many other students would benefit greatly from the opportunity to orient their education toward acquiring specialized technical or trade skills (e.g., electrician, computer programming and repair, graphic arts). Technical and vocational careers are just as important as professional, white-collar careers, and in some instances, are vital to the welfare of our society.
> 15   I urge all of us to recognize the need for technical education in high school curricula and for more colleges to have courses of study related to technological and trade school career choice. Our education agenda should include vocational education as an alternative to high school students.

1. In line 8, "indispensable" means
   (A) inferior
   (B) essential
   (C) secretive
   (D) permanent
   (E) superfluous

2. Which of the following is the author most likely to discuss next?
   (A) ways in which international commerce benefits from technology
   (B) specific steps to make vocational education more accessible
   (C) reasons why vocational careers are better than technical ones
   (D) the particular ways in which professional careers benefit society
   (E) a personal story about making the decision to pursue a white-collar career

3. The author's primary purpose of the passage is to
   (A) entertain the reader with an amusing story
   (B) describe a meaningful personal experience
   (C) offer specific solutions to a general problem
   (D) list things that he believes are problems
   (E) explain the reasoning behind a particular point of view

4. According to the passage, the author most likely views which of the following as a problem?
   (A) an overemphasis on white-collar careers
   (B) a wide range of higher-education options
   (C) too many students becoming electricians
   (D) the cost of attending colleges and universities
   (E) the unprofitability of technical and vocational careers

Passage #11

Music education has a long history, dating back to Ancient Greece. As part of a standard education, music was used to teach math and deemed equally important to forming a balanced individual. As a former educator, I know that an important component to youth development and a key solution to youth violence is access to art and
5   music education in our schools. College Board studies have shown that students who play an instrument score significantly higher on their SAT than those who do not. High risk elementary students who participated in an arts program for one year gained eight percentile points on standardized language arts tests. Those who have exposure to music and art are less likely to have discipline problems. If we are serious about improving
10 student achievement and curtailing youth violence in our schools, we must find adequate funding to bring music and art education to our children.
        Because of the vast amount of research proving the benefits of music education, we need to invest in more programs which will spark student interest in music, such as the National Endowment for the Arts (NEA) sponsored "Challenge America" initiative,
15 which would provide $50 million to more than 1,100 communities and bring the arts and music to regions previously underserved by cultural programming.
        Music and art education remains important in the lives of children. From infants listening to classical music to facilitate brain development, to elementary students learning about music-related careers from their favorite musicians, to high school
20 instrument students who achieve above average SAT scores, the importance of music education cannot be denied. I urge my distinguished colleagues to continue to support music and art education programs such as "Challenge America" which contribute to the success of students as they become members of our democracy.

1. This passage was probably written to
   (A) explain how a tradition began
   (B) refute a different point of view
   (C) weigh one option against another
   (D) justify a particular course of action
   (E) commemorate an influential person

2. The author cites all of the following as benefits of arts education EXCEPT
   (A) higher scores on the SAT
   (B) advanced brain development
   (C) greater participation in the NEA
   (D) advice about jobs and career paths
   (E) better behavior and lower violence

3. The author draws on all of the following to support her central point EXCEPT
   (A) facts and figures
   (B) scientific studies
   (C) historical context
   (D) her personal experience
   (E) the Challenge America motto

4. According to the passage, it can be inferred that
   (A) "Challenge America" is an unproven initiative
   (B) the College Board gives generously to the NEA
   (C) art and music learning is not available to all students
   (D) cultural education is standardized across the country
   (E) politicians are eager to provide money for arts education

5. It is most reasonable to infer from the passage that the author would support which of the following initiatives?
   (A) a law making all students take the SAT
   (B) a pledge drive to raise money for physical education
   (C) a proposal to eliminate standardized tests like the SAT
   (D) a plan to reduce the amount of money given to the NEA
   (E) a rule banning violent students from cultural education programming

The Tutorverse

Passage #12

Our Nation has a grand tradition of conservation. When Yellowstone National Park was established in 1872, it was the world's first national park. The idea of a national park was an American invention of historic proportions that led the way for global conservation efforts. One of the earliest and most energetic conservationists was

5   President Teddy Roosevelt, who dedicated 194 million acres of national parks and national preserves.

Over one-third of America is public land. They are places of continuous discovery, where we go to find ourselves, to uncover our history, and to explore for new resources. We are not the only ones to visit our public lands: millions of tourists, many from

10   overseas, enjoy our national parks every year.

Our public lands are part of who we are and their diversity reflects our identity. In many areas, they provide timber, ore, and forage that are the economic bedrock of rural America. In other areas, Congress has designated them as wilderness, places "untrammeled by man, where man is a visitor who does not remain."

15   I want to recognize the thousands of Federal employees who manage these lands year-round. The Bureau of Land Management, Forest Service, Fish and Wildlife Service, National Park Service, and other Federal land management agencies ensure that public lands in Nevada meet the changing needs of our communities. They provide a vital, though rarely reported, service to our Nation, managing our public lands for our children

20   and grandchildren.

National Public Lands Day encourages volunteers to join in that service. Across Nevada, at places like the Black Rock Desert, Lake Mead, Boundary Peak, Sloan Canyon and the Truckee River, volunteers will work to improve our public lands. This year's focus is the defense of native species from invasive weeds. Noxious weeds are a serious

25   problem that has plagued the West for years. Exotic weeds push out native plants and provide plenty of fuel for wildfires. In Nevada, we know about this threat all too well. National Public Lands Day volunteers in Elko, NV, will help to repair the damage from last year's record-setting fire season.

The preservation of our public lands is a priority for me. Our public lands are part

30   of what makes the United States a great Nation. I voice my gratitude to all who will participate in National Public Lands Day this year.

1. All of the following are given as benefits of public lands EXCEPT
    (A) they attract tourists from overseas
    (B) they are important to the economy
    (C) they provide psychological benefits to visitors
    (D) they are a source for valuable natural resources
    (E) they are examples of an unchanged wilderness

2. The main purpose of the passage is to
    (A) relax government regulation over public lands
    (B) explain the importance of National Public Lands Day
    (C) celebrate those who work to preserve public lands
    (D) advocate for an increase in the amount of public lands
    (E) recommend a requirement that all citizens visit public lands

(continued on next page)

3. The passage was probably taken from
   (A) a novel
   (B) a politician's speech
   (C) a scientific research paper
   (D) an entry in an encyclopedia
   (E) the pages of an instruction manual

4. According to the passage, a major threat to conservation efforts are
   (A) unusually dry and hot weather
   (B) lack of funding from the government
   (C) a lack of public interest in public lands
   (D) non-native species of plants and animals
   (E) lack of human caretakers and volunteers

5. The author would most likely agree with which of the following ideas?
   (A) that the government charge fees for access to any public land
   (B) that the country's first priority should be to conserve more land
   (C) that the government give control over some public land to big companies
   (D) that the government expand the amount of land managed by the National Park Service
   (E) that the government prohibit international travelers from visiting public land

Passage #13

> Today, education is perhaps the most important function of state and local governments. Compulsory school attendance laws and the great expenditures for education both demonstrate our recognition of the importance of education to our democratic society. It is required in the performance of our most basic public
> 5 responsibilities, even service in the armed forces. It is the very foundation of good citizenship. Today it is a principal instrument in awakening the child to cultural values, in preparing him for later professional training, and in helping him to adjust normally to his environment. In these days, it is doubtful that any child may reasonably be expected to succeed in life if he is denied the opportunity of an education. Such an opportunity, where
> 10 the state has undertaken to provide it, is a right which must be made available to all on equal terms.

1. The author cites all of the following as ways in which education has positive effects on children EXCEPT that it
   (A) increases the chances for success
   (B) prepares them to join the workforce
   (C) makes them better-informed citizens
   (D) is a basic function of the government
   (E) helps instill certain morals and beliefs

2. From the passage, you can tell that the author would most likely
   (A) vote in favor of increasing a school's budget
   (B) vote against spending money on education
   (C) refrain from teaching students about ethical behavior
   (D) only allow people to vote who have completed a certain amount of schooling
   (E) support a movement to make education the responsibility of families, not the government

3. Which of the following is the author most likely to discuss next?
   (A) reasons why school should not be compulsory
   (B) the particular topics children should learn in school
   (C) why some children receive a better education than others
   (D) specific examples and statistics about how education is beneficial
   (E) the reasons why the government should reduce the amount spent on education

The Tutorverse

The Writing Sample

Overview

Before students begin the multiple-choice section of the Upper Level SSAT, they will be asked to complete a writing sample. This must be completed in 25 minutes. While this writing sample is **not** scored, it will be sent to the admissions officers at the schools to which students apply. The writing sample will be used by schools to assess a student's writing skills and learn more about him or her. A copy of the writing sample will **not** be included in the scores provided unless separately purchased from the SSAT.

On the Actual Test

Students will have a choice between two prompts: a creative piece, and an essay.

The creative prompt is intended to spark a student's imagination. It will ask the student to write a story based on a phrase. The essay prompt will ask the student to consider something academic, or to describe something about his or her life. Students should select the choice that speaks to him or her!

Students will have 25 minutes to write the sample. Consider mapping out time as follows:

> 3 minutes – *Plan*. Brainstorm ideas and jot down notes on the scrap paper that will be provided. Students should generally organize their samples into five paragraphs (introduction, body paragraphs, and conclusion).

> 20 minutes – *Write*. If students have planned well, the actual writing of the sample should be a breeze. Remember: big words and long sentences by themselves can't compensate for clearly and concisely communicated ideas!

> 2 minutes – *Proofread*. This is crucial! Reread the sample to look for and correct any punctuation, spelling, and grammar errors.

Tutorverse Tips!

Remember that the writing sample has two purposes. Schools want to see how well a student can write, but also want to learn something about the student as a person. Think of the writing sample as a written interview. If a student is asked to describe the best birthday party he or she has ever attended, the student may want to consider focusing on the experience itself and how it made him or her feel. Why was the birthday party special? How did the party make the student feel? Instead of focusing only on describing the events that happened, ask "So what?" – why were the events special?

Remember to plan thoroughly before writing and to proofread carefully when finished. The planning is important because admissions directors can identify well organized writing samples versus those samples that lack structure. Proofreading is important in order to remove careless mistakes – such as simple punctuation or spelling errors – that will reflect poorly on a student's writing skills.

The Tutorverse

How to Use This Section

Below are 10 essay prompts that have been grouped into 5 pairs. Treat each pair as a prompt you might see on the real test.

1. Set a timer for 25 minutes.
2. Choose one topic from the first pair. Think about which prompt allows you to best express yourself.
3. Make your notes on a separate piece of paper.
4. Write your essay on a separate sheet of lined paper.
5. Remember to proofread!

Schools would like to get to know you through an essay or story that you write. Choose one of the topics below that you find most interesting. Fill in the circle next to the topic of your choice. Then, write a story or essay based on the topic you chose.

Ⓐ If you could go back and correct one mistake you've made, what would it be?

Ⓑ He searched frantically, but couldn't find it.

Ⓐ Should all schools require students to wear school uniforms?

Ⓑ I barely saw it coming in time.

Ⓐ Should the voting age be lowered to thirteen?

Ⓑ I knew it was going to be a weird day.

Ⓐ If you were a journalist writing a newspaper article about a current event, what would you write about and why?

Ⓑ I couldn't bring myself to do it.

Ⓐ Tell about a lesson you learned from someone other than a teacher, and why it is important.

Ⓑ She opened the door slowly, knowing that it wasn't going to be good.

The Tutorverse

Practice Test (Form B)

Overview

The practice test is designed to assess a student's understanding of key skills and concepts. It is important to take the final practice tests after completing the diagnostic practice test and after the student has spent time studying and practicing.

Keep in mind that this practice test will be scored differently from the actual exam. On the actual Upper Level SSAT, certain questions will **not** count towards the student's actual score (i.e. the experimental section), and the student's score will be determined by comparing his or her performance with those of other students in the same grade. On this practice test, however, every question is scored in order to accurately gauge a student's current ability level. Therefore, this practice test should **NOT** be used as a gauge of how a student will score on the actual test. It should only be used to determine where students need additional practice.

Format

The format of this practice test is similar to that of the actual exam and includes 16 questions in a mock-experimental section. **For practice purposes only, treat the mock experimental section of the practice test as any other.**

The format of the practice test is below.

Scoring	Section	Number of Questions	Time Limit
Unscored Section (sent to schools)	Writing Sample	1	25 minutes
Scored Section	5-Minute Break		
	Section 1: Quantitative	25	30 minutes
	Section 2: Reading	40	40 minutes
	10-Minute Break		
	Section 3: Verbal	60	30 minutes
	Section 4: Quantitative	25	30 minutes
	Total Scored Exam (Sections 1-4)	**150**	**2 hours, 10 minutes**
Unscored Section	Section 5: Experimental	16	15 minutes

Answering

Use the answer sheet provided on the next page to record answers. Students may wish to tear it out of the workbook.

The Tutorverse

Section 1: Quantitative

1 Ⓐ Ⓑ Ⓒ Ⓓ Ⓔ	6 Ⓐ Ⓑ Ⓒ Ⓓ Ⓔ	11 Ⓐ Ⓑ Ⓒ Ⓓ Ⓔ	16 Ⓐ Ⓑ Ⓒ Ⓓ Ⓔ	21 Ⓐ Ⓑ Ⓒ Ⓓ Ⓔ
2 Ⓐ Ⓑ Ⓒ Ⓓ Ⓔ	7 Ⓐ Ⓑ Ⓒ Ⓓ Ⓔ	12 Ⓐ Ⓑ Ⓒ Ⓓ Ⓔ	17 Ⓐ Ⓑ Ⓒ Ⓓ Ⓔ	22 Ⓐ Ⓑ Ⓒ Ⓓ Ⓔ
3 Ⓐ Ⓑ Ⓒ Ⓓ Ⓔ	8 Ⓐ Ⓑ Ⓒ Ⓓ Ⓔ	13 Ⓐ Ⓑ Ⓒ Ⓓ Ⓔ	18 Ⓐ Ⓑ Ⓒ Ⓓ Ⓔ	23 Ⓐ Ⓑ Ⓒ Ⓓ Ⓔ
4 Ⓐ Ⓑ Ⓒ Ⓓ Ⓔ	9 Ⓐ Ⓑ Ⓒ Ⓓ Ⓔ	14 Ⓐ Ⓑ Ⓒ Ⓓ Ⓔ	19 Ⓐ Ⓑ Ⓒ Ⓓ Ⓔ	24 Ⓐ Ⓑ Ⓒ Ⓓ Ⓔ
5 Ⓐ Ⓑ Ⓒ Ⓓ Ⓔ	10 Ⓐ Ⓑ Ⓒ Ⓓ Ⓔ	15 Ⓐ Ⓑ Ⓒ Ⓓ Ⓔ	20 Ⓐ Ⓑ Ⓒ Ⓓ Ⓔ	25 Ⓐ Ⓑ Ⓒ Ⓓ Ⓔ

Section 2: Reading

1 Ⓐ Ⓑ Ⓒ Ⓓ Ⓔ	9 Ⓐ Ⓑ Ⓒ Ⓓ Ⓔ	17 Ⓐ Ⓑ Ⓒ Ⓓ Ⓔ	25 Ⓐ Ⓑ Ⓒ Ⓓ Ⓔ	33 Ⓐ Ⓑ Ⓒ Ⓓ Ⓔ
2 Ⓐ Ⓑ Ⓒ Ⓓ Ⓔ	10 Ⓐ Ⓑ Ⓒ Ⓓ Ⓔ	18 Ⓐ Ⓑ Ⓒ Ⓓ Ⓔ	26 Ⓐ Ⓑ Ⓒ Ⓓ Ⓔ	34 Ⓐ Ⓑ Ⓒ Ⓓ Ⓔ
3 Ⓐ Ⓑ Ⓒ Ⓓ Ⓔ	11 Ⓐ Ⓑ Ⓒ Ⓓ Ⓔ	19 Ⓐ Ⓑ Ⓒ Ⓓ Ⓔ	27 Ⓐ Ⓑ Ⓒ Ⓓ Ⓔ	35 Ⓐ Ⓑ Ⓒ Ⓓ Ⓔ
4 Ⓐ Ⓑ Ⓒ Ⓓ Ⓔ	12 Ⓐ Ⓑ Ⓒ Ⓓ Ⓔ	20 Ⓐ Ⓑ Ⓒ Ⓓ Ⓔ	28 Ⓐ Ⓑ Ⓒ Ⓓ Ⓔ	36 Ⓐ Ⓑ Ⓒ Ⓓ Ⓔ
5 Ⓐ Ⓑ Ⓒ Ⓓ Ⓔ	13 Ⓐ Ⓑ Ⓒ Ⓓ Ⓔ	21 Ⓐ Ⓑ Ⓒ Ⓓ Ⓔ	29 Ⓐ Ⓑ Ⓒ Ⓓ Ⓔ	37 Ⓐ Ⓑ Ⓒ Ⓓ Ⓔ
6 Ⓐ Ⓑ Ⓒ Ⓓ Ⓔ	14 Ⓐ Ⓑ Ⓒ Ⓓ Ⓔ	22 Ⓐ Ⓑ Ⓒ Ⓓ Ⓔ	30 Ⓐ Ⓑ Ⓒ Ⓓ Ⓔ	38 Ⓐ Ⓑ Ⓒ Ⓓ Ⓔ
7 Ⓐ Ⓑ Ⓒ Ⓓ Ⓔ	15 Ⓐ Ⓑ Ⓒ Ⓓ Ⓔ	23 Ⓐ Ⓑ Ⓒ Ⓓ Ⓔ	31 Ⓐ Ⓑ Ⓒ Ⓓ Ⓔ	39 Ⓐ Ⓑ Ⓒ Ⓓ Ⓔ
8 Ⓐ Ⓑ Ⓒ Ⓓ Ⓔ	16 Ⓐ Ⓑ Ⓒ Ⓓ Ⓔ	24 Ⓐ Ⓑ Ⓒ Ⓓ Ⓔ	32 Ⓐ Ⓑ Ⓒ Ⓓ Ⓔ	40 Ⓐ Ⓑ Ⓒ Ⓓ Ⓔ

Section 3: Verbal

1 Ⓐ Ⓑ Ⓒ Ⓓ Ⓔ	13 Ⓐ Ⓑ Ⓒ Ⓓ Ⓔ	25 Ⓐ Ⓑ Ⓒ Ⓓ Ⓔ	37 Ⓐ Ⓑ Ⓒ Ⓓ Ⓔ	49 Ⓐ Ⓑ Ⓒ Ⓓ Ⓔ
2 Ⓐ Ⓑ Ⓒ Ⓓ Ⓔ	14 Ⓐ Ⓑ Ⓒ Ⓓ Ⓔ	26 Ⓐ Ⓑ Ⓒ Ⓓ Ⓔ	38 Ⓐ Ⓑ Ⓒ Ⓓ Ⓔ	50 Ⓐ Ⓑ Ⓒ Ⓓ Ⓔ
3 Ⓐ Ⓑ Ⓒ Ⓓ Ⓔ	15 Ⓐ Ⓑ Ⓒ Ⓓ Ⓔ	27 Ⓐ Ⓑ Ⓒ Ⓓ Ⓔ	39 Ⓐ Ⓑ Ⓒ Ⓓ Ⓔ	51 Ⓐ Ⓑ Ⓒ Ⓓ Ⓔ
4 Ⓐ Ⓑ Ⓒ Ⓓ Ⓔ	16 Ⓐ Ⓑ Ⓒ Ⓓ Ⓔ	28 Ⓐ Ⓑ Ⓒ Ⓓ Ⓔ	40 Ⓐ Ⓑ Ⓒ Ⓓ Ⓔ	52 Ⓐ Ⓑ Ⓒ Ⓓ Ⓔ
5 Ⓐ Ⓑ Ⓒ Ⓓ Ⓔ	17 Ⓐ Ⓑ Ⓒ Ⓓ Ⓔ	29 Ⓐ Ⓑ Ⓒ Ⓓ Ⓔ	41 Ⓐ Ⓑ Ⓒ Ⓓ Ⓔ	53 Ⓐ Ⓑ Ⓒ Ⓓ Ⓔ
6 Ⓐ Ⓑ Ⓒ Ⓓ Ⓔ	18 Ⓐ Ⓑ Ⓒ Ⓓ Ⓔ	30 Ⓐ Ⓑ Ⓒ Ⓓ Ⓔ	42 Ⓐ Ⓑ Ⓒ Ⓓ Ⓔ	54 Ⓐ Ⓑ Ⓒ Ⓓ Ⓔ
7 Ⓐ Ⓑ Ⓒ Ⓓ Ⓔ	19 Ⓐ Ⓑ Ⓒ Ⓓ Ⓔ	31 Ⓐ Ⓑ Ⓒ Ⓓ Ⓔ	43 Ⓐ Ⓑ Ⓒ Ⓓ Ⓔ	55 Ⓐ Ⓑ Ⓒ Ⓓ Ⓔ
8 Ⓐ Ⓑ Ⓒ Ⓓ Ⓔ	20 Ⓐ Ⓑ Ⓒ Ⓓ Ⓔ	32 Ⓐ Ⓑ Ⓒ Ⓓ Ⓔ	44 Ⓐ Ⓑ Ⓒ Ⓓ Ⓔ	56 Ⓐ Ⓑ Ⓒ Ⓓ Ⓔ
9 Ⓐ Ⓑ Ⓒ Ⓓ Ⓔ	21 Ⓐ Ⓑ Ⓒ Ⓓ Ⓔ	33 Ⓐ Ⓑ Ⓒ Ⓓ Ⓔ	45 Ⓐ Ⓑ Ⓒ Ⓓ Ⓔ	57 Ⓐ Ⓑ Ⓒ Ⓓ Ⓔ
10 Ⓐ Ⓑ Ⓒ Ⓓ Ⓔ	22 Ⓐ Ⓑ Ⓒ Ⓓ Ⓔ	34 Ⓐ Ⓑ Ⓒ Ⓓ Ⓔ	46 Ⓐ Ⓑ Ⓒ Ⓓ Ⓔ	58 Ⓐ Ⓑ Ⓒ Ⓓ Ⓔ
11 Ⓐ Ⓑ Ⓒ Ⓓ Ⓔ	23 Ⓐ Ⓑ Ⓒ Ⓓ Ⓔ	35 Ⓐ Ⓑ Ⓒ Ⓓ Ⓔ	47 Ⓐ Ⓑ Ⓒ Ⓓ Ⓔ	59 Ⓐ Ⓑ Ⓒ Ⓓ Ⓔ
12 Ⓐ Ⓑ Ⓒ Ⓓ Ⓔ	24 Ⓐ Ⓑ Ⓒ Ⓓ Ⓔ	36 Ⓐ Ⓑ Ⓒ Ⓓ Ⓔ	48 Ⓐ Ⓑ Ⓒ Ⓓ Ⓔ	60 Ⓐ Ⓑ Ⓒ Ⓓ Ⓔ

Section 4: Quantitative

1 Ⓐ Ⓑ Ⓒ Ⓓ Ⓔ	6 Ⓐ Ⓑ Ⓒ Ⓓ Ⓔ	11 Ⓐ Ⓑ Ⓒ Ⓓ Ⓔ	16 Ⓐ Ⓑ Ⓒ Ⓓ Ⓔ	21 Ⓐ Ⓑ Ⓒ Ⓓ Ⓔ
2 Ⓐ Ⓑ Ⓒ Ⓓ Ⓔ	7 Ⓐ Ⓑ Ⓒ Ⓓ Ⓔ	12 Ⓐ Ⓑ Ⓒ Ⓓ Ⓔ	17 Ⓐ Ⓑ Ⓒ Ⓓ Ⓔ	22 Ⓐ Ⓑ Ⓒ Ⓓ Ⓔ
3 Ⓐ Ⓑ Ⓒ Ⓓ Ⓔ	8 Ⓐ Ⓑ Ⓒ Ⓓ Ⓔ	13 Ⓐ Ⓑ Ⓒ Ⓓ Ⓔ	18 Ⓐ Ⓑ Ⓒ Ⓓ Ⓔ	23 Ⓐ Ⓑ Ⓒ Ⓓ Ⓔ
4 Ⓐ Ⓑ Ⓒ Ⓓ Ⓔ	9 Ⓐ Ⓑ Ⓒ Ⓓ Ⓔ	14 Ⓐ Ⓑ Ⓒ Ⓓ Ⓔ	19 Ⓐ Ⓑ Ⓒ Ⓓ Ⓔ	24 Ⓐ Ⓑ Ⓒ Ⓓ Ⓔ
5 Ⓐ Ⓑ Ⓒ Ⓓ Ⓔ	10 Ⓐ Ⓑ Ⓒ Ⓓ Ⓔ	15 Ⓐ Ⓑ Ⓒ Ⓓ Ⓔ	20 Ⓐ Ⓑ Ⓒ Ⓓ Ⓔ	25 Ⓐ Ⓑ Ⓒ Ⓓ Ⓔ

Section 5: Experimental

1 Ⓐ Ⓑ Ⓒ Ⓓ Ⓔ	5 Ⓐ Ⓑ Ⓒ Ⓓ Ⓔ	9 Ⓐ Ⓑ Ⓒ Ⓓ Ⓔ	13 Ⓐ Ⓑ Ⓒ Ⓓ Ⓔ
2 Ⓐ Ⓑ Ⓒ Ⓓ Ⓔ	6 Ⓐ Ⓑ Ⓒ Ⓓ Ⓔ	10 Ⓐ Ⓑ Ⓒ Ⓓ Ⓔ	14 Ⓐ Ⓑ Ⓒ Ⓓ Ⓔ
3 Ⓐ Ⓑ Ⓒ Ⓓ Ⓔ	7 Ⓐ Ⓑ Ⓒ Ⓓ Ⓔ	11 Ⓐ Ⓑ Ⓒ Ⓓ Ⓔ	15 Ⓐ Ⓑ Ⓒ Ⓓ Ⓔ
4 Ⓐ Ⓑ Ⓒ Ⓓ Ⓔ	8 Ⓐ Ⓑ Ⓒ Ⓓ Ⓔ	12 Ⓐ Ⓑ Ⓒ Ⓓ Ⓔ	16 Ⓐ Ⓑ Ⓒ Ⓓ Ⓔ

The Tutorverse

Writing Sample

Schools would like to get to know you through an essay or story that you write. Choose one of the topics below that you find most interesting. Fill in the circle next to the topic of your choice. Then, write a story or essay based on the topic you chose.

Ⓐ What are three qualities that make a good friend?

Ⓑ I was on the verge of tears.

Use this page and the next page to complete your writing sample.

_____

_____

_____

_____

_____

_____

_____

_____

_____

_____

_____

_____

_____

_____

_____

_____

_____

_____

_____

_____

_____

_____

The Tutorverse

SECTION 1
25 Questions

There are five suggested answers after each problem in this section. Solve each problem in your head or in the space provided to the right of the problem. Then, look at the suggested answers and pick the best one.

<u>Note</u>: Any figures or shapes that accompany problems in Section 1 are drawn as accurately as possible EXCEPT when it is stated that the figure is NOT drawn to scale.

Sample Question:

$$11 \times 14 = \qquad ● \text{Ⓑ} \text{Ⓒ} \text{Ⓓ} \text{Ⓔ}$$

(A) 154
(B) 196
(C) 1,114
(D) 1,554
(E) 1,969

DO WORK IN THIS SPACE

1. If $17 + 3(1 - x) = 26$, what is the value of x?
   (A) −6
   (B) −2
   (C) 4
   (D) 2
   (E) 6

2. A can contains 6 red pencils, 7 black pencils, 9 white pencils, and 3 yellow pencils. A pencil is selected at random. What is the probability the pencil is red or white?
   (A) $\frac{6}{25}$
   (B) $\frac{9}{25}$
   (C) $\frac{12}{25}$
   (D) $\frac{3}{5}$
   (E) $\frac{4}{5}$

3. Half a pound of almonds costs $4.50. The cost of 4 pounds of almonds can be determined by multiplying $4.50 by which of the following?
   (A) $\frac{1}{2}$
   (B) 2
   (C) 2.25
   (D) 4
   (E) 8

GO ON TO THE NEXT PAGE.

The Tutorverse

DO WORK IN THIS SPACE

4. $150 - 6\frac{2}{7} =$

   (A) $144\frac{5}{7}$

   (B) $144\frac{4}{7}$

   (C) $143\frac{5}{7}$

   (D) $143\frac{2}{7}$

   (E) $142\frac{1}{7}$

5. Segments FC and EB are perpendicular. AD intersects FC at point B as shown. $\angle FBA$ measures 40°. What is the measure of $\angle EBD$?

   (A) 40°
   (B) 50°
   (C) 70°
   (D) 90°
   (E) 130°

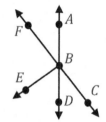

6. Three times Matt's age minus Abby's age equals 25. Four times Matt's age minus twice Abby's age equals 26. What is the difference between Matt's and Abby's ages?

   (A) 1
   (B) 2
   (C) 5
   (D) 7
   (E) 8

7. If $Q \div 3$ has a remainder of 2, what is the remainder of $6Q \div 3$?

   (A) 0
   (B) 1
   (C) 2
   (D) 3
   (E) 4

8. Find the area of the parallelogram with vertices at $(0, 0)$, $(6, 0)$, $(2, 8)$, and $(8, 8)$?

   (A) 16
   (B) 24
   (C) 32
   (D) 36
   (E) 48

9. What is the solution to the inequality $7(x - 2) + 3x < -12x - 3$?

   (A) $x < -\frac{2}{17}$

   (B) $x < -\frac{2}{7}$

   (C) $x < 2$

   (D) $x < \frac{1}{2}$

   (E) $x < -2$

GO ON TO THE NEXT PAGE.

The Tutorverse

DO WORK IN THIS SPACE

10. Which is the value of the expression $2(2^3 \times 3) - 3(5 + 3^2)$?
    (A) 6
    (B) 12
    (C) 86
    (D) 168
    (E) 384

11. A line with a slope of $\frac{1}{3}$ passes through the points $(k, 5)$ and $(9, k)$ on the coordinate grid. What is the value of k?
    (A) 12
    (B) 9
    (C) 8
    (D) 6
    (E) 5

12. If segment BC is one less than half of segment AD and $AB = CD$, what is the length of segment AB if $AD = 18$
    (A) 4.5
    (B) 5
    (C) 8
    (D) 9
    (E) 10

13. How many kilometers are there in 26 meters?
    (A) 0.026
    (B) 0.26
    (C) 2.6
    (D) 2,600
    (E) 26,000

14. What is the area, in square meters, of a circle with circumference 16π meters?
    (A) 8π
    (B) 16π
    (C) 32π
    (D) 64π
    (E) 256π

15. What is the greatest common factor of $6(x^2 - 16)$ and $9(3x^2 - 8x - 16)$?
    (A) $x - 16$
    (B) x^2
    (C) $x - 4$
    (D) $3x - 12$
    (E) $6x - 24$

GO ON TO THE NEXT PAGE.

The Tutorverse

DO WORK IN THIS SPACE

16. Gabby put $25 worth of gasoline into her car. Gas costs $2.50 per gallon. If Gabby's car can travel 30 miles per gallon, how many miles can she travel on $25 worth of gas?
    (A) 10
    (B) 30
    (C) 100
    (D) 250
    (E) 300

17. Richard takes his family to the movies, the prices for which are shown in the table. Which expression represents the total cost if Richard purchases a adult tickets and c children's tickets?
    (A) $12.5c + 8.75a$
    (B) $21.25(a + c)$
    (C) $12.5a + 8.75c$
    (D) $12.5a - 8.75c$
    (E) $12.5 + 8.75ac$

Ticket Type	Prices
Adult	$12.50
Children	$8.75

18. If you write out all the unique factors of 72 as a list, what is the median of the list?
    (A) 8.5
    (B) 9
    (C) 9.5
    (D) 10
    (E) 12.5

19. The sum of two positive integers is 40 while their difference is 8. Which is the larger of the two integers?
    (A) 16
    (B) 18
    (C) 20
    (D) 22
    (E) 24

20. Choose the inequality represented by the statement: "The difference of five times a number and 6 less than another number is greater than or equal to 54."
    (A) $5x - (y - 6) \geq 54$
    (B) $5 - x(y - 6) \geq 54$
    (C) $5x - (y - 6) \leq 54$
    (D) $5x - 6 + y \geq 54$
    (E) $6(5x) - y \leq 54$

GO ON TO THE NEXT PAGE.

The Tutorverse

DO WORK IN THIS SPACE

21. Jana ordered 4 pizzas for $12.50 each and 3 bottles of soda for $2.50 each. There is a 6% sales tax applied to the order. What is the cost of Jana's order after tax?
    (A) $57.50
    (B) $60.95
    (C) $65.45
    (D) $80.50
    (E) $92.00

22. In the addition of the three-digit numbers shown, the letters W, X, Y, and Z each represent a unique single digit. If W < X < Y < Z, then which of the following must be the sum of W + X + Y + Z?

    WYZ
    + XYZ
    ———
    678

    (A) 10
    (B) 13.5
    (C) 17
    (D) 21
    (E) 22

23. Which expression is equivalent to $\sqrt[3]{\sqrt{x^{18}}}$?
    (A) x^9
    (B) x^6
    (C) x^4
    (D) x^3
    (E) x

24. What is the union of Set M and Set P?

    Set M = {4, 5, 9, 12, 18}
    Set P = {4, 5, 13, 18, 20}

    (A) {4}
    (B) {4, 5}
    (C) {4, 5, 18}
    (D) {4, 5, 9, 12, 18}
    (E) {4, 5, 9, 12, 13, 18, 20}

25. Simplify the following expression: $(2^{-3})^2$
    (A) −12
    (B) $\frac{1}{64}$
    (C) $\frac{1}{2}$
    (D) 36
    (E) 64

STOP

IF YOU FINISH BEFORE TIME IS UP,
CHECK YOUR WORK IN THIS SECTION ONLY.
YOU MAY NOT TURN TO ANY OTHER SECTION.

The Tutorverse

SECTION 2
40 Questions

Carefully read each passage and then answer the questions about it. For each question, select the choice that best answers the question based on the passage.

All species of plants have unique chemical properties that assist in their survival. As it turns out, these same properties can also aid in the well-being of humans. Throughout history, human beings have turned to plants to treat a variety of illnesses. Thousands of years ago, our ancient ancestors ingested naturally occurring plants to help
5   cure disease and alleviate discomfort. Even today, many of those same herbal remedies line the shelves of drugstores worldwide. Ginger, aloe, and garlic are just some of the plants that have long been utilized in their unadulterated forms for health purposes.

Prescription medicines, on the other hand – pills, tablets, and serums, for example – bear little resemblance to their progenitors. Through a complex process of distillation,
10   scientists are able to isolate the rehabilitative chemical compounds found in plants. These isolated compounds are known as extracts. Because these extracts are so powerful, plant extracts can be found in some 40 percent of prescription medications in circulation. Menthol, a compound found in many throat lozenges, is known for relieving throat inflammation and is derived from the leaves of the mint plant. Salicin, a compound which
15   serves as the active ingredient in Aspirin, a widely-used pain reliever, derives from the bark of the willow tree. Quinine, a compound that fights malaria, a potentially fatal disease, is derived from the bark of cinchona tree.

1. The author is primarily concerned with
    (A) explaining a scientific process
    (B) listing significant diseases and their treatments
    (C) comparing modern medicine with herbal remedies
    (D) showing how plants can be used for medicinal purposes
    (E) documenting the different uses of certain chemical compounds

2. In line 9, "progenitors" most likely refers to
    (A) herbal remedies
    (B) types of illnesses
    (C) professional doctors
    (D) early human ancestors
    (E) modern prescription medicines

3. As mentioned in the passage, the main purpose of "distillation" (line 9) is to
    (A) cure life-threatening diseases
    (B) obscure the source of extraction
    (C) harness specific properties found in plants
    (D) create profitable prescription medication
    (E) provide an adequate alternative to herbal treatments

4. According to the passage, which of the following is NOT true?
    (A) The cinchona tree can help treat a deadly illness.
    (B) Plants with health benefits can be consumed raw.
    (C) Extracts are isolated compounds produced during distillation.
    (D) Plants produce certain chemicals primarily for the benefit of humans.
    (E) Consuming certain plants can have a positive effect on one's health.

5. It can be inferred from the passage that
    (A) prescription medication can only be developed through distillation
    (B) ancient human beings preferred ginger to other health remedies
    (C) plants are a necessity when developing cures for disease
    (D) the medical benefits of Salicin can only be achieved through distillation
    (E) both herbal remedies and prescription medications are viable solutions when treating illness

GO ON TO THE NEXT PAGE.

The Tutorverse

Pablo Picasso, widely considered to be one of the greatest artists of all time, once said: "Good artists borrow, great artists steal." But don't let his romanticized view of the artistic process fool you; there is nothing charming about the theft of intellectual property.

5   Where the theft of a physical object is pretty cut and dry, the theft of intangible things, like artistic ideas, is less so. "How," one might ask, "can anyone draw a distinction between being inspired by an artist and stealing from him?"

In Picasso's day, the ability to make an exact replica of a work of art was difficult, but not impossible. Today, making copies of art has never been easier, and can often be

10   accomplished with the push of a button. Consider the popular act of "sampling" – the taking of a portion of a someone else's song for use in one's own song. Sampling found its way into mainstream music in the hip-hop of the late 1970s. Hip-hop artists often used selections from older funk and soul records to form the backbone of their music.

Proponents of sampling claim that their work not only seeks to flatter the original

15   musician, but may even drive contemporary audiences to purchase the original recording. That may be so, but it does not excuse artists from failing to gain permission to use the sampled recording. Too often, self-interested musicians do not seek out "sample clearance." Instead, they choose to buck copyright law and take credit for another's intellectual property. In the process, they attempt to claim more than their fair share of a

20   song's profits.

If a musician truly wants to pay tribute to another artist's music, they should abide by sound recording copyright law. Failing to do so is not only immoral and illegal, but costly; recent lawsuits over sampling have resulted in musicians forfeiting millions of dollars in profits to owners of original recordings. Picasso may have seen artistry in theft,

25   but thankfully, the legal system does not.

6. The author would most likely respond to the question posed in lines 6-7 by claiming that
    (A) artists who pay tribute are not stealing
    (B) not getting permission is the same as theft
    (C) only Picasso could see such a difference
    (D) it is obvious when stealing has occurred
    (E) differences between thievery and inspiration are rarely noticed

7. It can be inferred from the passage that "sample clearance" (lines 17-18) refers to
    (A) determining if a sample has been stolen
    (B) mentioning the sampled artist as inspiration
    (C) getting the legal authority to use a sample
    (D) bypassing laws when creating art
    (E) the time spent recording a sample

8. Which of these is the best title for the selection?
    (A) Picasso's Stolen Art
    (B) The Legal Cost of Sampling
    (C) Stolen Art: Thievery in Sampling
    (D) The Problem with Artistic Inspiration
    (E) Deception and Lies in Hip Hop Music

9. To the author, musicians who sample illegally
    (A) are fans of Picasso's paintings
    (B) are exclusively hip-hop musicians.
    (C) cannot afford to obey copyright law
    (D) do not understand artistic inspiration
    (E) claim to be supporting other musicians

10. Without changing the author's meaning, "buck" (line 18) could be replaced by
    (A) defy
    (B) embrace
    (C) choose
    (D) question
    (E) suggest

11. According to the passage, what is a possible outcome of an illegal sampling lawsuit?
    (A) The original piece becomes more popular.
    (B) The sample owner is properly honored.
    (C) Laws are examined for fairness.
    (D) A sample clearance is obtained.
    (E) The musician turns over his money.

GO ON TO THE NEXT PAGE.

The Tutorverse

> Thou, too, sail on, O Ship of State!
> Sail on, O Union, strong and great!
> Humanity with all its fears,
> With all the hopes of future years,
> 5   Is hanging breathless on thy fate!
> We know what Master laid thy keel,
> What Workmen wrought thy ribs of steel,
> Who made each mast, and sail, and rope,
> What anvils rang, what hammers beat,
> 10   In what a forge and what a heat
> Were shaped the anchors of thy hope!
> Fear not each sudden sound and shock,
> 'Tis of the wave and not the rock;
> 'Tis but the flapping of the sail,
> 15   And not a rent made by a gale!
> In spite of rock and tempest's roar,
> In spite of false lights on the shore,
> Sail on, nor fear to breast the sea!
> Our hearts, our hopes, are all with thee,
> 20   Our hearts, our hopes, our prayers, our tears.
> Our faith triumphant o'er our fears,
> Are all with thee, are all with thee!

12. Which of the following best states the main idea of the poem?
    (A) Sea captains must possess bravery and skill.
    (B) A well-run ship needs a hard-working crew.
    (C) A ship is built from many different materials.
    (D) A citizen is hopeful of the future of his country.
    (E) Life is full of hardships that can be overcome with teamwork.

13. In the passage, the "false lights on the shore" (line 17) represent
    (A) coming of age
    (B) dim lighthouses
    (C) a group of people
    (D) a loss of innocence
    (E) challenges and difficulties

14. The "forge" and "heat" (line 10)
    (A) are metaphors for hope itself
    (B) refer to the way that ship anchors are made
    (C) are a warning against possible trials and ordeals
    (D) provide a solution to problems commonly faced by sailors
    (E) represent events from the past that have strengthened the country

15. The author's tone can be best described as which of the following?
    (A) urgent
    (B) fearful
    (C) soothing
    (D) inspirational
    (E) instructional

GO ON TO THE NEXT PAGE.

The Tutorverse

King Billy hurried into the bush till he came to a pond, and, stripping off his rags, he held up the coat. His jaw fell; the coat was incredibly threadbare, which, oddly, was inexplicable. He had never observed such in his life. He put it on, and, bending over the surface of the still pool, took a good look at the general effect. It was not bad from some
5   points of view, but Billy had his doubts as to whether he would be received with the respect due to his title if he went into Ballarat clothed thus. He tried to button it, but discovered that, if it had ever been intended for buttoning, he could not get it to meet across his chest. He picked up his discarded frock-coat, which was held together by the collar; then he felt the stuff of which the dress-coat was made, and the material pleased
10   him. "Oh, why," asked Billy, "had it not been made with front tails?" He saw at last that this coat and his high hat alone were insufficient for civilization. For full dress in a corroboree it might do. Unconsciously, he was so wrought upon by the purpose for which the coat had been built that he determined to reserve it for parties in the seclusion of the bush, where any merriment could be rightly checked by a crack from his baton. He
15   planted it carefully in a hollow log, and, having inserted himself with as much care into his discarded rags, he wandered off into the town.

16. The passage contains information to answer which of the following questions?
(A) What is Billy's destination?
(B) Who is Billy planning to meet?
(C) What town did Billy come from?
(D) Why does Billy have a high hat?
(E) How did Billy come across the dress-coat?

17. The narrator implies which of the following about a "corroboree" (line 12)?
(A) It is a type of job.
(B) It is a formal occasion.
(C) It is an informal occasion.
(D) It is a formal piece of clothing.
(E) It is an informal piece of clothing.

18. By the end of the passage, Billy
(A) wears the dress-coat into Ballarat
(B) hides the dress-coat and wanders back into the bush
(C) pulls on his old clothes and walks back into the wild
(D) puts his original clothes back on and goes to Ballarat
(E) rips up his frock-coat and puts the pieces on the dress-coat

19. You can tell that Billy feels both
(A) eager and poised
(B) curious and ecstatic
(C) confident and joyful
(D) venerable and powerful
(E) disappointed and self-conscious

20. The narrator uses the title "King" in front of Billy's name
(A) ironically
(B) disdainfully
(C) respectfully
(D) thoughtfully
(E) affectionately

The Tutorverse

Classical conditioning is a learning procedure that pairs a powerful biological stimulant with a neutral stimulant. The former provokes involuntary reactions in our bodies, while the latter does not. When we are hungry and smell food, for instance, we can't help but salivate. On the other hand, neutral stimulants have no such effect on our

5 biology. The ringing of a bell or the slamming of a door, for instance, does not elicit a predictable bodily response in humans. The effects of classical conditioning transpire when a biological stimulant and a neutral stimulant occur together over a long period of time. After a while, the neutral stimulant begins to provoke the same bodily response as the biological stimulant. If a person hears a bell ring every time he is served a meal, he

10 may begin to salivate whenever he hears the ringing of a bell, even if there is no food.

The scientist Ivan Pavlov demonstrated this special relationship in a famous experiment involving dogs. Over the course of a few weeks, Pavlov played the tick-tock sound of a metronome when he served the dogs their food. The dogs usually salivated when they smelled food, but after hearing the metronome playing during feeding time,

15 they soon began to salivate at the sound of a metronome as well. That the brain of animals could be conditioned in such a way was a striking discovery. Pavlov's research was so important that classical conditioning is often called Pavlovian conditioning.

The implications of classical conditioning go far beyond the behavior of dogs. For example, psychologists have used the tenets of classical conditioning to help patients

20 overcome unwanted habits. Take, as an example, a patient who snacks compulsively. In order to curtail this habit, a psychologist might expose the patient to an undesirable biological stimulant whenever the patient feels the need to snack. Over time, the desire to snack should elicit a negative response from the patient, causing the patient to lose the desire to snack entirely.

21. The author's primary purpose is to
(A) recommend ways to overcome bad habits
(B) profile the life of a famous scientist
(C) explain the biological reasons for hunger
(D) discuss the history and impact of a psychological discovery
(E) clarify the relationship between different types of stimuli

22. Without changing the author's meaning, "elicit" line 23 could be replaced by
(A) demonstrate
(B) follow
(C) illicit
(D) incite
(E) restrain

23. According to the passage, which of the following was used as a neutral stimulant in Pavlov's experiment?
(A) a high-pitch noise
(B) the smell of dog food
(C) the sound of a metronome
(D) the sound of a ringing bell
(E) the sound of a slamming door

24. Which of the following might result from classical conditioning?
(A) a person scratching an itch
(B) a cat purring when stroked
(C) a person crying when in physical pain
(D) a bird chirping at the sound of a chime
(E) a person yawning at the end of a long day

25. It can be inferred that the structure of Pavlov's experiment was based on what assumption?
(A) Negative habits can be conditioned.
(B) The smell of food is a powerful neutral stimulant.
(C) Only humans have involuntary reactions.
(D) Neutral stimulants naturally provoke biological responses.
(E) Metronomes do not typically arouse biological reactions in dogs.

26. The tone of the passage can best be described as
(A) conflicted
(B) defiant
(C) impartial
(D) outraged
(E) skeptical

GO ON TO THE NEXT PAGE.

The Tutorverse

Squire Green was the rich man of the town. He had inherited from his father, just as he came of age, a farm of a hundred and fifty acres, and a few hundred dollars.

The land was not good, and far from productive; but he had scrimped and saved and pinched and denied himself, spending almost nothing, till the little money which the
5   farm annually yielded him had accumulated to a considerable sum. Then, too, as there were no banks near at hand to accommodate borrowers, the squire used to lend money to his poorer neighbors. He took care not to exact more than six percent interest. However, it was generally understood that the borrower must pay an additional fee to secure a loan, which, added to the legal interest, gave him a very handsome consideration for the
10 use of his spare funds. So his money rapidly increased, doubling every five or six years through his shrewd mode of management, and every year he grew more economical. His wife had died ten years before. She had worked hard for very poor pay, for the squire's table was proverbially meager, and her bills for dress, judging from her appearance, must have been uncommonly small.
15   The squire had one son, now in the neighborhood of thirty, but he had not been at home for several years. As soon as he attained his majority he left the homestead, and set out to seek his fortune elsewhere. He vowed he wouldn't any longer submit to the penurious ways of the squire. So the old man was left alone, but he did not feel the solitude. He had his gold, and that was company enough. A time was coming when the
20 two must part company, for when death should come he must leave the gold behind; but he did not like to think of that, putting away the idea as men will unpleasant subjects.

27. Which of the following conclusions about Squire Green's wife can best be drawn from the passage?
(A) She was unlucky.
(B) She threw lavish parties.
(C) She died from being overworked.
(D) She squandered the family fortune.
(E) She did not spend money on luxuries.

28. Without changing the narrator's meaning, "attained his majority" (line 16) could be replaced by
(A) grew up
(B) got married
(C) found his fortune
(D) inherited the land
(E) paid back his debt

29. In line 18, the word "penurious" most nearly means
(A) stingy
(B) loving
(C) generous
(D) profitable
(E) unfortunate

30. The narrator portrays Squire Green as someone who
(A) looks down on others for being poor
(B) has an unhealthy obsession with money
(C) is a respected member of his community
(D) is altruistic about helping his neighbors
(E) cares more for personal relationships than for material possessions.

31. The narrator's primary concern in the passage is to
(A) argue that making a lot of money will lead to loneliness
(B) show that a rich person will always be an unhappy person
(C) describe how someone created a fortune out of nothing
(D) explain how someone can make money lending money
(E) share more about a person's values and how they came to be

GO ON TO THE NEXT PAGE.

The Tutorverse

Watching television shows used to be a shared cultural experience that happened in real time. Each week, millions would build their schedules around the air time of their favorite shows. Faithful viewers would tune-in to catch the latest episode and would go to work the next day eager to bemoan cliffhanger endings and speculate about the next

5   week's installment.

The rise of streaming services and on-demand programming has changed this experience. Binge-watching, or "bingeing," is the rapid consumption of televised content, and afflicts millions. For the same reason that cliffhangers are frustrating, bingeing is satisfying; in many cases, binge-watchers often view entire seasons' worth of content in

10   just a few days. Without realizing it, binge-watchers have traded the once-communal act of television watching for isolation and instant gratification. Viewers race through episodes on their own schedules and are out-of-sync with other watchers. And because binge-watchers move so quickly from show to show, there's little time for personal reflection, let alone discussion with fellow fans.

15   Indeed, binge-watching is antithetical to the medium itself. Long-form television programming often consists of meticulously planned seasons, which allow characters to develop and plots to twist over a period of time. Writers are careful to ensure that narratives unfold at the speed of life so that viewers can properly empathize with characters and understand subtle plot-points. When viewers binge-watch a television

20   show, they in fact prevent themselves from appreciating these nuances. Instead of spending time digesting the newest conflict in their favorite series, they immediately thrust themselves into the next episode. It's not surprising that bingeing a particularly dramatic series can lead to confusion, or even emotional exhaustion.

32. This passage was probably written to
   (A) provide a criticism of television writers
   (B) describe risks of a cultural phenomenon
   (C) recommend an innovative shift in viewing habits
   (D) list the positive aspects of an entertainment medium
   (E) highlight the advantages of a contemporary lifestyle

33. Without changing the author's meaning, "antithetical to" (line 15) could be replaced by
   (A) respectful of
   (B) indifferent to
   (C) the opposite of
   (D) not as important as
   (E) complementary toward

34. The author states that which of the following is a possible result of bingeing?
   (A) more meticulously planned shows
   (B) less respect for television show writers
   (C) greater empathy for television characters
   (D) a newfound appreciation for "cliffhangers"
   (E) the inability to properly process and absorb content

35. It can be inferred from the passage that the author sees "instant gratification" (line 11) as
   (A) an unpopular way to watch television shows
   (B) a tempting but unfavorable aspect of bingeing
   (C) an unavoidable change in television viewers' habits
   (D) a potentially dangerous habit for reckless viewers
   (E) an intended consequence created by television show writers

36. The passage suggests that binge-watchers
   (A) rarely finish an entire television series
   (B) are unaware of the repercussions of bingeing
   (C) prefer to watch shows with cliffhangers
   (D) are incapable of understanding complicated plotlines
   (E) prefer to watch television shows in isolation

GO ON TO THE NEXT PAGE.

The Tutorverse

> The jealousy of a free people ought to be constantly awake against the insidious wiles of foreign influence, since history and experience prove that foreign influence is one of the most baneful foes of democratic government. But to be useful, that jealousy must be impartial; otherwise, it becomes the instrument of the very influence to be avoided,
>
> 5   instead of a defense against it. Excessive partiality for one foreign nation and excessive dislike of another cause those who notice to see danger only on one side and serve to veil and even influence on the other. Real patriots who may resist the intrigues of the favorite are liable to become suspected and hated, while its tools and tricks commandeer the support and confidence of the people to surrender their interests.

37. As used in lines 1 and 3, "jealousy" most nearly means
    (A) bitterness
    (B) covetousness
    (C) envy
    (D) resentment
    (E) suspicion

38. The "it" (line 5) probably refers to
    (A) jealousy
    (B) confidence
    (C) impartiality
    (D) odious patriots
    (E) foreign influence

39. The author's tone can best be described as which of the following?
    (A) cautionary
    (B) condescending
    (C) evasive
    (D) inane
    (E) incensed

40. Which of the following best states the main idea of the passage?
    (A) Even allies can become enemies.
    (B) A republican government will have many enemies.
    (C) It is important for a country to have powerful allies.
    (D) It is difficult to tell between real patriots and usurpers.
    (E) A country's security depends on well-informed people making independent decisions.

STOP
IF YOU FINISH BEFORE TIME IS UP,
CHECK YOUR WORK IN THIS SECTION ONLY.
YOU MAY NOT TURN TO ANY OTHER SECTION

The Tutorverse

SECTION 3
60 Questions

There are two different types of questions in this section: synonyms and analogies. Read the directions and sample question for each type.

Synonyms

Each of the questions that follow consist of one capitalized word. Each word is followed by five words or phrases. Select the one word or phrase whose meaning is closest to the word in capital letters.

Sample Question:

HOT: ●ⒷⒸⒹⒺ

(A) warm
(B) sunny
(C) open
(D) enjoyable
(E) unfriendly

---

1. ANTIDOTE:
   (A) remedy
   (B) symptom
   (C) disease
   (D) illness
   (E) poison

2. CUSTODIAN:
   (A) powerful leader
   (B) self-promoter
   (C) grounds-keeper
   (D) hired employee
   (E) famous celebrity

3. MANUFACTURE:
   (A) glue
   (B) retrieve
   (C) believe
   (D) undo
   (E) assemble

4. COWER:
   (A) increase
   (B) tremble
   (C) cover
   (D) maintain
   (E) heal

5. CREDIBLE:
   (A) trustworthy
   (B) tireless
   (C) amiable
   (D) unbelievable
   (E) rich

6. OUTRAGEOUS:
   (A) anxious
   (B) furious
   (C) energetic
   (D) suitable
   (E) shocking

7. CHARACTERIZE:
   (A) dignify
   (B) befriend
   (C) confess to
   (D) describe as
   (E) hold responsible

8. MODIFY:
   (A) adjust
   (B) emerge
   (C) preserve
   (D) train
   (E) accept

GO ON TO THE NEXT PAGE.

9. RELEVANT:
   (A) unrelated
   (B) important
   (C) graphic
   (D) interesting
   (E) lofty

10. VERIFY:
   (A) ignore
   (B) add
   (C) link
   (D) confirm
   (E) integrate

11. ADHERE:
   (A) recoil
   (B) inquire of
   (C) follow closely
   (D) condemn
   (E) sway

12. GARGANTUAN:
   (A) volatile
   (B) enormous
   (C) insignificant
   (D) essential
   (E) weak

13. AUDIBLE:
   (A) perceptible
   (B) melodious
   (C) impermissible
   (D) enjoyable
   (E) contemptible

14. VACUOUS:
   (A) imperative
   (B) forceful
   (C) unlimited
   (D) magnificent
   (E) empty

15. VIRTUOSO:
   (A) expert
   (B) novice
   (C) philosopher
   (D) programmer
   (E) writer

16. SUCCINCT:
   (A) unspecific
   (B) remarkable
   (C) tasty
   (D) brief
   (E) radical

17. BOISTEROUS:
   (A) rowdy
   (B) unwise
   (C) supportive
   (D) fluent
   (E) fraudulent

18. FALLACY:
   (A) unusual redundancy
   (B) self-righteousness
   (C) common misconception
   (D) established fact
   (E) correction

19. ABSTAIN:
   (A) engage
   (B) collide
   (C) continue
   (D) refrain
   (E) solicit

20. LAUD:
   (A) attend
   (B) clap
   (C) announce
   (D) praise
   (E) specialize

21. ANTERIOR:
   (A) front
   (B) nearby
   (C) beneath
   (D) back
   (E) above

22. COGNIZANCE:
   (A) fanaticism
   (B) distinction
   (C) knowledge
   (D) responsibility
   (E) justification

GO ON TO THE NEXT PAGE.

The Tutorverse

23. AUTONOMY:
    (A) existence
    (B) revolution
    (C) sovereignty
    (D) forced servitude
    (E) motion sensing

24. BELLICOSE:
    (A) concerned
    (B) argumentative
    (C) peaceful
    (D) lenient
    (E) impeccable

25. FATUOUS:
    (A) hilarious
    (B) mountainous
    (C) meaningless
    (D) apathetic
    (E) massive

26. PARADIGM:
    (A) necessary change
    (B) strange inconsistency
    (C) animal-like ferocity
    (D) highest standard
    (E) false precision

27. COVERT:
    (A) clandestine
    (B) adept
    (C) public
    (D) prohibited
    (E) lethal

28. CREDULOUS:
    (A) dependable
    (B) conspicuous
    (C) corrupt
    (D) ambitious
    (E) shrewd

29. ACQUIESCE:
    (A) procure
    (B) quiet down
    (C) rebel against
    (D) get from
    (E) abide by

30. PORTEND:
    (A) establish
    (B) rebut
    (C) transport
    (D) assimilate
    (E) foreshadow

GO ON TO THE NEXT PAGE.

The Tutorverse

Analogies

The questions that follow ask you to find relationships between words. For each question, select the answer choice that best completes the meaning of the sentence.

Sample Question:

Dance is to dancer as: ●ⒷⒸⒹⒺ

(A) lesson is to teacher
(B) cat is to yarn
(C) fish is to water
(D) umbrella is to rain
(E) shovel is to snow

Choice (A) is the best answer because a dancer dances a dance, just as a teacher teaches a lesson. This choice states a relationship that is most like the relationship between dance and dancer.

31. Carpenter is to furniture as tailor is to
(A) clothing
(B) chair
(C) table
(D) body
(E) store

32. Magnificent is to ordinary as maternal is to
(A) paternal
(B) loving
(C) child
(D) heartless
(E) family

33. Lamp is to light as sun is to
(A) heat
(B) smell
(C) darkness
(D) bright
(E) calorie

34. Tripod is to stabilize as extinguisher is to
(A) inflame
(B) submerge
(C) refrigerate
(D) enable
(E) douse

35. Fragile is to sturdy as
(A) sick is to ill
(B) frail is to weak
(C) dog is to cat
(D) bizarre is to normal
(E) yellow is to orange

36. Music is to musician as painting is to
(A) painter
(B) technique
(C) style
(D) beauty
(E) paint

37. Peaches is to cream as
(A) lightbulb is to electricity
(B) sing is to sung
(C) night is to day
(D) color is to colorful
(E) dawn is to daybreak

38. Chef is to meal as
(A) builder is to house
(B) farmer is to livestock
(C) home is to family
(D) restaurant is to menu
(E) lunch is to dinner

GO ON TO THE NEXT PAGE.

The Tutorverse

39. Starved is to hungry as
    (A) burned is to toasted
    (B) thirsty is to water
    (C) famished is to satisfied
    (D) fed is to appetite
    (E) dried is to rejuvenated

40. Designer is to fabric as
    (A) veterinarian is to clinic
    (B) mechanic is to automobile
    (C) waiter is to dinner
    (D) journalist is to television
    (E) barber is to scissors

41. Sedan is to car as
    (A) yacht is to boat
    (B) vehicle is to van
    (C) automotive is to driver
    (D) candy is to taffy
    (E) battleship is to torpedo

42. Keyboard is to computer as
    (A) edit is to revise
    (B) chalk is to blackboard
    (C) eraser is to clean
    (D) transcribe is to type
    (E) mouse is to select

43. Mile is to foot as
    (A) pound is to ounce
    (B) liter is to gram
    (C) happy is to sad
    (D) race is to runner
    (E) track is to field

44. Correspond is to resemble as
    (A) aggregate is to collect
    (B) solicit is to irritate
    (C) conquer is to conqueror
    (D) defer is to prioritize
    (E) theorize is to scientist

45. Knife is to cut as
    (A) computer is to internet
    (B) telephone is to converse
    (C) letter is to envelope
    (D) fork is to slice
    (E) email is to type

46. Grove is to tree as
    (A) stalagmite is to cave
    (B) stream is to creek
    (C) volcano is to igneous
    (D) plateau is to ravine
    (E) archipelago is to island

47. Volume is to measurement as
    (A) professor is to philosophy
    (B) oak is to pine
    (C) orangutan is to gorilla
    (D) centimeter is to meter
    (E) regicide is to murder

48. Cowboy is to wrangle as
    (A) partner is to business
    (B) fan is to circulate
    (C) patient is to inject
    (D) enemy is to celebrate
    (E) friend is to reject

49. Resemblance is to parallel as
    (A) diligence is to sloppiness
    (B) guffaw is to bird
    (C) conceit is to conceited
    (D) ultimatum is to requirement
    (E) corruption is to politician

50. Bricklayer is to cement as
    (A) dramatist is to technology
    (B) soldier is to brigade
    (C) question is to command
    (D) judge is to gavel
    (E) protestor is to rally

51. Atom is to matter as
    (A) fiber is to cloth
    (B) reaction is to action
    (C) chemistry is to physics
    (D) journal is to parchment
    (E) pride is to lion

52. Began is to begun as
    (A) become is to became
    (B) beaten is to beat
    (C) blown is to blew
    (D) bit is to bitten
    (E) broken is to broke

GO ON TO THE NEXT PAGE.

The Tutorverse

53. Plentiful is to ubiquitous as
    (A) simple is to complex
    (B) trendy is to fashionable
    (C) likely is to inevitable
    (D) corrosive is to congenial
    (E) omnipresent is to rare

54. Kernel is to cob as
    (A) apartment is to furniture
    (B) trunk is to tree
    (C) lotion is to skin
    (D) organ is to vital
    (E) outlet is to socket

55. Needle is to yarn as
    (A) paycheck is to account
    (B) hammer is to nail
    (C) hair is to scissors
    (D) megaphone is to amplify
    (E) base is to dugout

56. Abominable is to snowman as
    (A) unicorn is to extinct
    (B) cavity is to fairy
    (C) stew is to steak
    (D) sunshine is to tornado
    (E) eager is to beaver

57. Magician is to perform as
    (A) philosopher is to contemplate
    (B) skyscraper is to capsize
    (C) compatriot is to antagonize
    (D) ocean is to sea
    (E) fanatic is to forgive

58. Thrown is to throw as
    (A) worn is to wear
    (B) wear is to wore
    (C) wore is to wearing
    (D) threw is to threwn
    (E) threw is to throwing

59. Meager is to copious as
    (A) heroic is to knight
    (B) miserly is to scrooge
    (C) cheap is to economical
    (D) plentiful is to abundant
    (E) clandestine is to exposed

60. Imagination is to figment as virtue is to
    (A) paragon
    (B) holiness
    (C) vice
    (D) antithesis
    (E) righteousness

STOP
IF YOU FINISH BEFORE TIME IS UP,
CHECK YOUR WORK IN THIS SECTION ONLY.
YOU MAY NOT TURN TO ANY OTHER SECTION

The Tutorverse

SECTION 4
25 Questions

There are five suggested answers after each problem in this section. Solve each problem in your head or in the space provided to the right of the problem. Then look at the suggested answers and pick the best one.

Note: Any figures or shapes that accompany problems in Section 1 are drawn as accurately as possible EXCEPT when it is stated that the figure is NOT drawn to scale.

Sample Question:

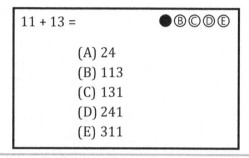

11 + 13 =   ●ⒷⒸⒹⒺ

(A) 24
(B) 113
(C) 131
(D) 241
(E) 311

DO WORK IN THIS SPACE

1. Let x be an integer such that $1 < x < 15$. What is the probability that x is divisible by 3, but NOT divisible by 2?
    (A) $\frac{2}{15}$
    (B) $\frac{2}{13}$
    (C) $\frac{1}{5}$
    (D) $\frac{2}{7}$
    (E) $\frac{1}{3}$

2. What is the quotient of 8.1 and 9?
    (A) 90
    (B) 9
    (C) 0.09
    (D) 0.9
    (E) 0.99

3. What is 0.7% written in scientific notation?
    (A) 7×10^{-4}
    (B) 7×10^{-3}
    (C) 0.7×10^{-3}
    (D) 0.7×10^{-2}
    (E) 7×10^{3}

4. The perimeter of a hexagon is 21 meters. If the length of each side of the figure is decreased by 2 meters, what is the perimeter of the new figure, in meters?
    (A) 6
    (B) 9
    (C) 11
    (D) 19
    (E) 23

GO ON TO THE NEXT PAGE.

The Tutorverse

DO WORK IN THIS SPACE

5. Which equation represents the result of solving $2x - y = 9$ for x?
    (A) $x = \frac{9-y}{2}$
    (B) $x = \frac{y+9}{2}$
    (C) $x = \frac{9}{2} - y$
    (D) $x = \frac{9}{2} + y$
    (E) $x = 9 - 2y$

6. If 40 percent of t is 14, what is 60 percent of $2t$?
    (A) 7
    (B) 28
    (C) 35
    (D) 42
    (E) 70

7. A restaurant has 5 appetizers to choose from, 4 main courses, and 5 desserts. How many different meals can be ordered if one orders one appetizer, one main course, and one dessert?
    (A) 5
    (B) 20
    (C) 25
    (D) 100
    (E) 500

8. What is the value of the hundreds digit in the standard form of 1.0258×10^4?
    (A) 8 hundred
    (B) 5 hundred
    (C) 2 hundred
    (D) 1 hundred
    (E) 0 hundred

9. Joe paints 1 room in 8 hours while Frank paints 1 room in 6 hours. What is the combined rate, in rooms per hour, at which they paint?
    (A) $\frac{1}{6}$
    (B) $\frac{7}{24}$
    (C) $\frac{24}{7}$
    (D) 6
    (E) 8

10. Estimate the value of $\sqrt{1,000 - 100} + \sqrt{1,000 \div 100}$.
    (A) 6
    (B) 13
    (C) 27
    (D) 33
    (E) 300

GO ON TO THE NEXT PAGE.

The Tutorverse

DO WORK IN THIS SPACE

11. Which of the following is equivalent to the expression
    $(3x^2 + 2x - 1) - (x^2 + 2x)$?
    (A) $2x^2 - 1$
    (B) $4x^2 + 4x - 1$
    (C) $3x^2 + 4x - 1$
    (D) $2x^2 + x - 3$
    (E) $3x^2 - 4$

12. Point S is reflected across the x-axis, then reflected across the y-axis. If its original coordinates were $(4, 3)$, what are the coordinates of the resulting point?
    (A) $(4, 3)$
    (B) $(3, 4)$
    (C) $(-4, 3)$
    (D) $(4, -3)$
    (E) $(-4, -3)$

13. According to the bar graph shown, how many students have at least 2 siblings?
    (A) 10
    (B) 15
    (C) 25
    (D) 60
    (E) 85

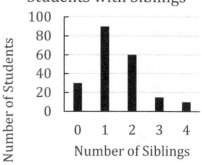

14. A metal pipe is $15\frac{1}{2}$ feet long, and is cut into three even pieces. How many inches long is one of the pieces?
    (A) $5\frac{1}{6}$
    (B) 62
    (C) 64
    (D) 66
    (E) 186

15. Manny launches a toy rocket into the air. The rocket's height, y, in feet with respect to time, x, in seconds can be modeled by the function $y = -2x^2 + 2x + 16$. What is the maximum height, in feet, of the rocket?
    (A) 8
    (B) $10\frac{1}{2}$
    (C) $16\frac{1}{2}$
    (D) 18
    (E) 20

GO ON TO THE NEXT PAGE.

The Tutorverse

DO WORK IN THIS SPACE

16. The sum of the integers from 20 through 30, inclusive, is
    (A) 50
    (B) 255
    (C) 275
    (D) 465
    (E) 930

17. If m and n are prime numbers, what is the least common multiple of $8m^2$, $10m^4n^6$, and $12n^8$?
    (A) $120m^4n^8$
    (B) $120m^2n^6$
    (C) $80m^4n^8$
    (D) $80m^2n^6$
    (E) $120m^4n^6$

18. A triangle has a base of 24 inches and two other sides that each measure 15 inches. What is the height of the triangle, in inches?
    (A) 9
    (B) 11
    (C) 15
    (D) 18
    (E) 24

19. Sheldon has b socks. Rachel has 9 more than twice as many socks as Sheldon. In terms of b, how many socks do Sheldon and Rachel have altogether?
    (A) $b + 3$
    (B) $2b + 9$
    (C) $2b - 9$
    (D) $3b + 9$
    (E) $b^2 + 9$

20. If the average of 3 consecutive integers is 23, what is the largest number?
    (A) 20
    (B) 22
    (C) 24
    (D) 25
    (E) 29

21. Which are the solutions to the equation $x^2 - 12x = -11$?
    (A) 1, 12
    (B) −11, −1
    (C) 1, 11
    (D) 6, 5
    (E) −1, 12

GO ON TO THE NEXT PAGE

The Tutorverse

DO WORK IN THIS SPACE

22. A company sells a can that is 5 cm high and 8 cm in diameter. They also sell a jar that has twice the volume as the can. If the radius of the jar and the can is the same, what is the height of the can in cm?
    (A) 4π
    (B) 10
    (C) 10π
    (D) 16
    (E) 18

23. What fraction is equivalent to $\sqrt{\frac{2x}{144}}$ when $x = 18$?
    (A) $\frac{1}{12}$
    (B) $\frac{1}{6}$
    (C) $\frac{1}{2}$
    (D) $\frac{3}{4}$
    (E) $\frac{9}{12}$

24. Consider the data set {9, 5, 2, 6, 5, 2, 1, 2}.
    Which number, if added to the set, will not change the range?
    (A) 0
    (B) 7
    (C) 11
    (D) 13
    (E) 16

25. Which expression is equivalent to $\frac{1}{a} - \frac{2}{b}$?
    (A) $\frac{2a-b}{ab}$
    (B) $\frac{-1}{a-b}$
    (C) $\frac{b-2a}{a-b}$
    (D) $\frac{b+2a}{ab}$
    (E) $\frac{b-2a}{ab}$

STOP
IF YOU FINISH BEFORE TIME IS UP,
CHECK YOUR WORK IN THIS SECTION ONLY.
YOU MAY NOT TURN TO ANY OTHER SECTION.

The Tutorverse

SECTION 5
16 Questions

For millennia, *Homo sapiens* lived almost exclusively as hunter-gatherers. All that changed around 9500 B.C. during a period known as the Agricultural Revolution. Thanks to certain environmental and technological developments, humans began to cultivate certain grains in greater quantities than ever before. What followed was a seismic shift in
5   the lifestyle of *Homo sapiens*.

Prior to the Agricultural Revolution, human beings lived nomadically as they foraged for their food. Small bands of humans hunted animals and collected a variety of grains and other edible vegetables. While this might sound difficult, hunting for food typically only took a few hours a day. Still, there was always uncertainty surrounding
10   food. Where would the next meal come from? And would there be enough food to go around? It was not uncommon for people to go without a meal for days at a time.

Some say that these concerns were put to rest during the Agricultural Revolution. When humans learned how to farm, they began to exert a greater control over their food supply. In addition, farming allowed *Homo sapiens* to give up a life of wandering and
15   create permanent settlements. This, in turn, led to the development of civilization itself – religion, customs, trade, and class. Still, there were drawbacks, not least of which was reliance upon a good harvest, which in turn relied upon favorable climate conditions. Furthermore, bodies that had evolved to climb trees and chase animals now had the difficult task of adapting to carrying water buckets and clearing fields. And while a good
20   harvest could yield enough food to last years, a single unsuccessful harvest could lead to widespread starvation.

The Agricultural Revolution was certainly revolutionary, but was it actually progress? Was it better to give up the uncertainty of foraging for the grueling task of harvesting crops? Thousands of years later, historians continue to debate whether a shift
25   to a farming-based society was ultimately in humanity's best interest.

1. According to the passage, the Agricultural Revolution was set in motion by
   (A) the end of widespread starvation
   (B) a continued reliance on foraging for food
   (C) the development of religion and newfound customs
   (D) the overhunting and extinction of many animal species
   (E) an ability to farm select grains on a large scale

2. Which is the best title for the passage?
   (A) A Revolution in Eating
   (B) The Dawn of Civilization
   (C) Back to Roots: The Beginning of Farming
   (D) The Agricultural Revolution: For Better or For Worse?
   (E) The Prehistoric Life of *Homo Sapiens*: Lessons for Modern Humans

3. The author's tone can best be described as which of the following?
   (A) partial
   (B) nostalgic
   (C) analytical
   (D) obsequious
   (E) inspirational

4. The passage contains information to answer which of the following questions?
   (A) Which tactics were most successful for growing crops?
   (B) Which grains provided the backbone of the *Homo sapiens* diet?
   (C) How did humans cope with unsuccessful harvests?
   (D) Was the Agricultural Revolution a sign of progress?
   (E) Why were *Homo sapiens* able to farm certain grains during the Agricultural Revolution?

GO ON TO THE NEXT PAGE.

The Tutorverse

5. The bodies of *Homo sapiens* likely evolved to "climb trees and chase animals" because
   (A) it was a form of entertainment for thousands of years
   (B) there were a variety of grains for humans to develop
   (C) they had grown accustomed to foraging and hunting for their food
   (D) it facilitated the development of religion, customs, trade, and class
   (E) their bodies were accustomed to carrying water buckets and clearing fields

6. EXAGGERATE:
   (A) publish
   (B) testify
   (C) embellish
   (D) list
   (E) embolden

7. BOORISH:
   (A) peerless
   (B) popular
   (C) mature
   (D) uncivilized
   (E) sophisticated

8. COSMOPOLITAN:
   (A) delicate
   (B) advanced
   (C) pedestrian
   (D) elementary
   (E) cultured

9. Jury is to juror as
   (A) horse is to race
   (B) chef is to kitchen
   (C) whole is to piece
   (D) dam is to river
   (E) army is to fort

10. Snows is to snowed as
    (A) plow is to plowed
    (B) plow is to plows
    (C) plows is to plow
    (D) plowed is to plow
    (E) plows is to plowed

11. Nose is to breathe as eye is to
    (A) vision
    (B) lash
    (C) ball
    (D) see
    (E) lid

12. Parachute is to rescue as shovel is to
    (A) spade
    (B) dig
    (C) garden
    (D) foot
    (E) metal

13. How many integers from 30 to 60, inclusive, are multiples of **neither** 2 nor 3?
    (A) 6
    (B) 10
    (C) 15
    (D) 20
    (E) 21

14. If x is a factor of a and y is a factor of b, which statement is true?
    (A) ab is a multiple of xy
    (B) a is a multiple of xy
    (C) b is a multiple of x
    (D) ab is a factor of xy
    (E) a is a factor of xy

15. If $x^2 + y^2 = 80$ and $2xy = 64$, what is the value of $(x + y)^2$?
    (A) 1.25
    (B) 8
    (C) 16
    (D) 144
    (E) 5,120

16. What is the degree measure of one angle in a regular octagon?
    (A) 45
    (B) 90
    (C) 120
    (D) 135
    (E) 1,080

Scoring the Practice Test (Form B)

Writing Sample – Unscored

Have a parent or trusted educator review the essay or story written for the writing sample. Important areas to focus on include organization, clarity of ideas, originality, and technical precision (spelling, grammar, etc.).

Sections 1-4 – Scored

Score the test using the answer sheet and referring to the answer key at the back of the book.

Step 1: For each section, record the number of questions answered correctly.

Step 2: For each section, record the number of questions answered incorrectly. Then, multiply that number by ¼ to calculate the penalty.

Section	Questions Correct
Quantitative *Section 1 + Section 4*	_____
Reading *Section 2*	_____
Verbal *Section 3*	_____

Section	Questions Incorrect	Penalty	
Quantitative *Section 1 + Section 4*	_____	x 1/4 =	_____
Reading *Section 2*	_____	x 1/4 =	_____
Verbal *Section 3*	_____	x 1/4 =	_____

Step 3: For each section, subtract the Penalty in *Step 2* from the Questions Correct in *Step 1*. This is the raw score. Note that the actual test will convert the raw score to a scaled score by comparing the student's performance with all other students in the same grade who took the test.

Section	Raw Score
Quantitative *Section 1 + Section 4*	_____
Reading *Section 2*	_____
Verbal *Section 3*	_____

> **Consider**: How certain were you on the questions you guessed on? Should you have left those questions blank, instead? How should you change the way you guess and leave questions blank?

Carefully consider the results from the practice test when revising a study plan. Remember, the Upper Level SSAT is given to students in grades 8-11. Unless the student has finished 11th grade, chances are that there is material on this test that he or she has not yet been taught. If this is the case, and the student would like to improve beyond what is expected of his or her grade, consider working with a tutor or teacher, who can help learn more about new topics.

Section 5 – Unscored

On the real test, the Experimental section will NOT be scored. Consider the student's performance on this section for practice purposes only. Did he or she do better on one section than other? Use this information along with the information from Sections 1-4 to reevaluate the study plan.

The Tutorverse

Final Practice Test (Form C)

Overview

The practice test is designed to assess a student's understanding of key skills and concepts. It is important to take the final practice tests after completing the diagnostic practice test and after the student has spent time studying and practicing.

Keep in mind that this practice test will be scored differently from the actual exam. On the actual Upper Level SSAT, certain questions will **not** count towards the student's actual score (i.e. the experimental section), and the student's score will be determined by comparing his or her performance with those of other students in the same grade. On this practice test, however, every question is scored in order to accurately gauge a student's current ability level. Therefore, this practice test should **NOT** be used as a gauge of how a student will score on the actual test. It should only be used to determine where students need additional practice.

Format

The format of this practice test is similar to that of the actual exam and includes 16 questions in a mock-experimental section. **For practice purposes only, treat the mock experimental section of the practice test as any other.**

The format of the practice test is below.

Scoring	Section	Number of Questions	Time Limit
Unscored Section (sent to schools)	Writing Sample	1	25 minutes
Scored Section	5-Minute Break		
	Section 1: Quantitative	25	30 minutes
	Section 2: Reading	40	40 minutes
	10-Minute Break		
	Section 3: Verbal	60	30 minutes
	Section 4: Quantitative	25	30 minutes
	Total Scored Exam (Sections 1-4)	**150**	**2 hours, 10 minutes**
Unscored Section	Section 5: Experimental	16	15 minutes

Answering

Use the answer sheet provided on the next page to record answers. Students may wish to tear it out of the workbook.

The Tutorverse

Section 1: Quantitative

1 Ⓐ Ⓑ Ⓒ Ⓓ Ⓔ	6 Ⓐ Ⓑ Ⓒ Ⓓ Ⓔ	11 Ⓐ Ⓑ Ⓒ Ⓓ Ⓔ	16 Ⓐ Ⓑ Ⓒ Ⓓ Ⓔ	21 Ⓐ Ⓑ Ⓒ Ⓓ Ⓔ
2 Ⓐ Ⓑ Ⓒ Ⓓ Ⓔ	7 Ⓐ Ⓑ Ⓒ Ⓓ Ⓔ	12 Ⓐ Ⓑ Ⓒ Ⓓ Ⓔ	17 Ⓐ Ⓑ Ⓒ Ⓓ Ⓔ	22 Ⓐ Ⓑ Ⓒ Ⓓ Ⓔ
3 Ⓐ Ⓑ Ⓒ Ⓓ Ⓔ	8 Ⓐ Ⓑ Ⓒ Ⓓ Ⓔ	13 Ⓐ Ⓑ Ⓒ Ⓓ Ⓔ	18 Ⓐ Ⓑ Ⓒ Ⓓ Ⓔ	23 Ⓐ Ⓑ Ⓒ Ⓓ Ⓔ
4 Ⓐ Ⓑ Ⓒ Ⓓ Ⓔ	9 Ⓐ Ⓑ Ⓒ Ⓓ Ⓔ	14 Ⓐ Ⓑ Ⓒ Ⓓ Ⓔ	19 Ⓐ Ⓑ Ⓒ Ⓓ Ⓔ	24 Ⓐ Ⓑ Ⓒ Ⓓ Ⓔ
5 Ⓐ Ⓑ Ⓒ Ⓓ Ⓔ	10 Ⓐ Ⓑ Ⓒ Ⓓ Ⓔ	15 Ⓐ Ⓑ Ⓒ Ⓓ Ⓔ	20 Ⓐ Ⓑ Ⓒ Ⓓ Ⓔ	25 Ⓐ Ⓑ Ⓒ Ⓓ Ⓔ

Section 2: Reading

1 Ⓐ Ⓑ Ⓒ Ⓓ Ⓔ	9 Ⓐ Ⓑ Ⓒ Ⓓ Ⓔ	17 Ⓐ Ⓑ Ⓒ Ⓓ Ⓔ	25 Ⓐ Ⓑ Ⓒ Ⓓ Ⓔ	33 Ⓐ Ⓑ Ⓒ Ⓓ Ⓔ
2 Ⓐ Ⓑ Ⓒ Ⓓ Ⓔ	10 Ⓐ Ⓑ Ⓒ Ⓓ Ⓔ	18 Ⓐ Ⓑ Ⓒ Ⓓ Ⓔ	26 Ⓐ Ⓑ Ⓒ Ⓓ Ⓔ	34 Ⓐ Ⓑ Ⓒ Ⓓ Ⓔ
3 Ⓐ Ⓑ Ⓒ Ⓓ Ⓔ	11 Ⓐ Ⓑ Ⓒ Ⓓ Ⓔ	19 Ⓐ Ⓑ Ⓒ Ⓓ Ⓔ	27 Ⓐ Ⓑ Ⓒ Ⓓ Ⓔ	35 Ⓐ Ⓑ Ⓒ Ⓓ Ⓔ
4 Ⓐ Ⓑ Ⓒ Ⓓ Ⓔ	12 Ⓐ Ⓑ Ⓒ Ⓓ Ⓔ	20 Ⓐ Ⓑ Ⓒ Ⓓ Ⓔ	28 Ⓐ Ⓑ Ⓒ Ⓓ Ⓔ	36 Ⓐ Ⓑ Ⓒ Ⓓ Ⓔ
5 Ⓐ Ⓑ Ⓒ Ⓓ Ⓔ	13 Ⓐ Ⓑ Ⓒ Ⓓ Ⓔ	21 Ⓐ Ⓑ Ⓒ Ⓓ Ⓔ	29 Ⓐ Ⓑ Ⓒ Ⓓ Ⓔ	37 Ⓐ Ⓑ Ⓒ Ⓓ Ⓔ
6 Ⓐ Ⓑ Ⓒ Ⓓ Ⓔ	14 Ⓐ Ⓑ Ⓒ Ⓓ Ⓔ	22 Ⓐ Ⓑ Ⓒ Ⓓ Ⓔ	30 Ⓐ Ⓑ Ⓒ Ⓓ Ⓔ	38 Ⓐ Ⓑ Ⓒ Ⓓ Ⓔ
7 Ⓐ Ⓑ Ⓒ Ⓓ Ⓔ	15 Ⓐ Ⓑ Ⓒ Ⓓ Ⓔ	23 Ⓐ Ⓑ Ⓒ Ⓓ Ⓔ	31 Ⓐ Ⓑ Ⓒ Ⓓ Ⓔ	39 Ⓐ Ⓑ Ⓒ Ⓓ Ⓔ
8 Ⓐ Ⓑ Ⓒ Ⓓ Ⓔ	16 Ⓐ Ⓑ Ⓒ Ⓓ Ⓔ	24 Ⓐ Ⓑ Ⓒ Ⓓ Ⓔ	32 Ⓐ Ⓑ Ⓒ Ⓓ Ⓔ	40 Ⓐ Ⓑ Ⓒ Ⓓ Ⓔ

Section 3: Verbal

1 Ⓐ Ⓑ Ⓒ Ⓓ Ⓔ	13 Ⓐ Ⓑ Ⓒ Ⓓ Ⓔ	25 Ⓐ Ⓑ Ⓒ Ⓓ Ⓔ	37 Ⓐ Ⓑ Ⓒ Ⓓ Ⓔ	49 Ⓐ Ⓑ Ⓒ Ⓓ Ⓔ
2 Ⓐ Ⓑ Ⓒ Ⓓ Ⓔ	14 Ⓐ Ⓑ Ⓒ Ⓓ Ⓔ	26 Ⓐ Ⓑ Ⓒ Ⓓ Ⓔ	38 Ⓐ Ⓑ Ⓒ Ⓓ Ⓔ	50 Ⓐ Ⓑ Ⓒ Ⓓ Ⓔ
3 Ⓐ Ⓑ Ⓒ Ⓓ Ⓔ	15 Ⓐ Ⓑ Ⓒ Ⓓ Ⓔ	27 Ⓐ Ⓑ Ⓒ Ⓓ Ⓔ	39 Ⓐ Ⓑ Ⓒ Ⓓ Ⓔ	51 Ⓐ Ⓑ Ⓒ Ⓓ Ⓔ
4 Ⓐ Ⓑ Ⓒ Ⓓ Ⓔ	16 Ⓐ Ⓑ Ⓒ Ⓓ Ⓔ	28 Ⓐ Ⓑ Ⓒ Ⓓ Ⓔ	40 Ⓐ Ⓑ Ⓒ Ⓓ Ⓔ	52 Ⓐ Ⓑ Ⓒ Ⓓ Ⓔ
5 Ⓐ Ⓑ Ⓒ Ⓓ Ⓔ	17 Ⓐ Ⓑ Ⓒ Ⓓ Ⓔ	29 Ⓐ Ⓑ Ⓒ Ⓓ Ⓔ	41 Ⓐ Ⓑ Ⓒ Ⓓ Ⓔ	53 Ⓐ Ⓑ Ⓒ Ⓓ Ⓔ
6 Ⓐ Ⓑ Ⓒ Ⓓ Ⓔ	18 Ⓐ Ⓑ Ⓒ Ⓓ Ⓔ	30 Ⓐ Ⓑ Ⓒ Ⓓ Ⓔ	42 Ⓐ Ⓑ Ⓒ Ⓓ Ⓔ	54 Ⓐ Ⓑ Ⓒ Ⓓ Ⓔ
7 Ⓐ Ⓑ Ⓒ Ⓓ Ⓔ	19 Ⓐ Ⓑ Ⓒ Ⓓ Ⓔ	31 Ⓐ Ⓑ Ⓒ Ⓓ Ⓔ	43 Ⓐ Ⓑ Ⓒ Ⓓ Ⓔ	55 Ⓐ Ⓑ Ⓒ Ⓓ Ⓔ
8 Ⓐ Ⓑ Ⓒ Ⓓ Ⓔ	20 Ⓐ Ⓑ Ⓒ Ⓓ Ⓔ	32 Ⓐ Ⓑ Ⓒ Ⓓ Ⓔ	44 Ⓐ Ⓑ Ⓒ Ⓓ Ⓔ	56 Ⓐ Ⓑ Ⓒ Ⓓ Ⓔ
9 Ⓐ Ⓑ Ⓒ Ⓓ Ⓔ	21 Ⓐ Ⓑ Ⓒ Ⓓ Ⓔ	33 Ⓐ Ⓑ Ⓒ Ⓓ Ⓔ	45 Ⓐ Ⓑ Ⓒ Ⓓ Ⓔ	57 Ⓐ Ⓑ Ⓒ Ⓓ Ⓔ
10 Ⓐ Ⓑ Ⓒ Ⓓ Ⓔ	22 Ⓐ Ⓑ Ⓒ Ⓓ Ⓔ	34 Ⓐ Ⓑ Ⓒ Ⓓ Ⓔ	46 Ⓐ Ⓑ Ⓒ Ⓓ Ⓔ	58 Ⓐ Ⓑ Ⓒ Ⓓ Ⓔ
11 Ⓐ Ⓑ Ⓒ Ⓓ Ⓔ	23 Ⓐ Ⓑ Ⓒ Ⓓ Ⓔ	35 Ⓐ Ⓑ Ⓒ Ⓓ Ⓔ	47 Ⓐ Ⓑ Ⓒ Ⓓ Ⓔ	59 Ⓐ Ⓑ Ⓒ Ⓓ Ⓔ
12 Ⓐ Ⓑ Ⓒ Ⓓ Ⓔ	24 Ⓐ Ⓑ Ⓒ Ⓓ Ⓔ	36 Ⓐ Ⓑ Ⓒ Ⓓ Ⓔ	48 Ⓐ Ⓑ Ⓒ Ⓓ Ⓔ	60 Ⓐ Ⓑ Ⓒ Ⓓ Ⓔ

Section 4: Quantitative

1 Ⓐ Ⓑ Ⓒ Ⓓ Ⓔ	6 Ⓐ Ⓑ Ⓒ Ⓓ Ⓔ	11 Ⓐ Ⓑ Ⓒ Ⓓ Ⓔ	16 Ⓐ Ⓑ Ⓒ Ⓓ Ⓔ	21 Ⓐ Ⓑ Ⓒ Ⓓ Ⓔ
2 Ⓐ Ⓑ Ⓒ Ⓓ Ⓔ	7 Ⓐ Ⓑ Ⓒ Ⓓ Ⓔ	12 Ⓐ Ⓑ Ⓒ Ⓓ Ⓔ	17 Ⓐ Ⓑ Ⓒ Ⓓ Ⓔ	22 Ⓐ Ⓑ Ⓒ Ⓓ Ⓔ
3 Ⓐ Ⓑ Ⓒ Ⓓ Ⓔ	8 Ⓐ Ⓑ Ⓒ Ⓓ Ⓔ	13 Ⓐ Ⓑ Ⓒ Ⓓ Ⓔ	18 Ⓐ Ⓑ Ⓒ Ⓓ Ⓔ	23 Ⓐ Ⓑ Ⓒ Ⓓ Ⓔ
4 Ⓐ Ⓑ Ⓒ Ⓓ Ⓔ	9 Ⓐ Ⓑ Ⓒ Ⓓ Ⓔ	14 Ⓐ Ⓑ Ⓒ Ⓓ Ⓔ	19 Ⓐ Ⓑ Ⓒ Ⓓ Ⓔ	24 Ⓐ Ⓑ Ⓒ Ⓓ Ⓔ
5 Ⓐ Ⓑ Ⓒ Ⓓ Ⓔ	10 Ⓐ Ⓑ Ⓒ Ⓓ Ⓔ	15 Ⓐ Ⓑ Ⓒ Ⓓ Ⓔ	20 Ⓐ Ⓑ Ⓒ Ⓓ Ⓔ	25 Ⓐ Ⓑ Ⓒ Ⓓ Ⓔ

Section 5: Experimental

1 Ⓐ Ⓑ Ⓒ Ⓓ Ⓔ	5 Ⓐ Ⓑ Ⓒ Ⓓ Ⓔ	9 Ⓐ Ⓑ Ⓒ Ⓓ Ⓔ	13 Ⓐ Ⓑ Ⓒ Ⓓ Ⓔ
2 Ⓐ Ⓑ Ⓒ Ⓓ Ⓔ	6 Ⓐ Ⓑ Ⓒ Ⓓ Ⓔ	10 Ⓐ Ⓑ Ⓒ Ⓓ Ⓔ	14 Ⓐ Ⓑ Ⓒ Ⓓ Ⓔ
3 Ⓐ Ⓑ Ⓒ Ⓓ Ⓔ	7 Ⓐ Ⓑ Ⓒ Ⓓ Ⓔ	11 Ⓐ Ⓑ Ⓒ Ⓓ Ⓔ	15 Ⓐ Ⓑ Ⓒ Ⓓ Ⓔ
4 Ⓐ Ⓑ Ⓒ Ⓓ Ⓔ	8 Ⓐ Ⓑ Ⓒ Ⓓ Ⓔ	12 Ⓐ Ⓑ Ⓒ Ⓓ Ⓔ	16 Ⓐ Ⓑ Ⓒ Ⓓ Ⓔ

The Tutorverse

Writing Sample

Schools would like to get to know you through an essay or story that you write. Choose one of the topics below that you find most interesting. Fill in the circle next to the topic of your choice. Then, write a story or essay based on the topic you chose.

Ⓐ If you could have dinner with any historical figure, who would it be?

Ⓑ He couldn't believe what he was seeing.

Use this page and the next page to complete your writing sample.

_____

_____

_____

_____

_____

_____

_____

_____

_____

_____

_____

_____

_____

_____

_____

_____

_____

_____

_____

The Tutorverse

SECTION 1
25 Questions

There are five suggested answers after each problem in this section. Solve each problem in your head or in the space provided to the right of the problem. Then, look at the suggested answers and pick the best one.

<u>Note</u>: Any figures or shapes that accompany problems in Section 1 are drawn as accurately as possible EXCEPT when it is stated that the figure is NOT drawn to scale.

Sample Question:

$11 \times 13 =$ ●ⒷⒸⒹⒺ

(A) 143
(B) 169
(C) 1,113
(D) 1,443
(E) 1,696

DO WORK IN THIS SPACE

1. All of the following products are equal EXCEPT
    (A) $2 \times \frac{1}{3}$
    (B) $2 \times \frac{2}{6}$
    (C) $3 \times \frac{2}{9}$
    (D) $4 \times \frac{1}{3}$
    (E) $4 \times \frac{1}{6}$

2. A certain number of gallons of 20% sodium chloride solution is to be mixed with a certain number of gallons of 15% sodium chloride solution to make 10 gallons of 16% sodium chloride solution. Which system of equations can be used to determine the number of gallons of 20% solution, x, and 15% solution, y, needed to make 10 gallons of 16% solution?
    (A) $x + y = 10$
    $0.2x + 0.15y = 1.6$
    (B) $x + y = 10$
    $0.2x + 0.15y = 0.16$
    (C) $x + y = 10$
    $2x + 15y = 16$
    (D) $x + y = 16$
    $2x + 15y = 10$
    (E) $x + y = 16$
    $0.2x + 0.15y = 10$

3. Jordan attempted 20 free throws. He made 13 of those free throws. What percent of the free throws attempted did Jordan make?
    (A) 15%
    (B) 45%
    (C) 65%
    (D) 75%
    (E) 00%

GO ON TO THE NEXT PAGE.

The Tutorverse

DO WORK IN THIS SPACE

4. Due to demand, the price, p, of a pound of coffee is increased by 175%.
   Which expression represents the new price?
   (A) $p + 175$
   (B) $p + \dfrac{175}{100}$
   (C) $p(1 + 0.75)$
   (D) $p(1 + 1.75)$
   (E) $1.75p$

5. Consider the data set {16, 17, 15, 18, 16, 14, 13, 18, 17, 14, 16, 15}.
   Which number, if added to the set, will not change the mode?
   (A) 13
   (B) 14
   (C) 15
   (D) 17
   (E) 18

6. Tim threw a football into the air. The football's height, y, in meters, with
   respect to time, x, in seconds, can be modeled by the function $y = -3x + 12x + 8$.
   What was the football's height, in meters after 1 second?
   (A) 12
   (B) 17
   (C) 20
   (D) 23
   (E) 28

7. What is the intersection of Set A and Set B?

   $$\text{Set A} = \{2, 7, 9, 14, 17, 20\}$$
   $$\text{Set B} = \{7, 10, 14\}$$

   (A) {7, 14}
   (B) {2, 7, 14}
   (C) {7, 14, 20}
   (D) {2, 7, 14, 20}
   (E) {2, 7, 9, 10, 14, 17, 20}

8. A machine can produce 80 toothpicks in 3 minutes. At the rate, how
   many toothpicks can the machine produce in 1 hour?
   (A) 225
   (B) 240
   (C) 1,600
   (D) 2,400
   (E) 4,800

9. Square $ABCD$ has an area of 49 square cm. Find the length of diagonal AC,
   in cm.
   (A) 7
   (B) $7\sqrt{2}$
   (C) 12.25
   (D) 14
   (E) 17

GO ON TO THE NEXT PAGE.

The Tutorverse

DO WORK IN THIS SPACE

10. A box contains 7 red markers, 2 green markers, 2 yellow markers, and 9 blue markers. If a marker is selected at random from the bag, what is the probability it will either be red or yellow?
   (A) $\frac{7}{190}$
   (B) $\frac{1}{10}$
   (C) $\frac{1}{5}$
   (D) $\frac{7}{20}$
   (E) $\frac{9}{20}$

11. Which expression is equivalent to $\sqrt{\sqrt{\sqrt{x^{72}}}}$?
   (A) x^8
   (B) x^9
   (C) x^{12}
   (D) x^{18}
   (E) x^{36}

12. Two adjacent angles in a parallelogram measure $(4x)°$ and $(6x)°$. What is the value of x?
   (A) 10
   (B) 12
   (C) 18
   (D) 24
   (E) 36

13. Jane kicks a soccer ball into the air. The ball's height, y, in feet, with respect to time, x, in seconds, can be modeled by the function $y = -x^2 + 4x + 5$. How many seconds does it take the ball to hit the ground after Jane kicks it?
   (A) −1
   (B) 1
   (C) 4
   (D) 5
   (E) 6

14. 18 is 5% of
   (A) 3.6
   (B) 9
   (C) 36
   (D) 90
   (E) 360

15. 13.6 liters of water are split evenly into four buckets. How many milliliters of water are in each bucket?
   (A) 3.2
   (B) 3.4
   (C) 320
   (D) 340
   (E) 3,400

GO ON TO THE NEXT PAGE.

The Tutorverse

DO WORK IN THIS SPACE

16. The fraction $\frac{5}{7}$ can be written as the repeating decimal $0.\overline{714285}$. What is the digit in the 100th decimal place?
    (A) 1
    (B) 2
    (C) 4
    (D) 5
    (E) 7

17. If y is a prime number, what is the least common multiple of $24y^4$ and $16y^3$?
    (A) $8y^7$
    (B) $8y^{12}$
    (C) $48y^3$
    (D) $48y^4$
    (E) $24y^5$

18. Estimate the decimal value of $\frac{48}{151} - \frac{99}{1198}$.
    (A) 0.3
    (B) 0.25
    (C) 0.2
    (D) 0.15
    (E) 0.1

19. The letters A, B, and C represent numbers on a number line. Zero is between B and C. Which statement must NOT be true?
    (A) $C = B^2$
    (B) $A = B^3$
    (C) B is the average (arithmetic mean) of A and C
    (D) $C = A^3$
    (E) $B = A^3$

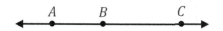

20. Which expression is equivalent to $\frac{2}{x+2} + \frac{6}{x-4}$?
    (A) $\frac{8x+4}{x^2+6x+8}$
    (B) $\frac{4}{x-1}$
    (C) $\frac{8}{2x-2}$
    (D) $\frac{4x+2}{x^2-x-4}$
    (E) $\frac{8x+4}{x^2-2x-8}$

21. Which is the slope of the line passing through the points $(4, 5)$ and $(-2, 0)$?
    (A) 6
    (B) $\frac{6}{5}$
    (C) $\frac{5}{6}$
    (D) $-\frac{5}{6}$
    (E) $-\frac{6}{5}$

GO ON TO THE NEXT PAGE.

The Tutorverse

DO WORK IN THIS SPACE

22. What is the length of the hypotenuse of the right triangle if its area is 30 cm²?

    (A) $\sqrt{61}$

    (B) $2\sqrt{34}$

    (C) $4\sqrt{34}$

    (D) 8

    (E) 68

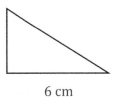

6 cm

23. Simplify the following expression: $\frac{a^3 b^5 c^7}{a^4 b^{-4} c^6}$

    (A) $\frac{a^7 c^{13}}{b^9}$

    (B) $\frac{ab^9}{c^{-1}}$

    (C) $\frac{ac}{b^9}$

    (D) $\frac{b^9 c}{a}$

    (E) $a^7 b c^{13}$

24. Which inequality represents all possible solutions of
    $24x - 3(8x + 2) > -2x - 10$?

    (A) $x > -8$

    (B) $x < -2$

    (C) $x > -2$

    (D) $x > 24$

    (E) $x < -8$

25. How many rectangles are in the figure shown?

    (A) 9

    (B) 14

    (C) 18

    (D) 24

    (E) 36

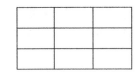

STOP
IF YOU FINISH BEFORE TIME IS UP,
CHECK YOUR WORK IN THIS SECTION ONLY.
YOU MAY NOT TURN TO ANY OTHER SECTION.

The Tutorverse

SECTION 2
40 Questions

Carefully read each passage and then answer the questions about it. For each question, select the choice that best answers the question based on the passage.

In three days the web was, with incredible diligence, completed; nor could I avoid thinking that the insect seemed to exult in its new abode. It frequently traversed it round, examined the strength of every part of it, retired into its hole, and came out very frequently. The first enemy, however, it had to encounter, was another and a much larger
5   spider, which, having no web of its own, and having probably exhausted all its stock in former labors of this kind, came to invade the property of its neighbor. Soon then a terrible encounter ensued, in which the invader seemed to have the victory, and the laborious spider was obliged to take refuge in its hole. Upon this I perceived the victor using every art to draw the enemy from his stronghold. He seemed to go off, but quickly
10 returned, and when he found all arts vain, began to demolish the new web without mercy. This brought on another battle, and, contrary to my expectations, the laborious spider became conqueror, and fairly killed his antagonist.

Now then, in peaceable possession of what was justly its own, it waited three days with the utmost patience, repairing the breaches of its web, and taking no sustenance that
15 I could perceive. At last, however, a large blue fly fell into the snare, and struggled hard to get loose. The spider gave it leave to entangle itself as much as possible, but it seemed to be too strong for the cobweb. I must own I was greatly surprised when I saw the spider immediately sally out, and in less than a minute weave a new net round its captive, by which the motion of its wings was stopped, and when it was fairly hampered in this
20 manner, it was seized, and dragged into the hole.

In this manner it lived, in a precarious state, and nature seemed to have fitted it for such a life, for upon a single fly it subsisted for more than a week.

1. The "stock" (line 5) refers to
    (A) a blue fly
    (B) a part of a plant
    (C) a wooden frame
    (D) an amount of food
    (E) an amount of material

2. According to the passage, what happens immediately after the larger spider begins to destroy the smaller spider's web?
    (A) The larger spider runs off only to return again.
    (B) The larger spider retreated into a hole.
    (C) The smaller spider retreated into a hole.
    (D) The smaller spider attacks the larger spider and wins.
    (E) The larger spider attacks the smaller spider and wins.

3. The author's attitude toward the smaller spider is best described as
    (A) perplexity
    (B) fascination
    (C) impatience
    (D) compassion
    (E) disillusionment

4. Which of these is the best title for the passage?
    (A) "When Spiders Attack"
    (B) "Spiders: Why We Need Them"
    (C) "A Day in the Life of a Spider"
    (D) "Spiders: Why They Do What They Do"
    (E) "Getting Over Your Fear of Spiders"

5. This passage is probably part of a larger piece of
    (A) a newspaper editorial
    (B) an encyclopedia entry
    (C) a journal or diary entry
    (D) a poem in a book of poetry
    (E) a critical review in a magazine

GO ON TO THE NEXT PAGE.

The Tutorverse

Suddenly I found myself lying awake, peering from my sandy mattress through the door of the tent. I looked at my watch pinned against the canvas, and saw by the bright moonlight that it was past twelve o'clock – the threshold of a new day – and I had therefore slept a couple of hours. The Swede was asleep still beside me; the wind howled
5 as before and something plucked at my heart and made me feel afraid. There was a sense of disturbance in my immediate neighborhood.

I sat up quickly and looked out. The trees were swaying violently to and fro as the gusts smote them, but our little bit of green canvas lay snugly safe in the hollow, for the wind passed over it without meeting enough resistance to make it vicious. The feeling of
10 disquietude did not pass however, and I crawled quietly out of the tent to see if our belongings were safe. I moved carefully so as not to waken my companion. A curious excitement was on me.

I was halfway out, kneeling on all fours, when my eye first took in that the tops of the bushes opposite, with their moving tracery of leaves, made shapes against the sky. I
15 sat back on my haunches and stared. It was incredible, surely, but there, opposite and slightly above me, were shapes of some indeterminate sort among the willows, and as the branches swayed in the wind they seemed to group themselves about these shapes, forming a series of monstrous outlines that shifted rapidly beneath the moon. Close, about fifty feet in front of me, I saw these things.
20 My first instinct was to waken my companion that he too might see them, but something made me hesitate – the sudden realization, probably, that I should not welcome corroboration; and meanwhile I crouched there staring in amazement with smarting eyes. I was wide awake. I remember saying to myself that I was *not* dreaming.

6. As used in the sentence, "smote" (line 8) most nearly means
   (A) bent
   (B) struck
   (C) terrified
   (D) outlined
   (E) frightened

7. The "green canvas" (line 8) probably refers to the
   (A) narrator's tent
   (B) color of the leaves
   (C) narrator's mattress
   (D) Swede's sleeping bag
   (E) shapes on the willows

8. The passage implies that the narrator "should not welcome corroboration" (lines 21-22) because
   (A) he is certain that he is dreaming
   (B) that would mean that ghosts are real
   (C) he does not want the Swede to think he is afraid
   (D) he does not want what he sees to be confirmed
   (E) what he sees is too fantastic and amazing to share

9. The mood of the passage is best described as
   (A) idyllic
   (B) cynical
   (C) mellow
   (D) indifferent
   (E) apprehensive

10. The imagery most important to this passage is
   (A) the sound of the wind
   (B) the outlines in the trees
   (C) the smell of the outdoors
   (D) the appearance of the tent
   (E) the temperature in the air

GO ON TO THE NEXT PAGE.

The Tutorverse

It may look innocuous, but the cigarette is one of the deadliest objects ever invented. According to the Centers for Disease Control and Prevention (CDC), 443,000 smoking-related deaths occur each year in the United States. Globally, smoking causes around six million deaths every year. It is hard to believe that while things like lead-based

5   paint and asbestos have been all but eliminated due to their health hazards, one of the biggest threats to human health can still be purchased at the local store. The legislation to curtail cigarette use that has thus far been passed is not enough. It is time to take a bolder stance on smoking.

The government has made an effort to curb the use of cigarettes by making them

10   expensive and difficult to purchase. Potential smokers must be at least 18 years old, and must pay high taxes when buying cigarettes. In addition, the government has launched expensive campaigns to raise awareness of the product's lethality; commercials and advertisements depict the effects of pneumonia, bronchitis, lung cancer, and emphysema – conditions that are prevalent among smokers. Yet, despite these deterrents, cigarette

15   use remains high; as of 2017, the CDC estimated that 46 million Americans age 18 years and older still smoke cigarettes.

Though some argue that well-informed adults should be allowed to smoke if they wish, the fact remains that doing so has considerable consequences for society. According to the CDC, the United States spends around 96 billion tax dollars each year covering the

20   costs associated with smoking-related health issues. What's more, secondhand smoke, or the smoke emitted into the air by smokers, can cause significant harm to non-smokers. Children exposed to secondhand smoke, for instance, are at a higher risk for infant death syndrome, middle ear infection, and asthma. Smoking also negatively affects the environment. Cigarette butts are a major source of land and water pollution, as the

25   chemicals from improperly discarded cigarettes seep into soil and bodies of water.

It's time to do what must be done and eliminate this scourge on our bodies, our societies, and our world.

---

11. In line 1, "innocuous" most nearly means
    (A) easy
    (B) lethal
    (C) harmless
    (D) complex
    (E) neutral

12. The author would most likely agree with which of the following statements?
    (A) Smokers usually quit smoking when they become ill.
    (B) The effects of smoking cigarettes are widely disputed.
    (C) The government should not use taxes to dissuade people from unhealthy habits.
    (D) Protecting personal freedoms is more important than safeguarding the public health.
    (E) Sometimes, people must be prevented from engaging in activities that harm themselves and others.

13. According to the passage, smoking can result in all of the following EXCEPT:
    (A) paying higher taxes
    (B) elimination of asbestos
    (C) high medical costs
    (D) infant mortality
    (E) lake pollution

14. In the author's opinion, anti-smoking campaigns are
    (A) not graphic enough
    (B) not worth the money
    (C) most effective on adults
    (D) most effective on children
    (E) not enough to stop people from smoking

GO ON TO THE NEXT PAGE.

The Tutorverse

Out of the night that covers me
Black as the Pit from pole to pole,
I thank whatever gods may be
For my unconquerable soul.

5   In the fell clutch of circumstance
I have not winced nor cried aloud
Under the bludgeonings of chance
My head is bloody, but unbowed.

Beyond this place of wrath and tears
10 Looms the Horror of the Shade,
And Yet the menace of the years
Finds, and shall find, me unafraid.

It matters not how straight the gate,
How charged with punishments the scroll,
15 I am the master of my fate;
I am the captain of my soul.

15. The author would most likely agree with which of the following statements?
   (A) Chance is violent, so you should make thorough plans.
   (B) If you lose control of yourself, you will face wrath and tears.
   (C) Death prevents people from acting how they want.
   (D) You should be adventurous, like the captain of a ship.
   (E) No matter how bad things get, you have to keep going.

16. In line 7, "bludgeonings" is an example of
   (A) allusion
   (B) simile
   (C) hyperbole
   (D) metaphor
   (E) paradox

17. When the speaker refers to the "Horror of the Shade" (line 10), he is
   (A) describing his fear of shadows
   (B) implying people are afraid of death
   (C) suggesting he prefers bright light
   (D) alluding to his own nickname
   (E) naming the place of wrath and tears

18. In the last stanza (lines 13-16), the author's tone can be best described as which of the following?
   (A) fearful
   (B) anxious
   (C) confident
   (D) dreary
   (E) doubtful

19. This passage was probably written to
   (A) encourage readers to be strong
   (B) help readers fall asleep at night
   (C) scare readers into staying complacent
   (D) instruct readers on how to overcome fate
   (E) warn readers about taking too many chances

GO ON TO THE NEXT PAGE.

The Tutorverse

Often ridiculed for its melodramatic tone and farfetched plotlines, the soap opera has actually been one of television's most enduring and profitable genres. Soap operas were first introduced in the 1930s as daytime radio broadcasts. Since then, they have evolved into a global phenomenon of televised, daytime dramas. Most other television
5   shows are considered highly successful if they air 100 episodes. Many soaps, however, are thousands of episodes long. Before finally being cancelled in 2009, *Guiding Light* – the most successful soap opera to date – aired a whopping 18,000 episodes.

Despite their historic success, soap operas appear to be on the brink of extinction. By 1998, only eleven daytime soap operas were in circulation in the United States. Nearly
10   twenty years later, only four remain, and rumors persist that more cancellations are imminent. So why has viewership declined? One reason is an increase in choice. As more cable channels invest in their own original dramas, viewers can look beyond soap operas for juicy storylines. Moreover, soaps have been eclipsed by the popularity of reality television, a cheaply produced genre notorious for its melodramatic narratives.
15   Perhaps most importantly, however, is that soap operas simply do not appeal to younger generations. Because soap operas cater to an older audience, they often lack content relevant to a younger demographic. In a culture inundated by social media, a constant stream of new smartphone apps, and the popularity of bite-sized, viral video clips, the soap opera just can't compete for a new generation of television viewers. How
20   can the dramatic exploits of two warring clans compete with cute cat videos?

20. Which of the following best states the main idea of the passage?
(A) A once successful television genre now struggles to stay relevant.
(B) New distractions mean people no longer care for dramatic narratives.
(C) The global popularity of a particular television show is an example of its widespread appeal.
(D) A younger generation of viewers share their parents' enthusiasm over a certain television genre.
(E) Cable channels are mostly responsible for changing television genres.

21. In line 13, the word "eclipsed" most nearly means
(A) darkened
(B) overshadowed
(C) enlightened
(D) surrounded
(E) eradicated

22. According to the passage, all of the following are true EXCEPT:
(A) Soap operas are no longer the only provider of melodramatic storylines
(B) Soap operas are now generally watched by an older demographic.
(C) Soap operas have not always been a genre exclusive to television.
(D) Reality television contributed to the declining popularity of the soap opera.
(E) Most successful television shows are able to produce thousands of episodes.

23. It can be inferred from the text that younger audiences
(A) are disinterested in radio broadcasts
(B) do not appreciate the over-the-top plotlines of soap operas
(C) are unable to connect with an older generation
(D) may dislike the length of soap operas
(E) are the intended audience for reality television

24. Which of the following conclusions can best be drawn from the passage?
(A) Soap operas are never viewed by younger audiences.
(B) Smartphone apps offer viewers another medium on which to watch soaps.
(C) Soap operas must become cheaper to make to remain popular.
(D) *Guiding Light* was ultimately cancelled due to changing viewing habits.
(E) Soap operas are only failing in the U.S.

GO ON TO THE NEXT PAGE.

The Tutorverse

I once decided to visit an acquaintance who had named his country place "The Elms." I went partly to punish him because his invitation was so evidently hollow and insincere.

5 He had "The Elms" worked on his clothes, and embossed on his stationery and blown in his glass, and it pained him to eat his food from table linen that didn't have "The Elms" emblazoned on it. He told me to come and surprise him any time, and shoot in his preserves, and stay until business compelled me to return to town again. He had no doubt heard that I never surprise anyone, and never go away from home very much, and so thought it would be safe. Therefore, I went. I went just to teach him a valuable lesson.

10 When I go to visit a man for a week, he is certainly thenceforth going to be a better man, or else punishment is of no avail and the chastening rod entirely useless in his case.

"The Elms" was a misnomer. It should have been called "The Shagbark" or "The Doodle Bug's Lair." It was supposed to mean a wide sweep of meadow, a vine covered lodge, a broad velvet lawn, and a carriage way, where the drowsy locust, in the sensuous

15 shadow of magnanimous elms, gnawed a file at intervals through the day, while back of all this the mossy and gray-whiskered front and corrugated brow of the venerable architectural pile stood off and admired itself in the deep and glassy pool at its base.

In the first place none of the townspeople for eight miles around knew that he called his old malarial tank "The Elms," so it was hard to find. But when I described the

20 looks of the lord of The Elms they wink at each other and wagged their heads and said, "Oh, yes, we know him," also interjecting well-known one syllable words that are not euphonious enough to print.

25. Which of the following describes the motivation behind the narrator's decision to visit "The Elms"?
(A) spite
(B) curiosity
(C) friendship
(D) magnanimity
(E) responsibility

26. The narrator's tone can best be described as which of the following?
(A) solemn
(B) reverent
(C) admiring
(D) concerned
(E) condescending

27. Without changing the author's meaning, the phrase "words that are not euphonious enough to print" (lines 21-22) can be replaced by
(A) verses
(B) praises
(C) promises
(D) directions
(E) profanities

28. Based on the narrator's description in lines 12-17, "The Elms" is most likely
(A) an insect farm with many dogs
(B) a stately property with a long carriage way
(C) an idyllic rural vacation home with a grand lawn
(D) a beautiful country estate with a vine covered building
(E) a property that is at best ordinary and not at all grand

29. When the narrator refers to his acquaintance as "lord of The Elms," (line 20), he does so
(A) proudly
(B) seriously
(C) reverently
(D) sarcastically
(E) embarrassedly

GO ON TO THE NEXT PAGE

The Tutorverse

Where "knowledge is power," that nation is the most powerful which has the largest population of intelligent men; for a nation to cramp and circumscribe the mental faculties of a class of its inhabitants is as unwise as it is cruel, since it, in the same proportion, sacrifices its power and happiness. The American people, in the light of this

5 reasoning, are at this moment, in obedience to their pride and folly, (we say nothing of the wickedness of the act,) wasting one sixth part of the energies of the entire nation by transforming three million of its men into beasts of burden. — What a loss to industry, skill, invention, (to say nothing of its foul and corrupting influence,) is Slavery! How it ties the hand, cramps the mind, darkens the understanding, and paralyses the whole man!

10 Nothing is more evident to a man who reasons at all, than that America is acting an irrational part in continuing the slave system at the South, and in oppressing its free colored citizens at the North. Regarding the nation as an individual, the act of enslaving and oppressing thus, is as wild and senseless as it would be for Czar Nicholas to order the amputation of the right arm of every Russian soldier before engaging in war with France.

15 We again repeat that Slavery is the peculiar weakness of America, as well as its peculiar crime; and the day may yet come when this visionary and oft-repeated declaration will be found to contain a great truth.

30. Without changing the author's meaning, "cramp and circumscribe" (line 2) could be replaced by
(A) allow
(B) dictate
(C) restrict
(D) liberate
(E) legalize

31. In order to have a powerful country, the author believes that America must
(A) unite the North and the South
(B) eliminate all malice and cruelty
(C) force more people into manual labor
(D) emulate the actions of Czar Nicholas
(E) allow everyone freedom and opportunity

32. According to the passage, which of the following is NOT true?
(A) Slavery wastes human potential.
(B) Slavery is a problem endemic to America.
(C) Unlike in the South, there is no inequality in the North.
(D) People who support slavery are missing the bigger picture.
(E) Freeing slaves would enable them to positively contribute to society.

33. Which of the following best states the main idea of the passage?
(A) Men are better off laboring than learning.
(B) Everyone should be entitled to education.
(C) The institution of slavery must be abolished.
(D) America is weak and needs to face difficult truths.
(E) Czar Nicholas was foolish to order the amputation of his soldiers' arms.

34. Which of the following is an example of allusion?
(A) "as unwise as it is cruel" (line 3)
(B) "ties the hand...the whole man" (lines 8-9)
(C) "Regarding the nation as an individual" (line 12)
(D) "for Czar Nicholas...with France" (line 13)
(E) "visionary and oft-repeated" (line 16)

35. The author's tone can best be described as which of the following?
(A) ironic
(B) ardent
(C) judgmental
(D) patronizing
(E) dispassionate

GO ON TO THE NEXT PAGE.

To judge from the conduct of the opposite parties, we shall be led to conclude that they will mutually hope to evince the justness of their opinions, and to increase the number of their converts by the loudness of their declamations and the bitterness of their invectives. An enlightened zeal for the energy and efficiency of government will be
5   stigmatized as the offspring of a temper fond of despotic power and hostile to the principles of liberty. An over-scrupulous jealousy of danger to the rights of the people, which is more commonly the fault of the head than of the heart, will be represented as mere pretense and artifice, the stale bait for popularity at the expense of the public good. It will be forgotten, on the one hand, that jealousy is the usual concomitant of love, and
10 that the noble enthusiasm of liberty is apt to be infected with a spirit of narrow and illiberal distrust. On the other hand, it will be equally forgotten that the vigor of government is essential to the security of liberty; that, in the contemplation of a sound and well-informed judgment, their interest can never be separated; and that a dangerous ambition more often lurks behind the specious mask of zeal for the rights of the people
15 than under the forbidden appearance of zeal for the firmness and efficiency of government. History will teach us that the former has been found a much more certain road to the introduction of despotism than the latter, and that of those men who have overturned the liberties of republics, the greatest number have begun their career by paying an obsequious court to the people; commencing demagogues, and ending tyrants.
20   In the course of the preceding observations, I have had an eye, my fellow-citizens, to putting you upon your guard against all attempts, from whatever quarter, to influence your decision in a matter of the utmost moment to your welfare, by any impressions other than those which may result from the evidence of truth.

36. The author's main intention is to
(A) profile historical despots
(B) provide an urgent warning
(C) describe the ideal government
(D) explain how tyrants come to power
(E) compare various forms of government

37. According to the author, the "over-scrupulous jealousy...of the people" (line 6) leads to
(A) the noble enthusiasm of liberty
(B) security and liberty for all people
(C) sound and well-informed judgment
(D) the desire to build an effective government
(E) leaders who amass power and reduce freedom

38. The phrase "paying an obsequious court to the people" (line 19) most nearly means
(A) prioritizing the needs of the country
(B) telling people what they want to hear to win popularity
(C) telling people what the need to hear, no matter how difficult
(D) making the difficult decisions needed as a leader of the country
(E) letting people change the government

39. As used in line 21, "quarter" probably refers to
(A) a source of information
(B) a particular neighborhood
(C) a certain percentage of people
(D) a person's individual opinions
(E) the government's official statements

40. In the author's opinion, political disagreements
(A) lead a country down the road to despotism
(B) are often more superficial than substantive
(C) should be avoided because they can be uncomfortable
(D) should only be the responsibility of well-educated citizens
(E) are primarily focused on how much power the government should have

STOP
IF YOU FINISH BEFORE TIME IS UP,
CHECK YOUR WORK IN THIS SECTION ONLY.
YOU MAY NOT TURN TO ANY OTHER SECTION.

The Tutorverse

SECTION 3
60 Questions

There are two different types of questions in this section: synonyms and analogies. Read the directions and sample question for each type.

Synonyms

Each of the questions that follow consist of one capitalized word. Each word is followed by five words or phrases. Select the one word or phrase whose meaning is closest to the word in capital letters.

Sample Question:

SMALL:　　　●ⒷⒸⒹⒺ

(A) tiny
(B) funny
(C) large
(D) cute
(E) pretty

---

1. DEFECT:
    (A) concept
    (B) creation
    (C) asset
    (D) product
    (E) flaw

2. OBSERVANT:
    (A) attentive
    (B) pitiable
    (C) careless
    (D) inaccurate
    (E) distracted

3. VOUCH:
    (A) crouch down
    (B) disclaim
    (C) recommend for
    (D) clean up
    (E) scribble around

4. LABYRINTH:
    (A) fame
    (B) maze
    (C) tyranny
    (D) anecdote
    (E) problem

5. DISCRIMINATE:
    (A) decorate
    (B) investigate
    (C) allow
    (D) differentiate
    (E) propose

6. RECEDE:
    (A) extend
    (B) annex
    (C) withdraw
    (D) expand
    (E) deliver

7. CRITERION:
    (A) review
    (B) reign
    (C) process
    (D) benchmark
    (E) appraisal

8. PERSPECTIVE:
    (A) potential
    (B) intellect
    (C) caution
    (D) proclamation
    (E) point of view

GO ON TO THE NEXT PAGE.

9. TRAIT:
   (A) smell
   (B) combination
   (C) traitor
   (D) friendly
   (E) attribute

10. PLUMMET:
   (A) fly
   (B) meet
   (C) plunge
   (D) increase
   (E) rise

11. AUTONOMOUS:
   (A) independent
   (B) alive
   (C) thinking
   (D) reliant
   (E) conscious

12. CULTIVATE:
   (A) reap benefits
   (B) limit
   (C) enjoy
   (D) work on
   (E) separate

13. CIVIL:
   (A) polite
   (B) indignant
   (C) heated
   (D) deadly
   (E) global

14. DESPONDENT:
   (A) miserable
   (B) well-informed
   (C) hesitant
   (D) immense
   (E) cordial

15. VORACIOUS:
   (A) conceited
   (B) gracious
   (C) vengeful
   (D) incessant
   (E) ravenous

16. EVANESCENT:
   (A) frantic
   (B) fleeting
   (C) delicious
   (D) untimely
   (E) bubbly

17. DIVULGE:
   (A) make known
   (B) keep secret
   (C) split up
   (D) luxuriate
   (E) consolidate

18. INFERENCE:
   (A) purpose
   (B) contrast
   (C) interpretation
   (D) comparison
   (E) affluence

19. RESCIND:
   (A) lower towards
   (B) grant permission
   (C) hint to
   (D) raise up
   (E) make null and void

20. ADVERSITY:
   (A) hospitality
   (B) commercial
   (C) relaxation
   (D) hardship
   (E) persistence

21. CIRCUMSPECT:
   (A) direct
   (B) suspicious
   (C) careless
   (D) inept
   (E) round

22. EMINENCE:
   (A) holy artifact
   (B) prestige
   (C) total anonymity
   (D) strong intuition
   (E) replica

GO ON TO THE NEXT PAGE.

The Tutorverse

23. BENEVOLENT:
    (A) theological
    (B) intolerant
    (C) compassionate
    (D) violent
    (E) infernal

24. DELETERIOUS:
    (A) innumerable
    (B) harmful
    (C) removable
    (D) misanthropic
    (E) indescribable

25. LOQUACIOUS:
    (A) neighboring
    (B) heartrending
    (C) obligatory
    (D) talkative
    (E) regrettable

26. LACONIC:
    (A) legitimate
    (B) potent
    (C) convivial
    (D) curt
    (E) famous

27. ENHANCE:
    (A) control
    (B) contrive
    (C) augment
    (D) muddle
    (E) taper

28. REPUDIATE:
    (A) enlist
    (B) collapse
    (C) reject
    (D) humanize
    (E) advance

29. ACRID:
    (A) unpleasant
    (B) amicable
    (C) abrupt
    (D) trivial
    (E) peak

30. DEFERENCE:
    (A) condescending impatience
    (B) generous donation
    (C) unreasonable delay
    (D) humble submission
    (E) nervous hesitation

GO ON TO THE NEXT PAGE.

The Tutorverse

Analogies

The questions that follow ask you to find relationships between words. For each question, select the answer choice that best completes the meaning of the sentence.

Sample Question:

> Shelf is to book as: ●ⒷⒸⒹⒺ
>
> (A) closet is clothes
> (B) kitchen is to bathroom
> (C) house is to neighborhood
> (D) sidewalk is to shoe
> (E) cloth is to table

Choice (A) is the best answer because a shelf is used to store a book, just as a closet is used to store clothes. This choice states a relationship that is most like the relationship between shelf and book.

---

31. Motive is to ulterior as holidays is to
    (A) motivation
    (B) secret
    (C) happy
    (D) emergency
    (E) sailboat

32. Makeup is to lipstick as
    (A) peanut is to shell
    (B) lamp is to lightbulb
    (C) canteen is to bottle
    (D) copy is to template
    (E) weapon is to dagger

33. Quiet is to mute as loud is to
    (A) cry
    (B) whisper
    (C) muffled
    (D) inaudible
    (E) deafening

34. Consistent is to erratic as
    (A) insane is to unstable
    (B) constant is to forever
    (C) unimportant is to immaterial
    (D) crucial is to trivial
    (E) rude is to mean

35. Catastrophe is to disaster as
    (A) dearth is to lack
    (B) expansion is to contraction
    (C) hygiene is to bath
    (D) incompetence is to competitive
    (E) mandate is to mandatory

36. Sent is to send as shone is to
    (A) get
    (B) set
    (C) shiny
    (D) shine
    (E) shines

37. Chapter is to novel as
    (A) fork is to knife
    (B) fabric is to sofa
    (C) desk is to tabletop
    (D) dish is to sink
    (E) chair is to leg

38. Calendar is to event as
    (A) journal is to memory
    (B) pen is to pencil
    (C) chair is to sit
    (D) eat is to table
    (E) date is to day

GO ON TO THE NEXT PAGE.

The Tutorverse

39. Notebook is to sheet as
    (A) postcard is to stamp
    (B) ruler is to line
    (C) card is to tag
    (D) memo is to memorandum
    (E) keyboard is to key

40. Practice is to perfection as
    (A) vigor is to apathy
    (B) ecstasy is to elation
    (C) carelessness is to accident
    (D) training is to regimen
    (E) happiness is to sadness

41. Wind is to cyclone as
    (A) sand is to surf
    (B) water is to wave
    (C) pebble is to boulder
    (D) tunnel is to funnel
    (E) tornado is to vortex

42. Ledger is to entry as
    (A) money is to cash
    (B) profit is to business
    (C) withdrawal is to loss
    (D) advice is to help
    (E) language is to word

43. Fireplace is to heat as
    (A) mop is to floor
    (B) separate is to fence
    (C) refrigerator is to preserve
    (D) freezer is to oven
    (E) flame is to lighter

44. Freefall is to gravity as
    (A) melt is to freeze
    (B) weight is to heaviness
    (C) trajectory is to route
    (D) speed is to velocity
    (E) shock is to electricity

45. Singer is to choir as
    (A) brick is to wall
    (B) cement is to wet
    (C) band is to drummer
    (D) carpet is to ceiling
    (E) plywood is to tree

46. Stunt is to publicity as
    (A) movie is to movies
    (B) breath is to bated
    (C) steal is to pirate
    (D) publicist is to actor
    (E) affect is to cause

47. Collusion is to complicity as
    (A) hostility is to hospitality
    (B) demise is to surmise
    (C) ferocity is to cowardice
    (D) gusto is to windy
    (E) consistency is to stability

48. Salary is to employee as
    (A) interest is to savings
    (B) supervisor is to bonus
    (C) promotion is to raise
    (D) money is to gift
    (E) demotion is to advancement

49. Thief is to pilfer as
    (A) witness is to attest
    (B) ambush is to armada
    (C) betrothed is to divorce
    (D) devout is to blaspheme
    (E) surgeon is to hospital

50. Benefactor is to alms as
    (A) benevolent is to kind
    (B) charity is to nonprofit
    (C) malefactor is to maleficent
    (D) philanthropist is to donation
    (E) benefit is to event

51. Ox is to plow as
    (A) hour is to clock
    (B) target is to dummy
    (C) machete is to blade
    (D) arrow is to arrowhead
    (E) sponge is to dish

52. Wool is to sheep as
    (A) cotton is to denim
    (B) shepherd is to herd
    (C) leather is to cow
    (D) calf is to lamb
    (E) male is to ram

GO ON TO THE NEXT PAGE.

The Tutorverse

53. Raptor is to dinosaur as
   (A) omnivore is to carnivore
   (B) ode is to farewell
   (C) government is to monarchy
   (D) reptile is to mammal
   (E) giraffe is to herbivore

54. Smallpox is to disease as geometry is to
   (A) algebra
   (B) math
   (C) school
   (D) teacher
   (E) student

55. Docile is to wild as
   (A) reliable is to trustworthy
   (B) tame is to domesticated
   (C) monotonous is to repetitive
   (D) outlandish is to valiant
   (E) mundane is to exotic

56. Identify is to logo as
   (A) devotee is to revile
   (B) rule is to mob
   (C) substantiate is to claim
   (D) antidote is to solve
   (E) befuddle is to cipher

57. Catholicism is to religion as
   (A) doctor is to surgeon
   (B) biography is to nonfiction
   (C) agriculture is to farming
   (D) municipality is to nation
   (E) rendition is to sketch

58. Hypothesis is to hypotheses as
   (A) larvae is to larva
   (B) memoranda is to memorandum
   (C) crisis is to crises
   (D) syllabi is to syllabus
   (E) curricula is to curriculum

59. Fencer is to saber as
   (A) inferno is to arsonist
   (B) knitter is to needle
   (C) earthenware is to potter
   (D) horse is to equestrian
   (E) proprietor is to owner

60. Chameleon is to adapt as eagle is to
   (A) talon
   (B) beak
   (C) noble
   (D) soar
   (E) rabbit

STOP
IF YOU FINISH BEFORE TIME IS UP,
CHECK YOUR WORK IN THIS SECTION ONLY.
YOU MAY NOT TURN TO ANY OTHER SECTION.

The Tutorverse

SECTION 4
25 Questions

There are five suggested answers after each problem in this section. Solve each problem in your head or in the space provided to the right of the problem. Then look at the suggested answers and pick the best one.

Note: Any figures or shapes that accompany problems in Section 1 are drawn as accurately as possible EXCEPT when it is stated that the figure is NOT drawn to scale.

Sample Question:

11 – 13 =	●ⒷⒸⒹⒺ

(A) –2
(B) 0
(C) 1
(D) 2
(E) 3

DO WORK IN THIS SPACE

1. What is the value of $(1 \times 0.01)^2$?
   (A) 10
   (B) 0.01
   (C) 0.001
   (D) 0.0001
   (E) 0.00001

2. What fraction of the students scored between a 90 and 100 on the test?
   (A) $\frac{1}{25}$
   (B) $\frac{2}{15}$
   (C) $\frac{4}{15}$
   (D) $\frac{1}{4}$
   (E) $\frac{2}{7}$

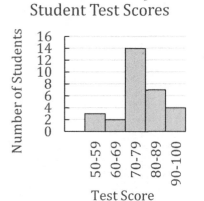

Student Test Scores

3. Which expression is equivalent to $4x^2 - 32x + 48$?
   (A) $(x - 8)(x - 6)$
   (B) $(x - 4)(x - 12)$
   (C) $4(x - 3)(x - 4)$
   (D) $4(x - 2)(x - 6)$
   (E) $4x(x - 2)(x - 6)$

GO ON TO THE NEXT PAGE.

The Tutorverse

DO WORK IN THIS SPACE

4. A store offered a 40% discount on all items over one weekend. After the weekend, all items returned to their original price. By what fraction of the discounted price of an item did the price increase after the weekend?
   (A) $\frac{1}{5}$
   (B) $\frac{1}{3}$
   (C) $\frac{2}{5}$
   (D) $\frac{3}{5}$
   (E) $\frac{2}{3}$

5. Which expression is equivalent to $(x^2 - 3x - 7) + (x^2 - 4x - 9)$?
   (A) $2x^2 + 7x + 16$
   (B) $7x + 16$
   (C) $-1x - 2$
   (D) $2x^2 - x - 2$
   (E) $2x^2 - 7x - 16$

6. What is the value of $-15 + 48 - 31 + 17$?
   (A) -19
   (B) 19
   (C) 39
   (D) 47
   (E) 49

7. A plane travels at a steady velocity in non-windy conditions. It takes 2 hours to travel 600 miles directly against a wind current and 5 hours to travel 3,200 miles in the same direction as the wind current. How many hours will it take the train to travel 1,880 miles in non-windy conditions? (*Note: distance = velocity × time*)
   (A) 2 hours
   (B) 4 hours
   (C) 6 hours
   (D) 10 hours
   (E) 15 hours

8. If a and b are distinct integers, and $\frac{a}{b}$ is a negative integer, then which statement must be true?
   (A) The sum of a and b is even
   (B) The sum of a and b is odd
   (C) The difference of a and b is positive
   (D) The difference of a and b is negative
   (E) The reciprocal $\frac{b}{a}$ is greater

GO ON TO THE NEXT PAGE.

The Tutorverse

9. Which of the following gives the number of cents in x pennies, y nickels, and z dimes?
   (A) $x + 5y + 10z$
   (B) $0.01x + 0.05y + 0.1z$
   (C) $x + y^5 + z^{10}$
   (D) xyz
   (E) $x - y - z$

10. What is the greatest common factor of 18 and 24?
    (A) 2^4
    (B) 3^3
    (C) 2×3
    (D) $2^3 \times 3^2$
    (E) $2^4 \times 3^3$

11. The formula for converting Fahrenheit to Celsius is $F = \frac{9}{5}C + 32$. Which equation is the result of solving for C?
    (A) $C = \frac{9F+32}{5}$
    (B) $C = 32 - \frac{9}{5}F$
    (C) $C = (\frac{9}{5})(F + 32)$
    (D) $C = (\frac{5}{9})(F - 32)$
    (E) $C = (\frac{9}{5})(F - 32)$

12. If the average of 6 consecutive odd integers is 32, what is the largest number?
    (A) 27
    (B) 29
    (C) 31
    (D) 35
    (E) 37

    $x + x+2 + x+4 + x+6 + x+8 + x+10$
    $6x + 30 = 32$
    $x + 5 = 32$
    $x = 27$

13. Which is the value of the expression $30 \div 6 \times (8 + 4)$?
    (A) $\frac{5}{12}$
    (B) 36
    (C) 44
    (D) 60
    (E) 64

14. The equation of the line graphed as shown is
    (A) $y = 2x + 4$
    (B) $y = \frac{1}{2}x + 2$
    (C) $y = -\frac{1}{2}x + 4$
    (D) $y = -2x - 4$
    (E) $y = -2x + 2$

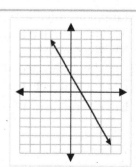

GO ON TO THE NEXT PAGE.

The Tutorverse

DO WORK IN THIS SPACE

15. What shape is made by the cross-section of the cone taken as shown?
    (A) Circle
    (B) Ellipse
    (C) Parabola
    (D) Hyperbola
    (E) Triangle

16. Which are the solutions to the equation $3x^2 + 4x + 1 = 0$?
    (A) $-4, 1$
    (B) $-1, -\frac{1}{2}$
    (C) $0, 1$
    (D) $-1, 1$
    (E) $-1, -\frac{1}{3}$

    $3x^2 + x + 3x + 1 = 0$
    $x(3x+1) + 1(3x+1)$
    $(3x+3)(x+1)$
    $(x+1)(\frac{1}{3}x+1))$

    $3x+3 <$
    $x+1 =$

17. Which line has no points in common with $y = 2x + 3$?
    (A) $y = -2x + 3$
    (B) $y = \frac{x}{2} + 3$
    (C) $y = -\frac{x}{2} + 5$
    (D) $4x + 2y = 10$
    (E) $-4x + 2y = 7$

18. Which fraction is equivalent to $\sqrt[3]{\dfrac{27}{72x}}$ when $x = 3$?
    (A) $\frac{1}{2}$
    (B) $\frac{1}{3}$
    (C) $\frac{1}{4}$
    (D) $\frac{1}{6}$
    (E) $\frac{1}{8}$

19. Point V (2, 3) is reflected across the line $y = 7$, then reflected across the line $x = 5$. What are the coordinates of the resulting point?
    (A) $(5, 7)$
    (B) $(-3, 1)$
    (C) $(8, 11)$
    (D) $(2, 11)$
    (E) $(8, 7)$

20. A pizza delivery person takes between 45 and 50 minutes to make a 15-mile round trip. The average speed, in miles per hour, must be between
    (A) 3 and $3\frac{1}{3}$
    (B) $3\frac{1}{3}$ and 6
    (C) 6 and 12
    (D) 12 and 18
    (E) 18 and 20

GO ON TO THE NEXT PAGE.

The Tutorverse

DO WORK IN THIS SPACE

21. The probability that it will rain on Monday is 0.55 and the probability that it will rain on Thursday is 0.7. The probability of rain on Monday is independent of the probability of rain on Thursday. What is the probability it does NOT rain on both Monday and Thursday?
    (A) 1.25
    (B) 1
    (C) 0.385
    (D) 0.25
    (E) 0.135

22. A rectangular prism has a square base and a height of 7 inches. If its volume is 252 cubic inches, find the length of one of the sides of the base, in inches.
    (A) 4
    (B) 6
    (C) 8
    (D) 12
    (E) 36

23. The sum of two positive integers is 78 while their difference is 6. Which is the smaller of the two integers?
    (A) 24
    (B) 28
    (C) 36
    (D) 38
    (E) 42

24. In a basketball league's season, each team plays 10 games. The league has 4 teams. Each game pits one team against one other team. How many total games does this season contain?
    (A) 5
    (B) 10
    (C) 20
    (D) 40
    (E) 80

25. What is the perimeter, in yards, of a right triangle which has an area of 12 yards² and one leg with length of 4 yards?
    (A) $\sqrt{52}$
    (B) 8
    (C) $10 + 2\sqrt{13}$
    (D) 12
    (E) 18

STOP
IF YOU FINISH BEFORE TIME IS UP,
CHECK YOUR WORK IN THIS SECTION ONLY.
YOU MAY NOT TURN TO ANY OTHER SECTION.

The Tutorverse

Final Practice Test (Form C) 225

SECTION 5
16 Questions

1. EMPHASIZE:
   (A) revise
   (B) erase
   (C) call attention to
   (D) hide away from
   (E) write down

2. ADAMANT:
   (A) muscular
   (B) stubborn
   (C) sympathetic
   (D) adaptable
   (E) pugnacious

3. ODIOUS:
   (A) static
   (B) hateful
   (C) fragrant
   (D) stinking
   (E) academic

4. Listless is to spirited as
   (A) spiritual is to religious
   (B) superstitious is to curious
   (C) decent is to evil
   (D) angel is to heaven
   (E) unorganized is to disheveled

5. Small is to miniscule as large is to
   (A) macroeconomic
   (B) average
   (C) terrifying
   (D) visible
   (E) colossal

6. Siren is to wail as horn is to
   (A) blare
   (B) car
   (C) angry
   (D) pedestrian
   (E) driver

7. Rooster is chicken as stag is to
   (A) party
   (B) male
   (C) gender
   (D) deer
   (E) venison

8. What is the value of $\frac{5.6 \times 10^4}{7.0 \times 10^{-3}}$?
   (A) 8.0×10^{-1}
   (B) 8.0×10^1
   (C) 8.0×10^6
   (D) 8.0×10^7
   (E) 8.0×10^8

9. What is the solution set to $4|3x - 5| - 7 < 1$?
   (A) $x < \frac{7}{3}$
   (B) $x > -1$
   (C) $x < 1$ or $x < \frac{7}{3}$
   (D) $1 < x < \frac{7}{3}$
   (E) $x < 1$

10. If $@x = 5x - 6$, what is the value of $@10$?
    (A) -34
    (B) -10
    (C) -1
    (D) 34
    (E) 44

11. Which of the following is equal to $\sqrt{36x^{36}}$?
    (A) $6x^6$
    (B) $6x^{18}$
    (C) $18x^6$
    (D) $18x^{18}$
    (E) $36x^6$

The Tutorverse

The explosive growth in our understanding and treatment of disease during the last century is a testament to a medical field that is relentless in its pursuit of ensuring human health. As scientists race to create remedies for human ailments, however, animal testing has become an unfortunate and immoral byproduct.

5   Many believe that testing experimental medications on animals is a safe alternative to performing those tests on humans. The hope is that by testing products on animals first, scientists will be better able to determine whether the treatments are safe for humans. The reality, however, is that animal testing consistently fails to predict human reactions, as responses to these chemical concoctions vary from species to

10 species. Penicillin, for instance, is a highly effective antibiotic when administered to humans that kills guinea pigs and has no effect on rabbits. Aspirin, a useful pain reliever for humans, kills cats and causes birth defects in rats, mice, dogs and monkeys. Unsurprisingly, a recent study on the efficacy of animal testing determined that only 19% of human side-effects could be predicted through animal testing. By some accounts, some

15 90% of medications judged to be effective after animal testing fail during human trials.

Even setting aside the question of animal testing effectiveness, the fact remains that animal testing can be a cruel process. Scientists cannot typically ensure the well-being of the animals being used in experiments, and are unable to anticipate how animals will react to medications intended for humans. In addition, scientists enjoy a great deal of

20 flexibility when it comes to the treatment of their animals. Lab animals, on the other hand, have few legal protections. Scientists are not required to provide pain relief to animals even if they know that a particular treatment will be painful.

Isn't it ironic that animal testing, a practice dedicated to the preservation of humanity, lacks just that?

12. Which of the following best states the passage's main idea?
(A) Animal testing is a primary source for developing human medications.
(B) The last century has seen a dramatic rise in medical discoveries.
(C) Animals are in need of greater legal protections.
(D) Animal testing is both ineffective and brutal.
(E) The science community behaves unethically.

13. It can be inferred from the passage that animal testing is a result of
(A) laws prohibiting human testing
(B) a desire to alleviate human illness
(C) medical discoveries like penicillin
(D) general scientific curiosity about animals
(E) the need to prevent unnecessary animal suffering

14. "Efficacy" (line 13) most nearly means
(A) practice
(B) stress
(C) frequency
(D) duress
(E) success

15. According to the passage, testing medicines on animals is largely ineffective because
(A) it is harmful to animals
(B) scientists are not limited by safety laws
(C) people are unaware of how lab animals are treated
(D) medicines have been developed without animal testing
(E) it doesn't mean the medicine will be effective in people

16. The author asks a question in lines 23-24 to
(A) transition to a new topic
(B) propose an alternate theory
(C) test the reader's knowledge
(D) support a growing body of evidence
(E) summarize a central idea of the passage

GO ON TO THE NEXT PAGE.

The Tutorverse

Scoring the Final Practice Test (Form C)

Writing Sample – Unscored

Have a parent or trusted educator review the essay or story written for the writing sample. Important areas to focus on include organization, clarity of ideas, originality, and technical precision (spelling, grammar, etc.).

Sections 1-4 – Scored

Score the test using the answer sheet and referring to the answer key at the back of the book.

Step 1: For each section, record the number of questions answered correctly.

Step 2: For each section, record the number of questions answered incorrectly. Then, multiply that number by ¼ to calculate the penalty.

Section	Questions Correct
Quantitative *Section 1 + Section 4*	_____
Reading *Section 2*	_____
Verbal *Section 3*	_____

Section	Questions Incorrect	Penalty
Quantitative *Section 1 + Section 4*	_____	x 1/4 = _____
Reading *Section 2*	_____	x 1/4 = _____
Verbal *Section 3*	_____	x 1/4 = _____

Step 3: For each section, subtract the Penalty in *Step 2* from the Questions Correct in *Step 1*. This is the raw score. Note that the actual test will convert the raw score to a scaled score by comparing the student's performance with all other students in the same grade who took the test.

Section	Raw Score
Quantitative *Section 1 + Section 4*	_____
Reading *Section 2*	_____
Verbal *Section 3*	_____

Consider: How certain were you on the questions you guessed on? Should you have left those questions blank, instead? How should you change the way you guess and leave questions blank?

Carefully consider the results from the practice test when revising a study plan. Remember, the Upper Level SSAT is given to students in grades 8-11. Unless the student has finished 11th grade, chances are that there is material on this test that he or she has not yet been taught. If this is the case, and the student would like to improve beyond what is expected of his or her grade, consider working with a tutor or teacher, who can help learn more about new topics.

Section 5 – Unscored

On the real test, the Experimental section will NOT be scored. Consider the student's performance on this section for practice purposes only. Did he or she do better on one section than other? Use this information along with the information from Sections 1-4 to reevaluate the study plan.

The Tutorverse

Answer Keys

This section provides the answer solutions to the practice questions in each section of the workbook except for the practice tests and writing sample sections. The answers to the practice tests immediately follow their respective tests. There are no answers provided to the writing sample section. Instead, consider having a tutor, teacher, or other educator review your writing and give you constructive feedback.

Remember: detailed answer explanations are available online at **www.thetutorverse.com**. Students should ask a parent or guardian's permission before going online.

Diagnostic Practice Test (Form A)

There is no answer key or explanation for the writing sample. Instead, have a parent or trusted educator review the essay or story written for the writing sample.

Section 1: Quantitative

1. D	5. D	9. C	13. D	17. E	21. C	25. E
2. C	6. D	10. A	14. A	18. B	22. C	
3. B	7. E	11. B	15. A	19. B	23. B	
4. C	8. E	12. D	16. A	20. B	24. C	

Section 2 – Reading

1. E	6. C	11. D	16. E	21. D	26. A	31. E	36. C
2. B	7. A	12. E	17. C	22. A	27. D	32. B	37. B
3. D	8. E	13. C	18. D	23. D	28. B	33. B	38. E
4. E	9. B	14. E	19. C	24. E	29. D	34. E	39. D
5. B	10. A	15. E	20. E	25. C	30. C	35. C	40. A

Section 3 – Verbal

1. E	9. B	17. A	25. C	33. D	41. A	49. D	57. D
2. B	10. D	18. D	26. C	34. E	42. A	50. C	58. D
3. B	11. B	19. B	27. A	35. A	43. D	51. E	59. C
4. A	12. C	20. C	28. B	36. A	44. C	52. C	60. C
5. C	13. D	21. E	29. C	37. A	45. E	53. D	
6. D	14. A	22. B	30. C	38. E	46. C	54. A	
7. A	15. B	23. A	31. B	39. A	47. E	55. D	
8. B	16. E	24. A	32. E	40. B	48. B	56. C	

Section 4 – Quantitative

1. C	5. A	9. E	13. A	17. D	21. D	25. C
2. A	6. D	10. D	14. C	18. E	22. A	
3. B	7. B	11. E	15. B	19. A	23. D	
4. E	8. A	12. B	16. B	20. D	24. B	

Section 5 – "Experimental"

1. A	3. D	5. D	7. A	9. A	11. E	13. B	15. B
2. D	4. C	6. D	8. C	10. C	12. E	14. B	16. D

The Tutorverse

Quantitative Reasoning & Mathematics Achievement

Number Concepts & Operations

Integers
| 1. D | 2. C | 3. B | 4. D | 5. E | 6. A | 7. E | 8. B |

Decimals
| 1. D | 3. D | 5. B | 7. E | 9. D |
| 2. B | 4. D | 6. A | 8. D | 10. E |

Fractions
| 1. D | 3. D | 5. A | 7. B | 9. C | 11. C | 13. B |
| 2. E | 4. C | 6. D | 8. C | 10. A | 12. D |

Percents
| 1. E | 3. A | 5. D | 7. E | 9. E | 11. A | 13. D | 15. D |
| 2. D | 4. C | 6. D | 8. B | 10. A | 12. A | 14. D |

Order of Operations
| 1. B | 3. B | 5. B | 7. B | 9. C |
| 2. C | 4. C | 6. C | 8. D | 10. A |

Number Theory
| 1. D | 2. D | 3. C | 4. A | 5. A | 6. A | 7. D | 8. A |

Rules of Divisibility
| 1. C | 2. E | 3. E | 4. C | 5. E | 6. D | 7. E | 8. C |

Place Value
| 1. E | 3. A | 5. E | 7. E | 9. D |
| 2. D | 4. A | 6. D | 8. D | 10. E |

Time/Money Concepts
| 1. A | 2. C | 3. B | 4. E | 5. C | 6. D | 7. C | 8. B |

Estimation
| 1. B | 3. B | 5. B | 7. D | 9. D |
| 2. E | 4. D | 6. A | 8. B | 10. B |

Unit Analysis
| 1. C | 2. C | 3. B | 4. E | 5. E | 6. E | 7. A | 8. C |

Computational Clue Problems
| 1. B | 2. C | 3. C | 4. D | 5. D | 6. D | 7. B | 8. E |

Sequences, Patterns, Logic
| 1. C | 3. C | 5. B | 7. C | 9. C | 11. D |
| 2. C | 4. D | 6. D | 8. A | 10. D | 12. D |

Algebra

Common Factor
| 1. A | 3. E | 5. A | 7. E | 9. A | 11. C | 13. C | 15. D |
| 2. B | 4. A | 6. E | 8. D | 10. A | 12. C | 14. E | 16. A |

Factoring
| 1. C | 3. D | 5. A | 7. C | 9. B |
| 2. A | 4. B | 6. E | 8. A | 10. C |

Ratio and Proportions
| 1. C | 3. D | 5. D | 7. D | 9. A | 11. A | 13. E |
| 2. D | 4. B | 6. C | 8. D | 10. C | 12. C |

Word Problems
1. B	4. B	7. E	10. B	13. E	16. D	19. C	22. D
2. C	5. C	8. E	11. B	14. E	17. D	20. B
3. E	6. E	9. C	12. A	15. C	18. B	21. E

The Tutorverse

Interpreting Variables

1. D	4. C	7. E	10. D	13. D	16. A
2. A	5. A	8. B	11. D	14. D	17. D
3. E	6. D	9. D	12. A	15. E	

Equations Based on Word Problems

1. A	3. E	5. B	7. E	9. A
2. E	4. C	6. D	8. B	

Equations Based on Illustrations

1. B	3. D	5. E	7. D	9. E
2. D	4. C	6. B	8. C	10. D

Rational Expressions

1. A	3. D	5. A	7. A	9. A
2. C	4. B	6. C	8. D	10. C

Exponential Expressions

1. A	3. B	5. D	7. C	9. E	11. E
2. C	4. A	6. E	8. D	10. B	

Radical Expressions

1. B	3. D	5. C	7. D	9. A	11. D	13. D	15. D
2. C	4. A	6. E	8. E	10. A	12. C	14. C	

Polynomial Expressions

1. D	3. C	5. C	7. E	9. D	11. B	13. E
2. A	4. B	6. E	8. B	10. C	12. B	

Solving Algebraic Equations for a Variable

1. B	4. E	7. E	10. A	13. D	16. E
2. C	5. C	8. D	11. C	14. C	17. C
3. A	6. E	9. A	12. D	15. D	

Quadratic Equations

1. A	3. A	5. E	7. B	9. E	11. B	13. D	15. D
2. B	4. C	6. D	8. A	10. E	12. D	14. B	16. B

Inequalities

1. A	4. C	7. D	10. E	13. C	16. D
2. D	5. E	8. B	11. D	14. B	17. C
3. C	6. E	9. D	12. B	15. C	

Scientific Notation

1. D	3. E	5. B	7. E	9. A	11. C
2. B	4. B	6. B	8. D	10. B	

Geometry & Measurements

Pythagorean Theorem

1. C	3. C	5. A	7. A	9. E	11. B
2. B	4. C	6. C	8. A	10. A	12. E

Perimeter, Area, Volume

1. D	4. C	7. C	10. D	13. D	16. D	19. C	22. E
2. B	5. D	8. E	11. B	14. D	17. B	20. C	
3. E	6. B	9. B	12. D	15. A	18. D	21. A	

Problems Using Shapes and Angles

1. A	4. A	7. C	10. E	13. D	16. D	19. A
2. C	5. E	8. E	11. E	14. D	17. D	
3. C	6. B	9. A	12. B	15. C	18. B	

Coordinates

1. A	3. A	5. C	7. C	9. C
2. C	4. B	6. B	8. E	10. D

Transformations

1. A	3. E	5. C	7. E	9. B	11. C
2. A	4. B	6. D	8. C	10. D	12. A

Slope

1. C	3. D	5. C	7. A	9. A	11. C
2. D	4. B	6. D	8. D	10. D	12. B

Spatial Reasoning

1. A	2. B	3. E	4. D	5. D	6. B	7. A	8. D

Data Analysis & Probability

Mean, Median, Mode

1. B	4. C	7. D	10. B	13. C	16. C
2. C	5. B	8. B	11. D	14. D	17. B
3. D	6. A	9. A	12. B	15. C	

Probability

1. D	3. D	5. D	7. C	9. C	11. E	13. B	15. D
2. D	4. A	6. D	8. D	10. E	12. D	14. B	

Counting

1. A	3. D	5. B	7. A	9. C	11. C
2. D	4. B	6. B	8. C	10. E	12. A

Set Theory

1. C	3. C	5. D	7. D	9. B	11. C	13. D
2. C	4. C	6. C	8. B	10. D	12. C	

Reading Charts & Graphs

1. A	3. C	5. C	7. D	9. A
2. B	4. E	6. B	8. D	10. D

Verbal – Synonyms

Introductory

1. D	7. B	13. D	19. E	25. D	31. B	37. B	43. D
2. B	8. A	14. B	20. B	26. E	32. A	38. A	44. D
3. A	9. E	15. A	21. C	27. D	33. E	39. E	45. B
4. C	10. E	16. C	22. D	28. E	34. C	40. D	46. A
5. A	11. B	17. C	23. A	29. B	35. B	41. C	47. D
6. D	12. E	18. C	24. A	30. E	36. E	42. B	

Intermediate

1. E	7. C	13. B	19. E	25. B	31. D	37. E	43. C
2. A	8. D	14. D	20. A	26. A	32. E	38. E	44. B
3. D	9. D	15. B	21. E	27. B	33. E	39. C	45. E
4. E	10. D	16. C	22. A	28. C	34. D	40. C	46. A
5. B	11. B	17. E	23. D	29. B	35. B	41. C	47. C
6. B	12. E	18. A	24. D	30. E	36. B	42. A	

Advanced

1. D	7. E	13. D	19. E	25. C	31. E	37. E	43. D
2. E	8. B	14. B	20. D	26. C	32. C	38. D	44. B
3. A	9. D	15. B	21. E	27. A	33. B	39. E	45. A
4. E	10. E	16. B	22. C	28. D	34. E	40. D	46. B
5. A	11. D	17. D	23. D	29. A	35. A	41. C	47. A
6. C	12. E	18. B	24. D	30. A	36. D	42. E	

The Tutorverse

Verbal – Analogies

Guided Practice – Antonyms

1. A	4. B	7. A	10. D
2. D	5. E	8. C	
3. D	6. A	9. C	

Guided Practice – Association

1. D	3. D	5. C	7. D	9. A
2. A	4. B	6. E	8. B	10. E

Guided Practice – Cause-and-Effect

1. D	3. A	5. C	7. A	9. C
2. E	4. E	6. C	8. A	10. A

Guided Practice – Defining

1. C	3. B	5. D	7. D	9. E
2. B	4. B	6. C	8. B	10. C

Guided Practice – Degree/Intensity

1. D	3. E	5. E	7. C	9. B
2. D	4. A	6. D	8. B	10. D

Guided Practice – Function/Object

1. A	3. A	5. B	7. A	9. D
2. D	4. C	6. C	8. D	10. E

Guided Practice – Grammar

1. C	3. D	5. A	7. D	9. B
2. A	4. A	6. A	8. C	10. B

Guided Practice – Individual/Object

1. B	3. E	5. B	7. C	9. B
2. A	4. E	6. C	8. E	10. D

Guided Practice – Noun/Verb

1. E	3. E	5. A	7. A	9. E
2. E	4. A	6. A	8. C	10. A

Guided Practice – Part/Whole

1. C	3. A	5. D	7. B	9. D
2. C	4. A	6. A	8. E	10. B

Guided Practice – Purpose/Object

1. A	3. C	5. C	7. B	9. A
2. E	4. C	6. D	8. D	10. A

Guided Practice – Type/Kind

1. A	3. D	5. A	7. D	9. D
2. B	4. C	6. A	8. A	10. D

Guided Practice – Whole/Part

1. C	3. E	5. B	7. D	9. E
2. D	4. B	6. E	8. A	10. A

Guided Practice – Synonym

1. E	3. A	5. D	7. E	9. E
2. E	4. B	6. E	8. E	10. C

Mixed Practice 1

1. E	3. A	5. E	7. B	9. A	11. E	13. C
2. E	4. E	6. B	8. A	10. B	12. A	14. C

Mixed Practice 2

1. B	3. D	5. B	7. D	9. A	11. A	13. C
2. A	4. E	6. E	8. E	10. A	12. A	14. A

The Tutorverse

Mixed Practice 3
1. B   3. B   5. C   7. E   9. C   11. E   13. A
2. A   4. A   6. E   8. E   10. C   12. A   14. D
Mixed Practice 4
1. A   3. B   5. C   7. B   9. A   11. C   13. E
2. B   4. D   6. D   8. E   10. A   12. E   14. A
Mixed Practice 5
1. C   3. D   5. B   7. D   9. C   11. A   13. C
2. A   4. C   6. A   8. D   10. D   12. B   14. B
Mixed Practice 6
1. A   3. E   5. E   7. C   9. C   11. D   13. B
2. D   4. C   6. E   8. E   10. D   12. C   14. C
Mixed Practice 7
1. E   3. E   5. D   7. E   9. E   11. D   13. D
2. B   4. D   6. A   8. E   10. D   12. A   14. A
Mixed Practice 8
1. A   3. B   5. A   7. D   9. B   11. D   13. E
2. D   4. C   6. B   8. D   10. B   12. E   14. A
Mixed Practice 9
1. E   3. B   5. B   7. B   9. E   11. D   13. D
2. B   4. E   6. D   8. B   10. E   12. E   14. C
Mixed Practice 10
1. B   3. A   5. C   7. B   9. B   11. E   13. E
2. B   4. C   6. E   8. A   10. B   12. D   14. E

Reading Comprehension – Fiction

Passage #1
1. A   2. D   3. B   4. B
Passage #2
1. A   2. B   3. A   4. E   5. E
Passage #3
1. E   2. E   3. C   4. C
Passage #4
1. B   2. D   3. B
Passage #5
1. C   2. A   3. A   4. B
Passage #6
1. E   2. E   3. A   4. B   5. A
Passage #7
1. C   2. E   3. D   4. A
Passage #8
1. B   2. E   3. C   4. A   5. E
Passage #9
1. D   2. C   3. E   4. B   5. C
Passage #10
1. D   2. E   3. D
Passage #11
1. D   2. A   3. A   4. D   5. D
Passage #12
1. A   2. B   3. D   4. C   5. A   6. E

The Tutorverse

Reading Comprehension – Non-Fiction

Passage #1
1. B   2. B   3. C   4. C   5. C

Passage #2
1. C   3. C   5. D
2. A   4. B   6. B

Passage #3
1. B   2. A   3. C   4. B   5. D

Passage #4
1. D   2. E   3. A   4. C   5. A   6. B

Passage #5
1. C   2. A   3. C   4. D

Passage #6
1. C   2. B   3. A   4. C

Passage #7
1. D   2. D   3. E   4. E   5. A

Passage #8
1. E   2. E   3. D   4. C   5. A

Passage #9
1. C   2. C   3. C   4. B   5. B   6. C

Passage #10
1. B   2. B   3. E   4. A

Passage #11
1. D   2. C   3. E   4. C   5. B

Passage #12
1. E   2. C   3. B   4. D   5. D

Passage #13
1. D   2. A   3. D

Practice Test (Form B)

There is no answer key or explanation for the writing sample. Instead, have a parent or trusted educator review the essay or story written for the writing sample.

Section 1: Quantitative

1. B	5. B	9. D	13. A	17. C	21. B	25. B
2. D	6. A	10. A	14. D	18. A	22. E	
3. E	7. A	11. D	15. D	19. E	23. D	
4. C	8. E	12. B	16. E	20. A	24. E	

Section 2 – Reading

1. D	6. B	11. E	16. A	21. D	26. C	31. E	36. B
2. A	7. C	12. D	17. C	22. D	27. E	32. B	37. E
3. C	8. C	13. E	18. D	23. C	28. A	33. C	38. E
4. D	9. E	14. E	19. E	24. D	29. A	34. E	39. A
5. E	10. A	15. D	20. A	25. E	30. B	35. B	40. E

Section 3 – Verbal

1. A	5. A	9. B	13. A	17. A	21. A	25. C	29. E
2. C	6. E	10. D	14. E	18. C	22. C	26. D	30. E
3. E	7. D	11. C	15. A	19. D	23. C	27. A	31. A
4. B	8. A	12. B	16. D	20. D	24. B	28. A	32. D

The Tutorverse

33. A	37. C	41. A	45. B	49. D	53. C	57. A
34. E	38. A	42. B	46. E	50. D	54. B	58. A
35. D	39. A	43. A	47. E	51. A	55. B	59. E
36. A	40. E	44. A	48. B	52. D	56. E	60. A

Section 4 – Quantitative

1. B	5. B	9. B	13. E	17. A	21. C	25. E
2. D	6. D	10. D	14. B	18. A	22. B	
3. B	7. D	11. A	15. C	19. D	23. C	
4. B	8. C	12. E	16. C	20. C	24. B	

Section 5 – "Experimental"

| 1. E | 3. C | 5. C | 7. D | 9. C | 11. D | 13. B | 15. D |
| 2. D | 4. E | 6. C | 8. E | 10. E | 12. B | 14. A | 16. D |

Final Practice Test (Form C)

There is no answer key or explanation for the writing sample. Instead, have a parent or trusted educator review the essay or story written for the writing sample.

Section 1: Quantitative

1. D	5. A	9. B	13. D	17. D	21. C	25. E
2. A	6. B	10. E	14. E	18. B	22. B	
3. C	7. A	11. B	15. E	19. D	23. D	
4. D	8. C	12. C	16. B	20. E	24. C	

Section 2 – Reading

1. E	6. B	11. C	16. D	21. B	26. E	31. E	36. B
2. D	7. A	12. E	17. B	22. E	27. E	32. C	37. E
3. B	8. D	13. B	18. C	23. D	28. E	33. C	38. B
4. C	9. E	14. E	19. A	24. D	29. D	34. D	39. A
5. C	10. B	15. E	20. A	25. A	30. C	35. B	40. B

Section 3 – Verbal

1. E	9. E	17. A	25. D	33. E	41. C	49. A	57. B
2. A	10. C	18. C	26. D	34. D	42. E	50. D	58. C
3. C	11. A	19. E	27. C	35. A	43. C	51. E	59. B
4. B	12. D	20. D	28. C	36. D	44. E	52. C	60. D
5. D	13. A	21. B	29. A	37. B	45. A	53. E	
6. C	14. A	22. B	30. D	38. A	46. B	54. B	
7. D	15. E	23. C	31. C	39. E	47. E	55. E	
8. E	16. B	24. B	32. E	40. C	48. A	56. E	

Section 4 – Quantitative

1. D	5. E	9. A	13. D	17. E	21. E	25. C
2. B	6. B	10. C	14. E	18. A	22. B	
3. D	7. B	11. D	15. B	19. C	23. C	
4. E	8. E	12. E	16. E	20. E	24. C	

Section 5 – "Experimental"

| 1. C | 3. B | 5. E | 7. D | 9. D | 11. B | 13. B | 15. E |
| 2. B | 4. C | 6. A | 8. C | 10. E | 12. D | 14. E | 16. E |

The Tutorverse

Made in United States
North Haven, CT
18 December 2023